Keep 2019 ✓

DATE DUE

Our Own Master Race:

Eugenics in Canada, 1885-1945

Angus McLaren

M&S

Cover photograph reproduced courtesy of Wellcome Institute Library.

Canadian Cataloguing in Publication Data

McLaren, Angus
    Our own master race

(The Canadian social history series)
Includes bibliographical references.
ISBN 0-7710-5544-7

1. Eugenics - Canada - History - 20th century.
I. Title. II. Series.

HQ755.5.C3M24 1990   363.9'2'0971   C90-093808-8

Printed and bound in Canada by John Deyell Company

McClelland & Stewart Inc.
The Canadian Publishers
481 University Avenue
Toronto, Ontario
M5G 2E9

Contents

Preface

In the depths of the Great Depression a number of Ontario's most respectable citizens came together to establish what they chose to call the Toronto League for Race Betterment. That such a name, conjuring up as it does today memories of the Nazis' horrific campaign of racial purification, should have been given to what was simply a birth control society might seem strange. In the interwar years, however, the employment of ethnic, nativist, and racist labels occasioned little public comment. The term "race" was casually employed by social commentators of every stripe and most assumed that the race could and should be "improved." Some thought progress would be made by changing the environment; others thought it could be best accomplished by encouraging the reproduction of the hereditarily superior and inhibiting that of the inferior. In practice there were few who completely denied the powers of either nature or nurture. But though a good deal has been written about Canadian social reformers' environmentalist arguments, next to nothing has been said about the eugenic theories advanced by the hereditarians.

Have the deeds and ideas of the eugenically minded escaped serious investigation simply because their influence was negligible? Some colleagues have assumed this was the case and on hearing of this study have protested that surely those who toyed with pseudo-scientific concepts of racial fitness must have never accounted for more than a tiny fringe group of kooks. Why devote a book to eccentrics who were inevitably doomed to failure? The ideas they played with were significant in the sad history of central Europe, but were not intelligent Canadians somehow immune to such concepts?

In way of response one might begin by asking where one would place the twenty-nine-year-old prairie student who in 1933 received an M.A. from McMaster University for a thesis on social hygiene and public health, which he later described as a topic in "Christian sociology." It was in fact a typical eugenic study that began with the popular hereditarian argument that the mentally and physically subnormal were not so much the victims but rather the causes of a good deal of the distress of the depression. They could be identified, asserted the author, as the low achievers on IQ tests, the delinquent, the venereally diseased, and the improvident. To determine the menace they posed society the student turned to the local asylum, where he traced the family trees of what he called twelve "immoral or nonmoral women." Whereas most decent citizens had two or three offspring, these dozen prostitutes and mental defectives had spawned ninety-five children and 105 grandchildren. The researcher was shocked that such misfits were caught in a wretched cycle of immorality, promiscuity, and improvidence, but he was more alarmed that in spreading disease, clogging up the school system, promoting crime and prostitution, burdening hospitals, and overwhelming charitable institutions they threatened the smooth functioning of society. The burden of the taxes that supported such degenerates was borne by the respectable. If they, too, were not to be pulled under by the economic crisis engulfing Canada the reproduction of the unfit had to be checked. How?

The author fell back on the remedies already popularized by hereditarians, who claimed that social problems had a biological basis – restriction of marriage to those holding certificates of health, segregation of the unfit on state farms where the sexes would be separated, limitation of some subnormal families by doctors' discreet provision of birth control information, and finally sterilization of the defective. The student was not indifferent to the necessity also of improving the environment, but the central thrust of his argument was that to protect itself society had to recognize that mental and physical misfits warranted no better treatment than that once reserved for lepers and criminals. Such a thorough exercise in victim-blaming sounds remarkably "un-Christian" to the modern ear, but in the 1930's this researcher was far from being the only Protestant who saw eugenics and Christianity complementing one another. He appeared to believe that the projected victims of the policies he advanced would not be affronted but actually would find some comfort in the notion that, "When education and legislation have failed there is still One who can take the broken earthenware from life's garbage heaps and make them vessels of honor in His temple of love."[1]

The research for this graduate thesis was carried out in Weyburn, Saskatchewan, by a young Baptist minister concerned as much with this life as with the next. The student was not some insignificant, heartless hereditarian; it was Tommy Douglas. The same year Douglas submitted his thesis on "The Problems of the Subnormal Family" to McMaster University he helped found the Co-operative Commonwealth Federation. He went on to serve as the CCF premier of Saskatchewan between 1941 and 1961 and became in 1961 the first leader of the federal New Democratic Party. He is probably best known for his long struggle in defence of state health care.

Why did Canada's most eloquent defender of socialism begin his career as a supporter of hereditarian theories? The short answer is that Douglas was fascinated with the eugenic message that stressed the primacy of scientific experts and planners. The Second World War, in revealing the horrors that resulted when biological solutions were sought for social problems, checked such early enthusiasms. The long answer is contained in the chapters that follow. The main point is that it is simply not sufficient to dismiss as a bizarre, individual quirk the interest expressed in eugenics by men and women like Douglas. Nor is it the historian's task to condemn them. The real goal is to understand what there was in the eugenics message that seemed to make good sense to many Canadians preoccupied by what they took to be the dangers of racial inefficiency, social inadequacy, and ill health.

Eugenics was preached throughout the Western world. Its arguments were used by both the political left and right; some policies, such as the legalization of birth control, were both defended and attacked on eugenic grounds. British eugenicists were primarily concerned with the issue of class and the ways that the threat of society being swamped by lower class "degenerates" might be prevented; American eugenicists, alarmed by the northward movement of free blacks and the arrival of millions of Southern and Eastern European immigrants, tended to be more racist in orientation.

Why such fears should have been felt and such responses made in Britain and the United States has been explained; the Canadian experience has not been examined. Most Canadians happily imagine that their country was spared the virulent racism and class consciousness of its neighbours. But cursory investigation reveals that Canada was not immune to eugenic preoccupations, which in the first half of the twentieth century coloured the discussion of a vast variety of topics ranging from sex instruction, intelligence testing, and special education to social welfare, immigration, and birth control. Indeed, English Canadians' fear of French-Canadian fertility gave the hereditarian debate in Canada a particular resonance. The fact that Canada did not produce an internationally recognized authority on eugenics, like Britain's Francis Galton or America's Charles Davenport, goes some way in explaining why intellectual historians have not provided an analysis of hereditarian thought in Canada. But just because they were not particularly original, the success of Canadian eugenicists in popularizing their creed is all the more remarkable and tells us a good deal about the social receptivity in Canada to theories of biological determinism. An examination of both the production of and the demand for such ideas promises to provide us with a fresh perspective on the country's past.

The nature-nurture debate has a long history. This study focuses on the believers in the primacy of heredity – most of whom described themselves as eugenicists – in late nineteenth- and early twentieth-century Canada. As noted, the history of eugenic thinking in Britain and the United States has recently received a good deal of attention and therefore the international context only has to be sketched in. Any study of eugenics must, however, begin as this one does, with a discussion of the "father" of eugenics, Francis Galton. Subsequent chapters are devoted to Canadian eugenic and hereditarian concerns as they were related to public health, immigration, birth control, care of the feeble-minded, and genetics. When appropriate, Canadian preoccupations are placed in the context of international eugenic concerns to clarify the ways in which this country's experience differed.

Although genetics and eugenics were closely linked, this study makes no attempt to provide an up-to-date history of genetic research. Some have suggested that the real heyday of eugenics was in the decade prior to the outbreak of World War One because geneticists, who increasingly understood the complexities of heredity, turned away from the simplistic policies of the eugenicists after 1915. But the general public was not made aware of the declining scientific respectability of eugenics; in fact, in Canada it enjoyed its greatest triumphs in the 1930's when the depression drove a desperate generation in search of scientific panaceas. A chapter of the book is devoted to Canada's leading human geneticist, but readers in search of an account of the evolution of genetics might best begin with Daniel J. Kevles's *In the Name of Eugenics: Genetics and the Use of Heredity* (1985).

A chapter is also devoted to the Eugenics Society of Canada, but the book is not primarily concerned with the activities of the members of an organized movement. Although mainline or traditional eugenics appealed chiefly to those frightened by the social changes of the turn of the century, some optimistic radicals were also attracted to the idea of wedding biology and politics. Eugenics could mean different things to different people. The present study, to illustrate the variety of ways in which assumptions about heredity might be manifested, provides fairly detailed biographical accounts of the different sorts of Canadians drawn to eugenics, the most important of whom were undoubtedly the public health pioneer Helen MacMurchy and the aggressive geneticist Madge Thurlow Macklin.

The eugenic crusade in Canada was never a unified movement. This book was not written to chronicle the activities of the small number of individuals who formally became members of the Eugenics Society of Canada but to explain the broad appeal of some of the particular strands of thought they embraced, and to account not so much for the hereditarians' specific social policy victories as for their success in popularizing a vocabulary and terminology that even their opponents employed. The goal is to understand the circumstances that led so many respectable Canadians, imagining the race to be threatened with "degeneration," to turn to eugenics as a guide for defensive action.

In carrying out this study I was aided directly and indirectly by many friends and colleagues. Brian Dippie, Ramsay Cook, Greg Kealey, Sam Shortt, and Nikki Strong-Boag generously took time out from their hectic schedules to read the entire manuscript and make helpful suggestions. I would also like to thank for their help: Garland Allen, Donna Andrew, Paul Bator, Lesley Biggs, David Keane, Jane Lewis, Jack Little, Janice Dicken McGinnis, Indiana Matters, Edward Phelps, Roy Porter, Fred Possmayer, James Snell, Hubert Soltan, Norman C. Staub, Richard Soloway, and Paul Weindling. I am especially grateful for unpublished material provided by Timothy J. Christian, John Griffin, Lyle Hutton, Bert Hansen, Janice Newton, Barry Mehler, James Reed, Theresa Richardson, William Schneider, and Mariana Valverde.

This is also an appropriate place to acknowledge the generous hospitality offered me over the years by Michael Finn and Elizabeth Park in Toronto; Richard Cox, Susannah Ginsberg, and Michael and Aimée Birnbaum in London; Marguerite Garling in Paris; and Brian and Donna Dippie in Victoria.

Thanks are also offered to the audiences subjected to portions of the study at the University of Guelph, Queen's University, the Ontario Institute for Studies in Education, and the annual meetings of the Canadian Society for the History of Medicine in Montreal, the New Zealand Historical Association in Palmerston North, and the Western History Association in Los Angeles.

Efficient assistance was provided by the staffs of the National Archives of Canada, the Provincial Archives of British Columbia, Alberta, Saskatchewan, and Ontario, the City Archives of Vancouver, the Hamilton Public Library, the Brantford Public Library, the United Church of Canada Archives, the University of Toronto Archives, the Queen Street Mental Health Archives, the Woodward Medical Library and the Special Collections Library at the University of British Columbia, the Victoria Medical Library, the Library of the University of Victoria, the Dora Lewis Rare Book Room at the University of Waterloo, the Countway Library of Medicine in Boston, the Contemporary Medical Archives Centre at the Wellcome Institute for the History of Medicine, the British Library, the Library of Congress, the Ohio State University Archives, the Goucher Alumnae Association, the Rockefeller Archive Center, the American Philosophical Society, and the Social Welfare History Archives at the University of Minnesota.

Time was made available for writing the present work thanks to a Social Sciences and Humanities Research Council of Canada research time stipend and a half-sabbatical from the University of Victoria.

Portions of this study appeared under different guises in *Birth Control in Nineteenth Century England* (London: Croom Helm, 1978) and in a 1986 article in the *Canadian Historical Review*. I would like to thank the editors and publishers for permission to reprint this material.

And, finally, many thanks to the secretaries at the Department of History at the University of Victoria – June Bull, Dinah Dickie, and Gloria Orr – for all the help so cheerfully given.

This book has been published with the help of a grant from the Canadian Federation for the Humanities, using funds provided by the Social Sciences and Humanities Research Council of Canada.

1

The Birth of Biological
Politics

In 1919 W.L. Lochhead introduced the readers of the *Canadian Bookman* to the complexities of the new science of genetics. He traced its lineage back to Francis Galton, whose statistical work demonstrated the importance of inheritance, August Weismann, who destroyed the old theory of acquired characteristics, and Gregor Mendel, whose experiments on hybridization revealed the way in which characteristics were passed from generation to generation. The new science, according to Lochhead, promised to do more than rejuvenate plant and animal breeding; it also held out hopes of improving human reproduction.

> This latter phase is called Eugenics and has received considerable study, the result going to show that human characteristics behave in a Mendelian manner, and that it is quite possible to improve upon existing methods of production of human beings. Many careful investigations of family records reveal the fact that both good and poor qualities are inherited according to Mendelian laws. Many defects such as feeble-mindedness, epilepsy, deaf-mutism, and disposition to tuberculosis and other diseases are undoubtedly inherited, and to put no hindrance to the breeding of unfit and degenerate persons exposes our country to the gravest risk of regression, especially when it is recognized that the population is being largely recruited from inferior stocks. The Eugenist has proposed the following measures for the improvement of the race, – More stringent marriage laws; sexual segregation of defectives; stricter control of immigration; and measures of sterilization of dangerous defectives. He also advocates the improvement of social conditions that prevent the marriage of desirables, and a campaign to enlighten the public regarding the ideals of eugenics.[1]

It says something about the spirit of the age that Lochhead – professor of botany at MacDonald College, local authority on the Hessian fly, pea-weavil, and mushrooms, and author of *The Weeds of Ontario* – felt qualified to judge which of his fellow citizens should or should not reproduce. But such pretensions were common in Canada at the beginning of the century, and, as Lochhead asserted, they sprang directly from the activities of Francis Galton.

Galton (1822-1911) – founder of anthropometry, population genetics, and eugenics – was convinced that mental qualities were always determined more by nature than by nurture.[2] This in turn meant that his thought was marked by a profound pessimism; if the bearers of natural genius failed to reproduce he saw no way in which adequate compensation could be made by the less intelligent. To advance such ideas in the golden age of Victorian liberalism, when it was widely believed that training and education could overcome every obstacle, was to place oneself very much in advance of public opinion. Even Galton's famous cousin, Charles Darwin, shared the general belief in the malleability of humanity and at times employed a variant of the environmentalist notion of "acquired characteristics" to explain the appearance of variations. Galton rejected this Lamarckian theory, not because he had the sort of scientific evidence of the impossibility of influencing "germ plasm" that Weismann would advance in the 1880's, but because it violated his deep-seated conservative belief, a belief almost religious in nature, in the predominance of heredity over social environment.

An independently wealthy gentleman scholar, Galton forced himself on the public's attention by announcing in *Hereditary Genius* (1869) that intellectual abilities were transmitted over time.[3] He was the first to assert that "intelligence" was a scientifically meaningful concept and that it was inheritable. Accordingly, in the 1870's he concentrated on developing statistical and anthropometric techniques to demonstrate the importance of heredity. He never produced a satisfactory measurement of intelligence (and even the tests elaborated in the early twentieth century by the Frenchmen Binet failed to winnow out the influences of education and social standing), but he was unwavering in his belief that sophisticated measurement would ultimately prove the primacy of inheritance.

Galton produced a vast range of quantitative studies on subjects ranging from fingerprinting to "Statistical Inquiries into the Efficacy of Prayer." His dictum, "Whenever you can, count," which had a revolutionary impact on biology and psychology, reflected his mystical faith, and one shared by many late Victorians, in the explanatory powers of statistical analysis. Galton even confessed in an autobiographical passage to the habit of secretly counting and categorizing the women he passed in the street.

> Whenever I have occasion to classify the persons I meet into three classes, "good, medium and bad," I use a needle mounted as a pricker, wherewith to prick holes, unseen, in a piece of paper, torn rudely into a cross with a long leg. I use the upper end for "good," the cross arm for "medium," the lower end for "bad." The prick holes keep distinct, and are readily read off at leisure.[4]

Such disclosures could easily be given a Freudian interpretation; more than one historian has attributed the unhappily married and childless Galton's preoccupations with reproduction to his own personal problems.[5]

In 1883 Galton coined the term "eugenics" to describe "the study of the agencies under social control that may improve or impair the racial qualities of future generations, either physically or mentally," and asserted that the statistical approach, if used to encourage such selective breeding, could solve the social ills that beset Britain.[6] Breeders had already succeeded in developing improved strains of plants and animals; could not such techniques now be applied to human reproduction? As confidence in liberalism waned such ideas began to receive the serious attention of academics. From the 1870's on, the British upper and middle classes, unlike the lower orders, were clearly limiting family size, and, consequently, social commentators became worried; by the turn of the century some went so far as to predict that the nation faced "race suicide" and national degeneration. If a healthy demographic balance were to be maintained, they claimed, it would be necessary to entice the "fit" to breed or to take measures to restrict the births of the "unfit."

The upsurge in concern was triggered in part by the pioneering social investigations of Charles Booth and Seebohm Rowntree, which revealed the wretchedness of the lives of a substantial portion of the urban working class.[7] These reports supplemented those demonstrating that the poorest portions of the population were contributing the largest additions to the national birth rate. Political concerns were added to social fears by the Boer War crisis; the chronic ill health and physical weakness of the British working class revealed by the recruiting program and the subsequent 1904 Interdepartmental Committee on Physical Deterioration brought forcibly home to the public the seriousness of the situation. It was in this period of anxious reappraisal of the country's social policies that the eugenics movement first blossomed.

Galton, following the tables produced by Charles Booth, graded citizens according to their civic worth – desirable, passable, and unde-sirable. He hoped that a national biographical index could then be established, listing those – inmates of prisons, hospitals, and asylums – not fit to breed. He believed that criminality, alcoholism, and feeble-mindedness were, like intelligence, inherited. Among the fit, on whose fertility his hopes were set, he sought to elicit a "sentiment of caste," which in time the state would officially recognize by the provision of "eugenic certificates." "Negative eugenics" was Galton's term for policies aimed at restricting the breeding of the unfit; the goal of "positive eugenics" was to encourage the fertility of the fit. Needless to say, because he relied heavily on biographical encyclopedias and school statistics in determining who was most talented, he posited social success as a reliable indicator of physical and intellectual hered-itary fitness.

Galton's theory – that the first condition of any process of race selection was to determine the existence of differences – was taken up and made scientifically respectable by Karl Pearson, professor of applied mathematics and mechanics at University College, London.[8] Pearson developed the science of biometry by applying statistical methods to the study of biology. Between 1891 and 1906 he launched a series of investigations into such questions as differences in stature, cephalic index, eye colour, fertility, and longevity. At the same time he served as the statistician of the Evolution Committee of the Royal Society, which had been established by Galton and the biologist W.F.R. Weldon. Galton's and Pearson's mathematical studies, partic-ularly on regression and correlation, were to be vitally important to the emergence of modern statistics and its role in both the social and natural sciences. But such studies revealed little about the actual process of hereditary transmission.

The Galtonian eugenicists relied on statistical analysis to trace the influence of innate characteristics because the contribution of genes, the physical basis of heredity, was not understood until Mendel's theories were rediscovered at the turn of the century. The pioneering work in the 1860's of Gregor Mendel, an Austrian monk, had initially received scant attention. But in 1900 his findings, based on research on pea hybridization that each characteristic passed from one genera-tion to the next was determined by a combination of dominant and recessive elements, were simultaneously rediscovered by a number of scientists. The emergence of this rival method of explaining heredity, which William Bateson named "genetics," was viewed with some resentment by Galton.[9] In part due to the difficulty of working with Mendelian-minded biologists more interested in chance mutations and discontinuous evolution than in actuarial tables, he abandoned the Evolution Committee and established the Eugenics Record Office. This he handed over to Pearson in 1906 to form part of the Biometric Laboratory at University College. Its purpose was to make the academic reading public aware of the dangers of hereditary illnesses through two series of publications – "Studies in National Deterioration" and "Eugenic Laboratory Memoirs" – while the Eugenics Educational Society, established by Galton in the same year, was to serve as a propaganda instrument to bring the message to both the politicians and the general public.

The Galtonian biometricians and the Mendelian-minded biologists could heatedly disagree about the best way to analyse the transmission of characteristics over time, but they gave the public the impression that all scientists at least agreed that heredity was now determined to be more important than environment. In the 1880's the German August Weismann had hypothesized that, although an individual might be influenced by improved surroundings, the "germ plasm" passed on to the next generation could not undergo any such change. This theory was now used to support the most extreme hereditarian views. Not only was Lamarck's theory of acquired characteristics (popularly associated with the idea that giraffes acquired long necks by stretching for leaves) now viewed as laughable; so, too, were many of the environmentalist notions that underlay so much of nineteenth-century progressive reformism.[10]

The growing success of eugenics in popularizing fears of degeneration was a symptom of a decline of faith in nineteenth-century liberalism. Under the aegis of Herbert Spencer, who coined the term "survival of the fittest," mid-century liberals held that competition was the key in an age of greater specialization, differentiation, and interdependence.[11] Those who were poor and unsuccessful had, the theory went, proven themselves unfit for the struggle and would, by the free working of natural laws, be removed from the contest. Spencer's doctrine was – for the fit – basically optimistic, for he assured them that they would continue to prosper and had no need to seek assistance from the state.

The population theories of the mid-nineteenth century mirrored the model of the laissez-faire economy. It was generally accepted that it was only possible to *understand* the "laws" of population; such laws could not be countered by institutional interference. This line of argument was followed by pessimistic Malthusians envisaging a never-ending series of swings between over- and under-population and optimistic Spencerians prophesying the arrival of an equilibrium. Both accepted a passive approach because both believed that population arrived naturally at its correct level.

Darwin had similarly advanced a view of the world in which evolution slowly took place as a result of small variations emerging from the interplay of nature and environment. Old-fashioned social Darwinists were true to such beliefs and willing to let the struggle for existence continue; the eugenicists called for a halt. They took this step because the social investigations of the 1880's made it clear that the unfit were not being eliminated; a glance at the birth rate revealed that it was the fit who were failing to reproduce. Whereas previous social commentators had only concerned themselves with the quantity of the population, the eugenicists of the 1900's concerned themselves with its "quality." The question was not if some survived, but who survived; the process of selection, not elimination, had to be controlled.[12] The Malthusian and utilitarian concept of "static adjustment" was thus replaced by the eugenicists with an evolutionary model in which heredity and environment, rather than reasoned self-interest, fired the engine of progress. The eugenicists argued that decisions on breeding could no longer be left to individual whim or chance; an outside agency was required to monitor actions that affected the entire community.[13]

This belief that some order had to be brought to the question of breeding motivated not only hereditarians; social scientists and politicians were also shifting away from the Malthusian hedonistic model and the atomistic individualism of Spencer and turning toward "collectivist" or "interventionist" approaches to social problems.[14] This new activism was a sign, first, of an optimistic belief in the possibility of social manipulation shared by socialists, radical Tories, "new" liberals, and eugenicists. A radical strand of thought in eugenic thinking was rooted in a belief in perfection that could be traced back to Rousseau and Condorcet. The triumphs of the industrial revolution furthered the faith in the ability to create new men. In the 1830's, Robert Owen, industrialist and utopian socialist, had speculated on the possibility of the state supervising births to attain "improvements of the organization of man." In America in the 1850's the perfectionist preacher John Humphrey Noyes defended the notion of improving the human race by "judicious breeding."[15]

The eugenicists' activism was a sign, also, of a new fear of the lower classes. Terrified by the prospect of the unfit multiplying thoughtlessly while the prudent restricted family size, the eugenicists called for state controls. The Malthusians had attributed the poverty of the poor to their lack of foresight and had addressed moral appeals to them, but the eugenicists attributed their plight to environmental and hereditary factors that could not be attenuated by individual prudence. The poor were not demoralized; they were degenerate.[16] If their degeneration was due to environmental causes it could be cured by social programs; if heredity was the cause the state could only limit the problem by restricting their breeding. According to the older liberal interpretation, the poor were seen as morally irresponsible but at least it was presumed that they could, if they saw the evil of their ways, escape their lot. The eugenicists adopted a more brutal attitude – if lack of fitness was attributed to hereditary taint there was no reprieve.[17]

Francis Galton's goal was to make eugenics both a science for measuring society's hereditary make-up and a movement to lobby for progressive policies to ensure better breeding. The "brutal pessimism" developed by most of his followers in their dealings with the working class seems at first glance at odds with the fact that Pearson and some others active in the English movement often described themselves as socialists. But for most, "socialism" was that system favouring a form of government that would empower the technocrat with means of social control. They believed they had found the scientific cure for a host of social problems and viewed themselves as enlightened reformers. Though at times sounding radical – in particular when criticizing the older landed elite, of which they were not part – the middle-class eugenicists sought to promote the values, virtues, and social structure of the society in which they had a vested interest.[18]

Galton and Pearson were close in spirit to the American "progressives" who felt threatened by the rise of both big business and organized labour. Like these Americans, they claimed to be protecting the "quality" of the race, but they failed to acknowledge that their criterion of "fitness," namely socio-economic status, predisposed them to categorize the lower classes in general as genetically inferior.[19] Those seeking to trace hereditarian influences prior to the discovery of chromosomes naturally had to rely heavily on appearances, but the importance of recessive characteristics indicated by Mendel's work should have alerted them to the deceptiveness of outward show. Eugenics did draw some adherents from the left, but in providing scientific "proof" of the inferiority of the lower classes it was primarily a product of a turn-of-the-century surge in anti-democratic and anti-egalitarian sentiment.

There was also an obvious anti-feminist element in eugenics. This was made apparent in the opposition voiced by Galton and Pearson to birth control. "I protest," wrote Galton in *Hereditary Genius*, "against the abler races being encouraged to withdraw in this way from the struggle for existence."[20] Pearson, in replying to an appeal for support made by the Malthusian League (the first public movement in favour of family limitation), declared:

> I am certainly in favour of rational limitation. None the less, I believe in the efficiency of society largely depending on the selection of better stocks, the removal or destruction of the less fit stocks. Now my grave difficulty about Neo-Malthusianism is simply this. It tends to act in the better, in the physically or mentally fitter, ranks of society, among the educated and thrifty of the middle and working classes. It does not act, so far as I can see, at all on Mr. Booth's "Class B." . . . While limiting the population we must, at the same time, ensure that the worst stock is the stock which is first and foremost limited.[21]

Even within the small family of the upper classes Pearson detected a danger. In "On the Handicapping of the First Born," he argued that it was statistically provable that the eldest child did not do as well as its siblings; if family size was limited and the percentage of first-born children increased, so did the danger of degeneration.[22]

To those like John Stuart Mill who defended "voluntary motherhood" and woman's right to advance as far as her individual capacities admitted, the eugenicists replied that sex differences were based on biological facts that could not be overridden by appeals to justice.[23] Woman's role was determined by her reproductive function. Biology, not politics, subjected her to man. If she was unhappy the answer was not to wrench her from her natural calling and plunge her into an unequal contest from which she could only emerge defeated and embittered; the answer was to provide her with the support necessary to permit her to fulfil more adequately her function as childbearer. In one of his earliest essays Pearson asserted that before woman's "rights," such as the right to vote, were debated it was first necessary to turn to the science of "sexualology" to establish her physical capacities.

> We have first to settle what is the physical capacity of woman, what would be the effect of her emancipation on her function of race production, before we can talk about her "rights," which are, after all, only a vague description of what may be the fittest position for her, the sphere of her maximum usefulness in the developed society of the future.

Higher education could, for example, raise the intelligence of women or lead to their degeneration. Feminists had the duty to advance their ideas with caution.

They must face sex-problems with sexualological and historical knowledge, and solve them, before they appeal to the marketplace with all the rhetorical flourish of "justice" and of "right." They must show that emancipation will tend not only to increase the stability of society and the general happiness of mankind, but will favour the physique and health of both sexes.[24]

Of course, no such demonstrations had been required before working men were given the vote in 1867 and 1884, but woman's emancipation, insisted the eugenicists, had to be judged on the grounds of its social and physiological utility.

In the eyes of the hereditarians the greatest anti-social act committed by the better type of women was the avoidance of pregnancy. Pearson lamented the tragic fact that the finer females, in restricting family size, were snuffing out strains of hereditary intelligence. He was willing to recognize that some women regarded childbearing as a form of subjection, but insisted that it had to be accepted as a price paid for the "race instinct for reproduction." In the future, he predicted, women would be rewarded and honoured for their sacrifice.

It will be simply based upon the recognition that women's childbearing activity is essentially a part of her contribution to social needs; that it ought to be acknowledged as such by the State; that society at large ought to insist, exactly as in the case of labour, that the condition under which it is taken shall be as favourable as possible, that *pro tanto* it shall be treated as part of woman's work for society at large.[25]

Pearson regretted that not everyone in the woman's movement responded positively to such an offer, that some refused to calculate women's rights against the measure of "general social efficiency," and that some were "out and out individualists."

The belief that feminism actually posed a danger to the eugenics movement was shared by many of its adherents. Galton was a well-known anti-feminist, a supporter of the Anti-Suffrage Society, and a defender of the Contagious Diseases Acts that permitted the forcible medical inspection of prostitutes. W.C.D. Whetham, the Cambridge scientist and agriculturalist, wrote that it was no coincidence that the feminist movement emerged as the birth rate of the upper classes fell; the better sort of woman was shirking her maternal duty.[26] C.W. Saleeby, the leading English popularizer of eugenic doctrines, led an all-out attack in *Woman and Womanhood: A Search for Principles* (1911) on the "dysgenic consequences" of women's education, the "intolerable evil" of married women's work, and the high rate of *male* infant mortality, which he referred to as "infanticide." He called for a "Eugenic Feminism" that would lure back to their natural roles the "incomplete and aberrant women" who were "ceasing to be mammals." The real divisions in society, according to Saleeby, were not along class or sex lines; they divided parents and non-parents. "Women's rights" could only be considered after those of, first, mothers and, second, fathers.[27]

In the writings of Havelock Ellis, the "sexual sage" of Edwardian England, one finds perhaps the most determined attempt to balance the demands of eugenicists and feminists. Fertility control he declared to be a fact and indeed a concomitant of a higher civilization.[28] The claim that it threatened "race suicide" was countered by the argument that it prevented unwanted births and infant deaths. But what most interested Ellis was the possibility of achieving "selection in reproduction." The campaign for women's suffrage he considered unimportant. He was more enthusiastic about the "Mutterschutz" movement in Germany in which the defence of motherhood was given priority over political questions.[29] Ellis believed that Galton and the Swedish feminist Ellen Key had arrived independently at the same conclusion as to the religious importance of procreation. As long as there were no children, lovers could love as they pleased; once offspring appeared the state had an obligation to intercede. Only in eugenics could the competing claims of the race and the individual be reconciled.[30]

Most English eugenicists were less indifferent than Ellis to the dangers posed by birth control. They attempted by a variety of schemes to encourage the breeding of the best stock. Galton suggested that a policy of "befriendment" of thriving families be adopted to promote the reproduction of the fit. Whetham proposed that old age pensions be based on the number of children raised, that scholarships be set aside for the children of the middle class, and that posts in the empire be guaranteed for sons of the gentry. The discussions of the "endowment of motherhood" and child welfare in the first decade of the twentieth century similarly attracted the attention of a host of hereditarians. Such aid, stated Pearson, could only be socially useful if care were taken that the right sorts of families were supported: "Yet time is approaching when real knowledge must take the place of energetic but untrained philanthropy in dictating the lines of feasible social reform."[31]

The problem with the "positive eugenics" stance was that it was more difficult to determine who should breed than who should not. Moreover, the danger of the growth of degeneracy excited attention, as apparently documented by the Boer War crisis, not the possibility of more conscientious breeding by the middle classes. By the time of his 1901 Huxley Lecture, Galton was calling for negative forms of eugenics, including the segregation and sterilization of the "undesirable." Pearson sounded the same note in his 1903 lecture; social reform could not repair the defects of heredity: "No scheme of wider or more thorough education will bring up in the scale of intelligence hereditary weakness to the level of hereditary strength."[32]

The direction the English eugenicists were taking was made clear by their studies, many of which appeared in the appropriately named series, "Studies in National Deterioration." Alien immigration, feeble-mindedness, alcoholism, insanity, and women's work were all presented by researchers as having a nefarious influence on fertility. The eugenicists did not all respond in the same way to such threats. Some, out of a fear of a contagion of tainted "germ plasm," called for campaigns against alcoholism and venereal disease. Others adopted the opposite tack, arguing against preventive medicine on the grounds that it kept alive the diseased and the debauched who would inevitably infect the innocent.[33]

As flawed and self-serving as the science of eugenics might in hindsight appear, it had an enormous appeal in both Britain and North America. In 1912 when the first international eugenics congress met in London, it was presided over by Leonard Darwin, a son of Charles Darwin, and listed among its vice-presidents Winston Churchill, Charles Eliot, former president of Harvard University, and two of Canada's most famous sons – the inventor Alexander Graham Bell and the renowned physician Sir William Osler. Over 700 delegates from around the world attended, including Dr. J.G. Adami from McGill University and Professor Ramsay Wright from the University of Toronto.[34] In fact, few scientists or doctors in early twentieth-century Canada were not drawn to the notion that the breeding of humans followed the same Mendelian laws and was as predictive in nature as that of other sexually reproducing organisms. Blood typing, colour blindness, and several metabolic diseases were in fact found to follow a strict Mendelian inheritance pattern and it was but a short step to assert that further research would ultimately furnish proof of the inheritability of criminality, promiscuity, feeble-mindedness, and alcoholism.

Such notions were abroad in Canada even before Galton's work was popularized by the Eugenics Education Society. Dr. Alexander Peter Reid, superintendent of the Nova Scotia Hospital for the Insane, informed the Institute of Natural Sciences in 1890 that action had to be taken to stave off national degeneration. Dividing society up into the three categories of the good, the bad, and the irresponsible, Reid declared that the "ulcerous and diseased outgrowths on society" could not be permitted to reproduce. Insanity, he informed his audience, was in 60 to 80 per cent of cases inherited. An education in sanitary laws and Darwinism was required, he argued, to lead society to recognize the right of the child to be well born.[35] In 1908, in fact, Nova Scotia was to be home of the League for the Care and Protection of Feeble-Minded Persons, which was also known as Canada's first "eugenical movement."[36]

Reid had received his M.D. from McGill, which served as an important conduit for English hereditarian ideas into Canada. Between 1897 and 1909 the Cambridge educated E.W. McBride was the university's Strathcona Professor of Zoology. McBride's class biases were given full force when he moved from his specialty – studies of sea urchins – to eugenics. Mental defectives were, he declared, a mutation created in the slums. In an earlier age they would have perished, "But nowadays, with the growth of a maudlin, unthinking sentimentality, strenuous efforts are made not only to keep all their offspring alive but to allow them to breed at the expense of the more competent members of the community." What was needed, in McBride's view, was a "weeding" out of prostitutes, criminals, and drunkards via sterilization. "All attempts to favour the slum population by encouraging their habits of reckless reproduction in throwing the support of their children on the State," he warned, "places a heavier burden on the shoulders of the Nordic race, who form the bulk of the taxpayers."[37]

Carrie Derick, assistant professor of botany at McGill, in 1891 the first woman on the faculty, and a prominent Montreal feminist, set out to stave off the sorts of dangers that McBride referred to. In 1904 she sought to interest the city of Montreal in special classes so that the feeble-minded could be prevented from contaminating normal students, and she repeatedly attempted to have "genetic" displays included in the city's annual Child Welfare Exhibitions.[38] The sort of information such displays would carry was indicated by a study Ina W. Cole carried out under Derick's direction at the Hervey Institute for Dependent Citizens. Of eighty inmates, Cole reported, twenty-six were normal, thirty-four feeble-minded, and twenty retarded. The question that such data posed, according to Derick, was not how social deprivation contributed to deviancy, but how society might free itself of the "menacing shadow" of the mental defective.[39]

Canadians did not restrict themselves to speculating on means of limiting the reproduction of the unfit; they also pondered ways of inducing the fit to reproduce. In 1911 M.M. Boyd of Bobcaygeon, Ontario, suggested in the columns of the *Journal of Heredity* that what was needed was "a system of numbering individuals of the human family." It was his contention that numbers should replace names, as the former offered a more precise designation and that over time pride in one's digit would be developed.[40] Dr. J.G. Adami, professor of pathology at McGill and delegate to the 1912 and 1921 International Congresses of Eugenics, had a similar idea. What eugenicists wanted, he avowed, was a new aristocracy. It was difficult to police or repress the breeding of the unfit, but one could at least reward the reproduction of the fit. World War One had revealed the possibilities of testing and grading recruits; it was only necessary to extend this policy to the public as a whole. Once a "human stud book" was created and "A1" men and women given preferential treatment throughout life, the quality and efficiency of the population would be assured.[41]

McGill's success in recruiting British hereditarians continued on into the interwar years. In the mid-1930's the Strathcona Professor of Zoology was the well-known English eugenicist and racist H.B. Fantham. Fantham was of the opinion that his studies of animal parasites qualified him as an expert in human genetics. It is more likely that years of teaching in South Africa provided him with the impetus to broach the issue of heredity. His views on race relations were concisely summed up in the ominous assertion: "When once chromosomes of Bantu origin get mingled in white families they cannot be bred out, as is so often popularly supposed, but will exhibit themselves in unfortunate ways and at unfortunate times throughout the ages."[42] Such statements did at least bring home to scientists like Lancelot Hogben (who also taught briefly at McGill before becoming one of Britain's leading critics of eugenics) the alarming extent to which genetics could be tainted by prejudice.[43]

Despite the presence at McGill of prominent defenders of eugenics the science did not find much favour among French Canadians. Quebec nationalists did, of course, refer constantly to "race" and "blood," but they were talking about the cultural attributes of a common language and religion.[44] They could not help but see that Francophones would necessarily do poorly when judged according to eugenic measurements. Their early indifference to eugenics could also be attributed in part to the declared hostility of the Catholic Church to all schemes aimed at interfering with reproduction. Étienne Parent, the nationalist journalist, had in the nineteenth century asserted that God determined level of intelligence and denied the claim that mental ability was inherited.[45] Moreover, in France itself even anticlerical intellectuals were never as drawn to pessimistic eugenic theories as were their English, American, and German counterparts. This could be largely attributed to France's long adherence to optimistic neo-Lamarckian beliefs in the possibility of improving humanity by changing the environment.[46]

The western provinces provided a more hospitable climate for the growth of hereditarian doctrines. Alice Ravenhill, prior to World War One, was British Columbia's most noted authority on the subject. An expert in household science and child hygiene, Ravenhill had arrived in Canada in 1910 after having played an active role in English eugenic circles. In British Columbia, both as a popular public speaker and as editor of the *Women's Institute Quarterly*, she spread the eugenic message. Perusers of the *Quarterly* in 1915 found among the recipes for bread and pickles and advice on the dressing of poultry and the canning of strawberries the bellicose declaration:

> The next enemies of the Empire will need to be even better prepared than the Germans, for the women are leaving nothing undone. Their soldiers are to be well-born, for they are making a study of eugenics. They are to be well-bred, for they have their domestic science and they are solving moral problems.[47]

The assertion of Archbishop Cody of Toronto that the state had a duty "to prevent the propagation of the feebleminded" was likewise approvingly reported by the *Quarterly* in 1916.[48]

On the Prairies eugenics found a place in university courses. "What physical defects warrant sterilization?" and "If defectives constitute 10% of the population and intellectuals 10% and the differential birth rate be 4:1, what will be the proportions of each in the third generation?" were the sorts of problems V.M. Jackson, professor of zoology, set his students at the University of Manitoba in the 1930's. His idea of comic relief was to include in his lessons a poem satirizing the handicapped.

> Two deaf mutes, a priest and the bans,
> Solemnized the prompting of glands;
>   Children seen, not heard,
>   Was the unspoken word
> And some seven now talk on their hands.[49]

It is difficult to imagine that Jackson, author of *Rat Ranching in Manitoba*, could have been competent to contribute anything meaningful to the discussion of human reproduction. But the fact that the hereditarian speculations of Jackson and so many other academics were seriously reported and pondered demonstrates that there existed a demand for scientific confirmations of natural inequality, which the universities dutifully fulfilled. As early as 1922 H.S. Patton, a University of Alberta economist, was complaining that the rise of eugenics was one symptom of the new reign of the professional experts who sought to control scientifically every aspect of life. "Whether, indeed, we shall be born at all or not is becoming a matter of eugenic research and scientific birth control."[50]

In Canada, as in Britain and America, the rise of eugenics symptomized a shift from an individualist to a collectivist biologism by those who sought to turn to their own purposes the fears raised by the threat of "degeneration." Individualism, materialism, feminism, and socialism were said to be rampant. The purported surges in venereal disease, tuberculosis, alcoholism, divorce, and labour unrest were pointed to by the nervous as evidence of the erosion of traditional values. Early Victorian science had reassured the middle class of the harmony of religious and scientific truths and the possibility of social peace and industrial harmony.[51] This vision had been momentarily lost. The sudden emergence of experimental biology and psychology with their natural concerns for hereditarian forces appeared to provide some answers. The argument was going to be increasingly made that only experts adequately schooled in the importance of heredity could possibly cope with the complex problems of rationally planning and controlling immigration, education, and a range of programs supporting the birth and rearing of healthy, fit children. In 1914 Dr. Helen MacMurchy, Ontario's leading public health expert, felt it necessary to provide an explanation of just what eugenics stood for; in 1915 she spoke of its tenets being "universally" accepted.[52]

2

Public Health and Hereditarian Concerns

The main support of eugenics, in Canada as elsewhere, came from those who believed that an understanding of heredity could improve *public* health. This in turn meant that in Canada, as in Britain and the United States, the most vocal defenders of eugenics were to be found in the ranks of the medical profession.[1] Why physicians sought to link hereditarian concerns to the public health issue and the extent to which such attempts affected social policies warrant close analysis.

In the early 1800's doctors enjoyed a relatively low status vis-à-vis other professionals. The working class either could not afford their help or shunned their services (associated as they were with the charity hospital); middle-class patients frequently had more confidence in home remedies than in the ministrations of physicians, who might well be their social and educational inferiors. By the late nineteenth century, however, the doctor-patient relationship was dramatically tilted in favour of physicians. Even in advance of therapeutic breakthroughs Canadian doctors proved themselves adept at securing what was close to a monopoly in providing medical services. At the turn of the century they simply extended their power in benefiting from the startling advances made in the biological sciences, which stressed more and more the complex processes underlying the spread of disease.[2]

Earlier, in the mid-nineteenth century, the belief in the primary importance of environmental forces on physical well-being was such that laymen and women often played the predominant roles in public health movements. Doctors appeared to have little more to contribute to such agitations when clean streets and fresh water supplies were obviously best provided by engineers and public works officials.[3] But the discovery and popularization of the germ theory at the end of the nineteenth century finally supplied doctors with the sort of evidence they needed to support their contention that only they were scientifically qualified to pronounce on the *real* causes of disease.[4] Discoveries in microbiology and pathology, they argued, provided the basis for accurate diagnosis and prognosis, which both individuals and the state could only ignore at their peril. The laity reluctantly felt it had to give ground to medical professionals when presented with evidence that even the clean and apparently healthy citizen could harbour deadly microbes.

The contention made by eugenicists that many complaints were, as well, hereditary and thus impervious to environmental influence was seen by some doctors as having the potential of further strengthening the power of the medical profession. It is thus not surprising that doctors provided the single largest group of eugenic advocates.[5] The interest they took in the forces of heredity was as much fueled by preoccupations with professional power as by disinterested scientific curiosity. Of course, not all medical practitioners were attracted to the eugenic cause. Probably there were as many who were more concerned that all the talk about innate roots of disease implied that medicine was helpless before the forces of heredity. Others, such as Dr. J.G. Adami, who worried that medicine would be stripped by eugenicists of its moralizing message, felt obliged to combat the view "that the race does not directly suffer from the follies of individuals."[6] Even most outright eugenicists were too sophisticated simply to dismiss the need for continued improvements in living conditions. But eugenicists would be the most strenuous defenders of the notion, supported by nearly all doctors, that there were limits to what could be accomplished by social improvements and that only they were in a position to judge the relative impact on public health of environmental and hereditary forces.

If doctors came to play an ever more important role in social planning, it was not simply due to their own efforts. They were increasingly turned to by those in authority who hoped that the medical sciences could provide more efficient methods of social management. That the state required such new methods seemed to be demonstrated by the threats posed by urbanization, industrialization, declining Anglo-Saxon fertility, and massive foreign immigration. Just as industry was acknowledging the benefits of scientific studies, so, too, the state was beginning to accept the need of employing professionals to deal with threatening social problems.[7] World War One offered doctors a golden opportunity to show the variety of ways in which they could make themselves useful to government in providing a healthy, disciplined military; they came out of the experience confident that in the future they would enjoy positions of leadership in civilian society.[8]

Throughout the Western world the early twentieth century witnessed the triumph of medical authority and a corresponding rise in the social and political power of the doctor. In Canada the medical "expert" who would play an increasingly powerful role in public health reform and government service was personified by four doctors preoccupied by hereditary defect – Peter H. Bryce, Charles Hastings, Charles Kirke Clarke, and Helen MacMurchy. In succeeding chapters on the subjects of immigration and mental testing we will return to Bryce, Hastings, and Clarke. For the purposes of investigating the links of eugenics and public health, this chapter will focus on the career of MacMurchy.

Helen MacMurchy probably did more than any other individual in Canada in the first third of the twentieth century to alert the public to the dangers posed to public health. She played a particularly important role in focusing attention on three crucial issues – infant mortality, maternal mortality, and feeble-mindedness. In each case her concern was motivated more by the threat disease posed the "race" than by empathy for the individual. Her humanitarianism – manifested in her support for a number of badly needed public health reforms – was always held in check by her conviction that innate biological inequality could never be overcome. There came a point, in her view, where doctors simply had to accept the fact that individuals were responsible for their own fates.

MacMurchy was clearly convinced of her own superiority, an opinion based on her remarkable success in winning recognition in the two traditionally male-dominated realms of medicine and the civil service. She was a member of the second generation of Canadian women doctors, attending the Women's Medical College and then the University of Toronto, where she earned her M.D. in 1901. She was the first woman in the Department of Obstetrics and Gynaecology at Toronto General Hospital, with a cross-appointment as lecturer at the university, and also the first woman to be accepted by the Johns Hopkins University medical school for post-graduate study.[9]

After a short stint of private practice, MacMurchy moved into the public service, working for the Ontario government from 1906 to 1919 and then for the federal government's Department of Health from 1920 to 1934. She served as medical inspector for the Toronto schools from 1910 to 1911 but was forced to resign because of clashes with the educational authorities, and between 1906 and 1916 she was the inspector of the feeble-minded in Ontario. In 1914 she also served as first inspector of auxiliary classes, established by the government in response to her proddings. Appointed as the first chief of the Division of Maternal and Child Welfare in the newly established Department of Health in 1920, she held the position until her retirement in 1934.[10]

In each of her areas of interest MacMurchy more than balanced her concern for the individual with her preoccupation with the overarching needs of the "race." While not unaware of the impact environment had on physical and mental health, she inevitably reverted back to the argument of "individual inadequacy" to explain the main threats to public health. Society was not responsible for the nation's ills; individuals were. The answers she offered for each problem were at bottom always the same. First, certain minimal standards of public health were to be established. Second, the "well-intentioned but ignorant" were to be instructed by doctors on the rules of hygiene and sent on their way. The issue of whether or not social conditions might make it impossible to follow such advice was usually skirted. Third, the "vicious or hopelessly deficient" – those incapable of following instructions – were to be segregated and institutionalized.

In turning to MacMurchy's work on infant mortality one is presented with a good example of the ways she sought to sort out social and individual responsibilities for ill health. Toronto had an appallingly high infant mortality rate that varied between 140 and 180 deaths per thousand infants in the decade prior to the First World War.[11] The rate in a progressively administered city such as Rochester, New York, was 50 per cent lower. MacMurchy showed real anger that so many Canadian babies went to an early grave. But in referring to the "infant soldier" who died in his first battle, she made it clear that she was more concerned by the loss suffered by the nation rather than that suffered by the individual family.[12] Appointed to investigate the situation by her friend William J. Hanna, the Ontario Provincial Secretary, MacMurchy produced reports on provincial infant deaths in 1910, 1911, and 1912.[13]

MacMurchy concluded that social inequalities were reflected in differential mortality rates: "The destruction of the poor is their poverty. The rich baby lives, the poor baby dies."[14] She focused particular attention on the failure of local governments to guarantee healthy supplies of milk that could have attenuated the scourges of diarrhea and enteritis.[15] But after cataloguing the shortcomings of the social system that gave rise to a high infant mortality rate, she cruelly proceeded to blame the victims. It was, she argued, the ignorance of mothers that sustained the high death rate. "Poverty, of course, is not a simple but a complex condition. It probably means poor health, inefficiency, lack of energy, less than average intelligence or force in some way, not enough imagination to see the importance of details."[16]

What was needed was instruction of women: "we teach reading, and we leave parenthood to come by chance. It does not so come."[17] The medical expert, according to MacMurchy, had to save the poor from themselves and in particular instruct women on the nature of their "natural" role. Breastfeeding was ordered while women's work outside the home was condemned.

Blaming "ignorant mothers" for infant deaths was part of MacMurchy's message that doctors had to insist that women's first duty was to remain in the home. For the mother to work or to shirk the nursing of her baby was in effect to "sign its death warrant."[18] "Where the mother works, the baby dies. Nothing can replace maternal care."[19] There was a certain irony in such pronouncements. One of the architects of the bureaucratic state was informing her sisters that despite the fact that almost every other aspect of life was becoming institutionalized, the rearing of children was to remain confined to individual households. "It has been shown again and again, and cannot be emphasized too much, that the institution for a baby is a fatal failure compared with a home. We should set our faces against institutions in Canada except for the very few Canadians, insane, feeble-minded, chronic criminals etc. who cannot make good outside an institution."[20] This, of course, meant that children's deaths would inevitably be attributed to their mothers' failures, not society's.

Just how much help even the expert could provide was a moot point. There were some, MacMurchy argued, who were beyond assistance. "The efficient person, the adequate and strong character, the person of principle and affection, will succeed where the weakling, the unemployable, untidy, unthrifty, good for nothing will never succeed."[21]

MacMurchy's interpretation of the problem of maternal mortality paralleled in a number of ways her analysis of infant mortality.[22] With the provision of improved milk supplies infant deaths declined quite dramatically after 1914, but in the first third of the twentieth century deaths of mothers in childbirth remained more or less constant at a rate of about 5.5 per 1,000.[23] This was surprising since families were smaller, women were having fewer pregnancies, and mothers were younger. Canada's maternal mortality rate was high, 20 per cent higher than Britain's and about twice that of the Scandinavian countries.[24] In the 1920's this meant that about twenty-four mothers died each week; the numbers began to edge upward even more in the early years of the depression.

In 1923 MacMurchy, as head of the Maternal and Child Welfare Division of the Department of Health, produced a first report on the situation in Canada. As a eugenicist her starting assumption was that the nation needed healthy children and, therefore, to save babies one had to start by saving their mothers.[25] MacMurchy's initial findings prompted the Canadian Medical Association to call for a national inquiry, which MacMurchy proceeded to provide.[26] The report, based on statistics garnered between 1925 and 1926, finally appeared in 1928 entitled *Maternal Mortality in Canada*.

MacMurchy's study was extremely important in focusing public attention on the tragic loss of mothers' lives due to puerperal sepsis, hemorrhage, toxemias, and other accidents of childbirth.[27] More problematical were her opinions on why so many women were dying. MacMurchy pretended that her report was simply providing statistical data and that it was up to others to interpret her findings.[28] In fact, she clearly communicated her views throughout her assessment. Maternal deaths, according to her, primarily resulted from a lack of medical care. Women were either ignorantly favouring the inadequate services of midwives or were cut off by distance or lack of economic resources from the services of doctors. Particularly at risk were rural women and members of ethnic minorities. Such women were chided by Mac-Murchy for their ignorance, indifference, and apathy. She called on doctors to take a more serious interest in the problem, and the state was asked to provided greater resources. What was necessary, asserted MacMurchy, was the extended medicalization of childbirth from pre-natal clinics to hospitalization of labour to follow-up postnatal care.[29]

Many doctors thought birth too mundane a process to take very seriously, but MacMurchy's interventionist message naturally won the support of the "progressives" in the profession. Dr. W.B. Hendry, professor of obstetrics and gynaecology at the University of Toronto, criticized those content to leave things to nature. Women, he insisted, had to be taught to rely on their doctor.[30] Dr. W. Benge Atlee made the same argument in an article entitled "Are Women Sheep?"[31] He called on women to organize to demand "better obstetrical care on the part of their medical attendants" in order to survive the "menace of maternity."[32] Women, continued Atlee, having confided to males the important decision-making tasks, should then retreat to their primary role of childbearing and rearing. "Every realist will concede that so long as the home is to remain the ideal of this civilization, woman's part in the communal life must be different from man's. It is the man's place to build and subsidize the home; the woman's place to rear the young in it."[33]

MacMurchy's message was also strongly supported by the National Council of Women. The women's movement, which in the late nineteenth century had been very supportive of midwives, in the post-

World War One period deferred almost completely to the male-dominated medical profession. Doctors were thus proving successful in
convincing women that maternity was a painful and menacing experience that could only be survived by relying on medical supervision.

A careful reading of the maternal death rate figures can lead,
however, to conclusions opposite to those arrived at by MacMurchy.
The first is that the high rate of puerperal septicemia suggests that there
was too much rather than too little instrumental interference by doctors
in childbirth cases. Such conclusions were supported by the figures,
which showed that home births were safer than hospital births and the
rural death rate lower than the urban.[34] Dr. E.W. Montgomery revealed
in a study of the maternal deaths in Manitoba between 1921 and 1927
that the rate in hospitals was 8.6 per 1,000 as compared to a rate of 2.6
per 1,000 women outside hospitals.[35] The more that medical care was
available, the greater the interference and the higher the mortality rate.
As the figures for the 1930's indicated, hospitalization in and of itself
clearly was not the best way to lower the maternal mortality rate. It
was, however, a good way to ensure the centralization and monopoli-
zation of medical care by physicians; it accordingly received their
active support.

A second conclusion emerging from the data is that MacMurchy
clearly downplayed the social and economic causes of maternal mortality. She did not, for example, give enough attention to the fact that
toxemia was associated with malnutrition and poverty. In fact, over
half of the women who died in MacMurchy's sample were destitute or
suffering from economically related complaints.[36] Even if prenatal
care had been available they would have had neither the time nor the
money to take advantage of it.

The third conclusion is that in her discussion of maternal mortality
MacMurchy cloaked the impact of abortion. This was not due to her
ignorance of the issue. In a 1910 article about the "unfit mother," whom
MacMurchy presented as thinking more of bridge games and automo-
biles than childbearing, she had broached the subject of "the crime
against the unborn . . . . There is the husband who never thinks of the
other person's point of view, till the poor wife flies for some help and
consideration to the dispensary or the doctor, or to the abortionist."[37]
But MacMurchy said little of the impact of abortion on maternal death
rates.[38] J. Wyllie noted in a 1933 article in the *Canadian Public Health
Journal* that there was reason to believe that self-induced abortions
were keeping the maternal mortality rate high.[39] In 1934 Drs. Jackson
and Jeffries confirmed these suspicions by publishing their findings
that in Manitoba between 1928 and 1932 17.1 per cent of maternal

deaths were due to abortion.[40] Drs. Phair and Sellers reported that in Ontario the rate of abortion-related deaths was 14 per cent.[41]

The significance of bungled abortions resulting in deaths was further highlighted by the discovery that the maternal death rate of single women was 40 to 100 per cent higher than that of the married. In 1935 a study of a special committee of the Division of Maternal and Child Hygiene estimated that from one in five to one in seven of all pregnancies were being terminated.[42] Obviously, the medicalization of childbirth was not going to help women who were actively seeking to *avoid* giving birth. What they needed was contraceptive information or access to safe abortion. MacMurchy gave the issue of induction of miscarriage short shrift because for both moral and professional reasons she was clearly hostile to the idea that social and legal reforms would ultimately be required to end maternal deaths.[43]

MacMurchy chose to present maternal mortality as a simple medical problem that could be solved by increasing the amount of medical intervention in childbirth. A reappraisal of the relevant data suggests, however, that if anything medical interventionism was *part* of the problem. In supporting a vast educational campaign aimed at indoctrinating Canadians with the belief that only a reliance on doctors could lower death rates, she was thus deflecting attention from the social, legal, and economic causes of maternal mortality. When maternal mortality rates did drop in the 1940's it was a result not simply of changes in obstetrical care but of marked improvements in socio-economic conditions.[44]

MacMurchy's penchant for championing the pretensions of the medical profession can be traced back to her early experiences in the public health service. She first won notoriety by her clashes with the Toronto school board. Shortly after her appointment in Toronto as medical inspector of the schools in 1910, she publicly attacked the existing system as a "farce."[45] It was ridiculous, she argued, for medical personnel to be directed in their duties by lay officials. The struggle over school inspection was important for three reasons. First, it was a key part of the struggle by doctors for political power and recognition. MacMurchy argued that the independence of the medical inspectors was essential so that, as professionals, they (like the lawyers hired by the school board) could be free to pursue their legitimate concerns.[46] Medical personnel could then turn their full attention to the welfare not only of the school but of the larger community. The school nurse was presented by Florence Huestis, a fervant supporter of MacMurchy, as "the teacher of the parents, the pupils, the teachers, and the family in applied practical hygiene."[47] MacMurchy returned again and again to this key theme – the need for the patient and the general community to have "faith" in the doctor. "The school doctor *knows*," wrote MacMurchy.[48] The professional demanded that the non-professionals trust their betters.

School medical inspection was important for a second reason – it promised to provide a healthier and more orderly working class under the surveillance of scientific observers. This movement in pursuit of greater social efficiency had begun in Europe in the mid-nineteenth century and in the 1890's spread to Britain and America. In 1906 Montreal was the first Canadian city to adopt the measure.[49] As a 1907 article by Dr. A.P. Knight, professor of physiology at Queen's University, made clear, great hopes were held out that such inspections would play a central role in the growth of preventive medicine. He cited Herbert Spencer's line, "People are beginning to see that the first requisite to success in life is to be a good animal" and Francis Galton's affirmation that "A collection of living magnates in various branches of intellectual achievements is always a feast to my eyes, being as they are, such massive, vigorous, capable animals."[50] What now was needed, according to Knight, was "to see to it that our boys and girls get as adequate instruction in the laws of health as our farmers get in the rearing of pigs and cattle." Given his metaphorical bent, he made his suggestion for annual September examinations sound very much like a fall roundup. "When a child deviates much from the normal, the parents should be seen by the medical inspector, and suggestions should be made for remedying the defects that have been observed."[51]

The sort of preventive measures envisaged by Knight and MacMurchy were as much educational as medical. They accused lay officials of "ignorance or callous indifference" and parents of "ignorance" in the care and feeding of their children. But they promised that in return for acceptance of medical dictates great rewards could be reaped. Dr. Charles Hastings, the Toronto medical health officer, similarly asserted that medical intervention in home life was well warranted. "Psychologists assure us that mental, moral and physical degeneration go hand in hand. This is well attested by observations made in the children's courts in the various cities. Insufficient and improper feeding, badly ventilated homes, environments of filth and dirt constitute the very hot-beds in which criminals are bred."[52]

Just how far medical inspectors should be permitted to go in such policing of private households was questioned by some doctors. In 1913 members of the Toronto Academy of Medicine protested against the actions of Commissioner Star of the Juvenile Court, who was apparently levying fines against parents who did not comply with the orders of nurses and medical inspectors to have their children's tonsils and adenoids removed. Dr. A.W. Young argued that such oppressive interference could only have the effect of creating a popular backlash against the medical profession. In response, Florence Huestis and Dr. Margaret Patterson (later to be first magistrate of Toronto's Women's Court) asserted that it was perfectly legitimate for medical authority to be supported by the full weight of the law.[53]

The third reason advanced by MacMurchy to justify school inspection was that it would permit the separation of the "normal" pupils from the "abnormal."[54] The parents of the former would receive advice on nutrition and clothing. As for the latter, medical inspectors could, according to Knight, "point out minor defects in the mind and body and recommend treatment where the children do not deviate too far from the normal; but in graver cases, medical inspection can do a great deal at least for society, though not for the individual. It can point out the youthful pauper, insane, or criminal, and indicate what should be done with them in order to lessen their baneful influence in the community."[55] MacMurchy and Huestis were convinced that too many deviants were "at large."[56] They thereby acknowledged that medical examination and mental testing were aimed more at the labelling and segregating of the handicapped than at providing for their special needs.[57]

This fear of the feeble-minded was based on the assumption made by a large number of turn-of-the-century commentators that mental deficiency was a cause of a host of social ills.[58] For the middle class, of course, it was a comforting notion to think that poverty and criminality were best attributed to individual weaknesses rather than to the structural flaws of the economy. This explains why so many otherwise intelligent humanitarians supported the labelling, the segregation, and ultimately the sterilization of those they designated subnormal.

The National Council of Women was the first organized group to take up the campaign for the more effective segregation of the feeble-minded.[59] The early Canadian women's movement was, as a number of historians have noted, frequently preoccupied by the issues of race regeneration and moral purity.[60] It was a "progressive" movement concerned by what it took to be the multiplication of unhealthy families. Its middle-class Anglo-Saxon members tended to interest themselves in medicine, social Darwinism, positivism, and elitist centralization that appeared to offer the respectable some promise of protection from the social threats of the day. These women supported a variety of interventionist policies manifested in schools, hospitals, and asylums. Although the more liberal reformers within their ranks tried to spotlight environmental causes of social misery, the eugenic-minded clearly gained ground in the first decades of the twentieth century. Constance Hamilton, the leading conservative feminist, demanded that alcoholic mothers be prevented from filling "cradles with degenerate babies."[61] Carrie Derick of McGill, later in her career a professor of evolution and genetics, attacked as nonsense the idea that social legislation could improve the degenerate.[62] Mrs. M.K. Stead pointed out that "Contagious diseases have long been controlled by legislation, but this more deadly, transmittable disease of feeblemindedness is still uncontrolled."[63] The attitude of the NCW toward the feeble-minded was summed up in 1901 at its eighth annual meeting:

> Left to yourself you are not only useless, but mischievous. I have tried punishing, curing, reforming you, as the case may be: and I have failed. You are an uncurable, a degenerate, a being unfit for free, social life. Henceforth I shall care for you, I will feed and clothe you, and give you a reasonably comfortable life. In return you will do the work I set for you and you will abstain from interfering with your neighbour to his detriment. One other thing you will abstain from, – you will no longer pro-create your kind; you must be the last member of your feeble and degenerate family.[64]

The National Council of Women provided MacMurchy with regular support, and other groups, such as the Social and Moral Reform League and the YWCA, also interested themselves in the feeble-minded. Partly as a result of such pressure the Ontario government sent MacMurchy in 1905 to meet with the British Royal Commission on Mental Defectives and subsequently received her report on the extent of feeble-mindedness in the province.[65]

During the nineteenth century, asylums had been built to house the mentally ill who were considered curable, but next to nothing had been done for the mentally retarded, who were considered beyond remedy. The shift of attention toward the needs of the retarded was in part a direct result of their being "discovered" by teachers as mass education was made compulsory.[66] One of the unexpected consequences of the greater attention given to the care and rearing of children in the early twentieth century was the establishment of arbitrary norms of intellectual achievement. Those who did not meet them were increasingly viewed not simply as unfortunate but as a real "menace" to the normal.[67] M.C. Maclean of the Educational Division of the Dominion Bureau of Statistics cautioned that adverse social and economic conditions accounted for most aspects of retardation, but the hereditarians' stress on innate mental deficiency proved a far simpler and more easily understandable explanation, complementing as it did the liberal ideology of self-help.[68]

MacMurchy's annual reports on feeble-mindedness between 1907 and 1918 did much to impress upon medical and political leaders the extent of mental deficiency. Her 1920 popular account, *The Almosts: A Study of the Feeble-Minded*, brought home to vast numbers of lay readers the problems posed society by the subnormal. MacMurchy coloured both types of reportage with a curious mixture of compassion and cold-heartedness.

On the positive side MacMurchy presented herself and all like-minded medical professionals as deeply moved by the plight of the mentally deficient. These affectionate, good-natured, child-like beings could, she argued, prove to be productive workers if patiently trained. What they most needed were kind guides capable of discerning their strengths and limitations. It followed, she argued, that "if the mentally defective are cared for and sheltered from childhood up, their tastes remain the simple and innocent tastes of childhood."[69] Such care necessitated the creation of services that would be "preventive, progressive, and educational rather than penal or merely custodial in character."[70] Unthinking charity, asserted MacMurchy, had done nothing in the past to eradicate defectiveness; to get to the roots of the problem required a combination of the insights of business, science, and Christianity.

On the negative side, while arguing that the subnormal deserved "justice and a fair chance," MacMurchy concluded that they simply could not be treated like the normal. "It is the age of true democracy," she argued, "that will not only give every one justice, but will redeem the waste products of humanity and give the mental defective all the chance he needs to develop his gifts and all the protection he needs to keep away from him evils and temptations that he never will be grown-up enough to resist, and that society cannot afford to let him fall a victim to."[71] Shorn of its flowery language, this statement simply asserted that the feeble-minded had to be deprived of their freedom.

Such institutionalization cost money. But MacMurchy repeatedly protested that in calling for closer supervision of the feeble-minded the concerns for efficiency and economy were uppermost in her mind. Segregation in institutions ultimately paid for itself, she argued, because even greater expenses would be faced if the feeble-minded roamed free. Their education in public schools was "time, strength, and money wasted."[72] Their dissolute private lives resulted in illegitimacy and the spread of venereal disease. Once they acquired a taste for "evil things" they were led into lives of crime and prostitution. Unable to work, they burdened the tax roles and clogged the hospitals, industrial schools, and reformatories. Although the mental defectives accounted for only three to five per 1,000 of the population they were responsible, asserted MacMurchy with dubious statistical precision, for up to 60 per cent of its alcoholics, 66 per cent of its juvenile delinquents, 50 per cent of its unmarried mothers, and 29 to 97 per cent of its prostitutes! She declared that she shared the opinion of an American doctor that "every mental defective is a potential criminal."[73] In short, a relatively small minority was the source of most of society's woes.[74]

The hostility to feeble-mindedness was obviously based more on moral than on medical preoccupations. But the two issues were inextricably intertwined in the minds of most early twentieth-century commentators.[75] MacMurchy, for example, believed that feeble-mindedness was a great cause of venereal disease, illegitimacy, and infant mortality. Others believed that venereal disease created feeble-mindedness. Such eugenic preoccupations were clearly at play in the work of the Canadian National Council for Combating Venereal Disease, an organization directed from Toronto by Dr. Gordon Bates.[76] Such was the association of feeble-mindedness with venereal disease that MacMurchy could confidently assert in 1918 that "the social reformer, whether interested . . . in the cure of the so-called Social Evil, or in Venereal Disease knows that it is the cause, not the symptoms that we should attack, and no one cause of these great evils can be more completely proved than Mental Defect. It is not the only cause, but no other single cause is a greater obstruction to every effort towards Social Reform."[77]

Institutionalization offered double benefits. It prevented the feeble-minded from harassing society; even more importantly, it prevented them from reproducing. This desire to prevent the reproduction of the subnormal "tribe" was based on MacMurchy's eugenic assumption that mental deficiency was an inherited, "predictable" affliction. MacMurchy did not ignore the impact environmental forces might have in contributing to mental deficiency, but she placed primary responsibility on hereditary factors. "Heredity," she stated in her 1915 report, "is the cause in about eighty per cent or more of all cases."[78] She cited a Maryland official to the effect that, "It is impossible to calculate what even one feeble-minded woman may cost the public, when her vast possibilities for evil as a producer of paupers and criminals, through an endless line of descendants are considered."[79] Equally worrying to MacMurchy was the report of Pennsylvania investigators that the "clans" of social misfits had on average seven children per family while the normal had only three.[80] Closer to home, Professor A.P. Knight of

Queen's University titillated his readers with a secondhand account of the infamous Jukes family.[81] This New York dynasty in the course of seventy-five years, according to the feverish calculations of Richard Dugdale, had cost the community over a million dollars in public expenses and untold amounts of crime and pauperism. Concerns for "humanity and pity and business" demanded, according to Mac-Murchy, that such depredations be ended.[82] "We must not permit the feeble-minded to be mothers of the next generation," she insisted.[83] Ontario doctors, she informed the province's political leaders, "advise and beseech us to stop allowing mental defectives to produce children."[84]

This preoccupation with the feeble-minded swept the country. In Nova Scotia a League for the Care and Protection of Feebleminded Persons reported having fifty local branches by 1912.[85] In Manitoba the 1913 Conference of Charities and Corrections devoted much of its attention to the issue. Three years later J.S. Woodsworth produced a series of articles on mental defectives for the *Winnipeg Free Press* that purportedly resulted from his investigations for the Bureau of Social Research.[86] In fact, much of the material was taken straight out of MacMurchy's reports. In British Columbia in 1910 Dr. H.E. Young, secretary of the provincial board of health, established special classes for the retarded in the Vancouver school system.[87] In Ontario, due to MacMurchy's efforts, a deputation representing 200 municipalities petitioned in February of 1913 for improved inspection and examination of immigrants, recording of the numbers of the provincial mental defectives, greater care in the issuance of marriage certificates, prevention of the marriage of the feeble-minded, and the building of institutions and creation of training schools for their care.[88] In response the Ontario government passed in April a bill for the provision of auxiliary classes of which MacMurchy was to be the inspector.[89] At the same time Dr. C.K. Clarke in Toronto began to receive at the Social Service Clinic young people referred to him for psychiatric examination by Commissioner Boyd of the juvenile court.[90]

In 1914 and again in 1918 the *Public Health Journal* devoted special issues to mental health. Among the contributors, Dr. Elizabeth Shortt of the National Council of Women bewailed the heavy financial burden imposed by the subnormal, Lucy M. Brooking of Toronto's Alexandra Industrial School provided an account of the loose morals of female defectives, Dr. C.K. Clarke pointed to feeble-mindedness as the foundation of criminality, and Dr. Clarence Hincks called for the employment of the newly devised intelligence tests.[91]

Orchestrating this campaign was MacMurchy, who presented herself as a general in the "righteous war" against mental defectiveness.[92] By 1914 she was describing the sorts of "big plans" with which she sought to remove this "destructive social force" as "eugenic" in nature.[93] The mental defective, argued MacMurchy, was a poison in the body politic, sapping its energy and undermining its efficiency.

In 1908 MacMurchy optimistically asserted that 80 per cent of feeble-mindedness could be eliminated within a generation by segregation, but the ultimate weapon in this battle was sterilization of the feeble-minded.[94] Arguing that the financial burdens of institutionalization would soon become crushing, she suggested that only by sterilization could the prevention of the reproduction of the mentally deficient be economically achieved. MacMurchy was not alone. Dr. A.B. Atherton of Fredericton, although he blamed urban life, over-education of women, trashy novels, and sexual stimulation as partly responsible for degeneracy, concurred that defectives could not be allowed to breed.[95] R.W. Bruce Smith, Provincial Inspector of Hospitals and Public Charities, informed the 1907 Ontario Medical Association that notable British authorities such as Sir James Barr and Dr. Reid Rentoul agreed that "asexualization" could effectively end the propagation of tramps, prostitutes, unwed mothers, and perverts.[96] Dr. F. McKelvey Bell of Ottawa informed the readers of *Queen's Quarterly* that Dr. Lydston of Chicago provided evidence of the efficacy of "asexualization." Bell continued:

> Prevention is always better than cure. Institutions which will destroy the disease in its infancy are next in order of importance. Degeneracy underlies to a greater or lesser extent all social disease, therefore it must be our first aim to stamp out the degenerate. To do this we must begin at the beginning, i.e., with the control of marriage amongst criminals, degenerates and lunatics, in order that they shall not be able to procreate their kind.[97]

MacMurchy, however, was the best-known Canadian defender of the argument that sterilization was "perhaps better" than segregation as a way of dealing with the "menace" of feeble-mindedness and that its benefits should also be applied to the insane and the "chronic criminal."[98]

In 1910 the British American Medical Association heard a report on sterilization bills passed in Indiana and California. In Ontario a similar bill was presented to the legislature in 1912 by Dr. John Godfrey, member for West York. The proposed legislation would have allowed a board of surgeons to examine asylum inmates and "to perform operations which would prevent the procreation of children by those who might thus be declared unfit for marriage."[99] The *Canadian Law Journal*, in reporting the introduction of the bill, suggested that it have wider application, "as there are other institutions, such as havens, or refuges for fallen women, which have to harbour such characters, who should be subject to the same law as would apply to inmates of provincial institutions for the care of the insane, feeble-minded and epileptic."[100]

This fear of the breeding powers of the feeble-minded, initially sparked by Anglo-Saxon concerns about their own flagging fertility as contrasted to that of French Canadians, foreign migrants, and the subnormal, was heightened by the losses occasioned by World War One. The war seemed to run directly counter to the Darwinian law concerning the elimination of the unfit. The "best" young Canadians, according to English-Canadian writers, were going to their deaths in Flanders while the "worse" languished and reproduced at home.[101] It was thus not surprising that demands for their restriction should be made.[102] The conclusion to the 1917 report on *The Prevalence of Venereal Disease in Canada* included the request by William Goldie, professor of clinical medicine at the University of Toronto, for "supervision" of mental defectives. "It is from this class that the majority of prostitutes and moral perverts are recruited. This class should either become wards of the state, or be rendered innocuous by reverting to the logical but extreme measure of unsexing."[103]

It clearly took some time, however, before public opinion was won over to such measures. Dr. Godfrey's 1912 bill was withdrawn. Dr. A.P. Reid, the leading Nova Scotia public health officer, lamented in 1913 that most people would not discuss the most effective way of dealing with the "incubus" of mental defect.[104] J.S. Woodsworth noted in a 1916 article, "Sterilization has been proposed. But general sentiment is so strong against such a radical measure that its adoption is not practicable."[105] James Miller, head of the pathological laboratory at Queen's University, described the eugenicists of 1922 as wishing to "produce a healthy race by breeding from only healthy stock. There is much in this from the point of view of prevention of maternity in the mentally defective woman, in some cases by sterilization. But any wholesale legal control of marriage from this point of view will be disastrous."[106]

Even the reformers' plans for ever greater segregation of the feeble-minded could not be pushed too far, given the reluctance of all governments to embark on innovative policies and their even greater distaste for financing expensive new institutions. Municipal and provincial governments spent much of their energies accusing each other of refusing to accept their responsibilities in the care of the handicapped. MacMurchy's frustration with the slowness of reform in Ontario was such that in 1916 she attacked the provincial government for its timidity. She was supported by Dr. C.K. Clarke, who "castigated the government's policies for promoting 'the survival of the unfittest' and in particular . . . efforts to keep families together as promoting the 'raising up of families of imbeciles.' "[107]

MacMurchy was obviously not alone in turning to eugenics to explain the source of many of the public health problems plaguing Canada in the first third of the twentieth century. She was, however, the one person most responsible for winning for hereditarian concerns a central place on the agenda of the public health movement. Her writings on infant mortality, maternal mortality, and feeble-mindedness were all pervaded to a greater or lesser extent with the belief that personal inadequacies underlay much of the ill health of the nation. Her appointment in 1920 as the first chief of the federal Department of Health's Maternal and Child Welfare Division meant that she could continue to preach to Canadians on their need, first, to have an unquestioning faith in the directives of their doctors, and, second, to accept as given the notion that individual physical and mental deficiencies were the basis of most cases of disease.[108] She probably did more than any other doctor of her time to try to convince the Canadian public that a host of social problems were in fact medical issues that only physicians could competently deal with. She personified the medical profession's attempt to inculcate the idea that many diseases had individualistic and biological – not social – causes.[109]

After World War One the campaign for the sterilization of the feeble-minded was increasingly dominated by doctors who actually had some expertise in mental testing, psychiatry, or genetics. In her last book, *Sterilization? Birth Control? A Book for Family Welfare and Safety* (1934), MacMurchy continued to call for the forcible control of the reproduction of the feeble-minded. She argued once more that until sterilization was instituted good citizens would pay through their taxes for the "lawlessness, dependency, ill-health and incapacity" of the subnormal.[110] The availability of contraception, she continued, would in no way diminish the breeding of the handicapped. "There is a dead weight of unfitness for community and family life which costs us much in money and more in national prosperity and happiness. Can we expect the defective among us, who have the least capacity for self control, to rule one of the strongest urges of life?"[111]

Given her belief that the mentally deficient were reproducing at a prodigious rate, it followed that MacMurchy viewed the employment of family planning methods by the intelligent as socially disastrous. She thus carried on into the 1930's the pre-World War One preoccupation with "race suicide." She first sought to frighten her readers by asserting happily that contraceptives were not in any event foolproof: "no satisfactory, far less any ideal method is known."[112] She aimed as well to "medicalize" the whole issue of birth control by referring to users as "patients" who had to turn to doctors for advice. "It should not be undertaken or carried on except for clear, definite and grave reasons of a medical nature and under medical advice."[113] It clearly rankled her that neither of the world's most famous birth-controllers – Marie Stopes and Margaret Sanger – was a doctor. If birth control clinics had to be tolerated, they should "be organized in connection with hospitals and should conform to the ideals of hospital practice and of the medical profession."[114] But in fact she made it clear that she could not envisage how such a reconciliation could ever be made; birth control was wrong. "It is unnatural. It is contrary to one's higher instincts. It is repugnant to a member of the medical profession whose work and whose desire is to promote health and happiness."[115] Having established her right to pontificate on the lives of the deviant, MacMurchy was thus led to assert her right to dictate the reproductive duties of the normal.

3

Stemming the Flood
of Defective Aliens

At the 1914 Social Service Congress of Canada conference Helen MacMurchy rose to declare that the problem of defective children could only be solved if special education and medical inspection were complemented by restriction of immigration. "It is well known to every intelligent Canadian," she asserted, "that the number of recent immigrants who drift into institutions for the neuropathic, the feeble-minded and the insane is very great."[1] The same sentiments were expressed at the Congress's 1924 meeting, where it was asked:

> What are the eugenic effects of bringing in thousands of boys and girls, a considerable proportion of whom have sprung from stock which, whatever else may be said of it, was not able to hold its own in the stern competition in the motherland?

Such an influx, came the response, added to "our national burden of pauperism, vice, crime and insanity."[2]

For those Canadians preoccupied in the first decades of the twentieth century by what they chose to call "racial degeneration," there appeared to be two obvious threats: the first was the reproduction *in* Canada of the unfit; the second was the immigration *to* Canada of the unfit. Helen MacMurchy, as we have seen in the preceding chapter, was instrumental in raising the spectre of hordes of the unfit being born in Canada, but equally preoccupying to her and others was the prospect of the nation being swamped by waves of degenerate immigrants.

To put such concerns in context it has to be recalled that Canada was, in the first decades of the twentieth century, welcoming millions of immigrants. This necessarily frightened many Anglo-Saxons. Few non-British migrants came to Canada for most of the nineteenth century due to their preference for the United States. Indeed, so many native-born Canadians were lured south that the country's population scarcely grew. But in the 1890's the closing of the American frontier, the upturn in the Canadian economy, the completion of the transcontinental railway, and the launching of an aggressive immigration campaign by Laurier's Liberal government had dramatic results. Between 1896 and 1914 three million immigrants came to Canada. In the single decade between 1901 and 1911 the population jumped 43 per cent in what had become the world's fastest growing country. In 1913 alone over 400,000 immigrants arrived. What preoccupied their hosts was not so much the astonishing numbers as the fact that many (about 800,000 in the first decade of the twentieth century) came from the non-Anglo-Saxon world.[3]

In English-speaking Canada the arrival of newcomers fostered an ideology of "Canadianization" or what might more accurately be described as the goal of assimilating newcomers into Anglo-conformity. English Canadians assumed that white Anglo-Saxons were racially superior and immigrants were welcomed according to the degree to which they approached this ideal.[4] British and Americans were viewed as the most desirable, next northern and western Europeans, after them the central and eastern Europeans (including the Jews), and last of all the Asians and blacks. Thus one found in an eminently respectable history such as Sir G. Arthur Doughty and Adam Shortt's *Canada and Its Provinces* (1914-17) the Galicians presented as mentally slow; the Italians as devoid of shame; the Turks, Armenians, and Syrians as undesirable; the Greeks, Macedonians, and Bulgarians as liars; the Chinese as addicted to opium and gambling; and the arrival of Jews and Negroes as "entirely unsolicited."[5] James S. Woodsworth, the Social Gospeller and future founder of the CCF, followed a similar line of categorization (based on his reading of eugenics) when describing his mission work among the immigrants of pre-World War One Winnipeg. He contrasted the Scandinavians and Icelanders ("clean-bodied" and "serious-minded as a race") to the Slavs and Galicians ("addicted to drunken sprees" and "animalized").[6]

The government, however, was far more pragmatic in its view of immigrants' potential. Sir Clifford Sifton, who became Minister of the Interior in 1896, whatever his personal prejudices, was intent on having Canadian immigration agents ship out to Canada the thousands of central and eastern Europeans who seemed most willing and able to face the rigours of prairie winters.[7] Similarly, in British Columbia the railway companies brought in cheap and plentiful Chinese and Sikh labour. The practical political and economic concerns of the federal government and the railways in settling the West necessarily ran counter to the ideological preoccupations of many Anglo-Canadian intellectuals.[8] Most realized that Canada needed immigrants to do the hard, dirty work of building a country, but they worried about the sort of country that would result.

Opposition to the great wave of non-Anglo-Saxon immigration of the 1890's quickly surfaced. A virulent mix of nativism, racism, anti-radicalism, and anti-Semitism coloured most of the opposition to the arrival of the new Canadians. English Canadians paraded their concern for protecting "democratic institutions" and maintaining an Anglo-Saxon civilization. Such sentiments could manifest themselves in a variety of ways, ranging from the humanitarian concern to "Canadianize" and assimilate newcomers "for their own good" to the desire to shut Canada's borders and repatriate or deport troublemakers.[9] No one was embarrassed to speak of the need to protect the race; what was meant by "race," however, was not always made clear. Some used the term in the biological sense to refer to the purportedly fixed and permanent features that separated superior Anglo-Saxons from inferior groupings; others employed the concept in the cultural sense to refer to British traditions and customs that outsiders could, only with some difficulty, be taught.[10]

Such preoccupations had an effect on the debate over whether or not the Department of Immigration was doing enough to prevent the entry into Canada of the degenerate. J.R. Conn asserted in 1900 in an article in the *Queen's Quarterly* that a nation had the right to control its own fate: "This same right of the higher as against the lower types of life justifies the people of this continent in shutting out such alien elements of population as seem likely to lower rather than raise the general type of life." It was, he asserted, proven by the American experience that shipping in mere brute labour in the form of distinct races that could not be assimilated led to vice, crime, and pauperism. "Paupers and criminals are generally such because of inherent defects and no change of place can remedy these. A worthless character is a burden and obstacle wherever he goes."[11]

This argument that the federal government under Laurier and Sifton had shown a preference for the quantity rather than the quality of imported labour was parroted in 1901 by Alberta MP Frank Oliver. He accused easterners of swamping the West with Galician and Doukhobor migrants whose presence deterred the arrival of superior settlers. Canada, he continued to argue in 1903, if it was not to suffer a "deterioration in morality and intelligence," had to follow the American lead in elaborating a restrictive immigration program.[12] His colleague, E.N. Lewis, MP for West Huron, sought to press on the government the need to restrict immigration to northern Europeans "who have the same hereditary [*sic*] as ourselves." And reverting back to old racial slurs he concluded a 1914 attack on southern Europeans with the statement, "We do not want a nation of organ-grinders and banana sellers in this country."[13] Prejudice and discrimination thus could and did flourish in Canada without the assistance of hereditarian insights.

For all their talk of protecting the "race," the eugenicists did not see themselves as racists or nativists. Eugenics was, its followers claimed, both an international movement and a science. Most therefore made an effort to distance themselves from simple-minded nationalists. Calls for restriction of immigration based on eugenic arguments, so their proponents suggested, would not be based on prejudice, personal bias, or old-fashioned notions of patriotism but rather on progressive, sophisticated, and scientifically informed analyses of the worth of individual immigrants.

But in voicing their concern for sorting out the "degenerate," experts were making the unfounded assertion that they had the ability to identify accurately intellectual, moral, and physical strengths. In fact, in most cases it was appropriate cultural behaviour that they took as the best indicator of intelligence. MacMurchy, for example, in the midst of a plea for more sophisticated methods of medical examination and mental testing, made the amazing comment that she paid particular attention to an apparently dim-witted Scottish boy because she *knew* that Highlanders were shrewd.[14] Eastern and southern Europeans were not given the benefit of the doubt. In short, eugenic arguments provided apparently new, objective scientific justifications for old, deep-seated racial and class assumptions.

Eugenic concerns that the quality as opposed to the quantity of immigrants be the government's first priority moreover served specific class interests inasmuch as they enhanced the pretensions of the helping professions. Doctors, so the eugenicists argued, would necessarily play a key role in screening new arrivals because only physicians had the training that permitted the accurate determination of hereditary complaints. The leading eugenic reformers were, of course, doctors who could not help but appreciate the fact that their profession would gain if the government paid greater attention to their concerns. The federal Department of Health was only established in 1919, but for decades the government had relied on the medical profession in administering its immigration legislation. Eugenics-minded doctors in the early twentieth century therefore had real expectations that their lobbying for tougher immigration restrictions reflecting hereditarian concerns would meet with some success.[15] Many psychologists, social workers, and teachers would also be ultimately drawn to eugenics, in part because by embracing what they took to be a scientific approach to social problems they could enhance their professional standing.

Doctors took a leading role in employing eugenic arguments in the immigration debate. The belief that there existed real hereditarian differences that could not be overcome by an improvement of the environment was repeatedly expressed in the leading medical journals.[16] Dr. J.G. Adami, a Montreal expert on tuberculosis, appealed in 1912 to the Canadian Medical Association to combat the "puerile view" that "it is perfectly sound policy for this country to welcome as citizens those of degraded or depraved parentage."[17] An editorial in *Canada Lancet* for 1908-09 declared, along similar lines, "Degenerates among people are worse than bad weeds to a farmer."[18] Dr. Charles Hastings, medical health officer of Toronto, asserted that Canada was committing "race suicide" in sacrificing the well-being of its own youth to the care of newcomers. He informed the readers of the *Canadian Journal of Medicine and Surgery* that it cost the federal government

. . . nearly three quarters of a million annually for immigration purposes alone. Thousands are being imported annually of Russians, Finns, Italians, Hungarians, Belgians, Scandinavians, etc. The lives and environments of a large number of these have, no doubt, been such as is well calculated to breed degenerates. Who would think of comparing for a moment, in the interests of our country, mentally, morally, physically or commercially, a thousand of these foreigners with a thousand of Canadian birth?[19]

Eugenically inclined physicians claimed that they were providing a more sophisticated analysis than that of the older racists who denigrated all Slavs, Jews, Orientals, and blacks while trumpeting the virtues of all Anglo-Saxons. Indeed, hereditarians frequently pointed out that some of the worst sorts of immigrants were from Britain. Dr. Peter H. Bryce, for example, went out of his way to castigate the abilities of the "riotous Glasgow Jew" and the stroppy Cockney.[20] A 1909 editorial in the *Canadian Journal of Medicine and Surgery* asserted that Canada had become the "garbage pail of England, Ireland, and Scotland."[21] As professionals, eugenicist doctors were asserting that the old racial labels were too crude; the establishment of family pedigrees was required, as were sophisticated medical examination and mental testing. Only the specialist could determine the importance of such issues.

The hereditarians' assertion that foreigners were "inferior" was not original. Their most important contribution to the anti-immigration agitation was in specifying that it was the mental defectiveness of immigrants – a defectiveness that in 80 per cent of cases was inherited and could be scientifically determined – that justified their exclusion.[22] The country had the right to prevent itself from being swamped by carriers of hereditary feeble-mindedness. Helen MacMurchy, as the nation's expert on the subject, raised the alarm that the arrival of such degenerates threatened the fabric of Canadian society. In the same reports to the Ontario government that called for special education of the backward, she recommended as well that entry to the country of the feeble-minded be barred. In her *Fifth Report* (1910) she pointed out the need for the medical inspection of immigrants.[23] In her *Eighth Report* (1914) she lamented the fact that in 1913 forty-seven feeble-minded immigrants were detained but twenty-four were eventually released.[24] Basing her calculations on the work of Dr. Henry H. Goddard, who employed intelligence testing at the Vineland, New Jersey, Training School for Feeble-Minded Boys and Girls, she estimated that Canada was admitting more than a 1,000 feeble-minded immigrants a year. And as we have seen, MacMurchy claimed that feeble-mindedness was in turn responsible for poverty, unemployment, alcoholism, and prostitution.[25]

MacMurchy was not the first to claim that immigrants were swamping asylums, prisons, and hospitals. Dr. T.J.W. Burgess, superintendent of the Verdun Protestant Hospital, warned in his 1905 presidential address to the American Medico-Psychological Association that Canada was "flooded" with "defective immigrants."[26] Dr. Peter H. Bryce reported in *Canada Lancet* that the percentage of foreign-born in the hospitals had jumped from 20 per cent in 1903 to 30 per cent in 1906. "Whole families of degenerates have come out," he reported; at the Toronto Asylum they were overrepresented in the ranks of "sexual perverts, the criminal insane, slum degenerates, general paralytics and other types of weaklings."[27] Dr. J.D. Pagé, chief medical officer of the port of Quebec, informed the Public Health Association meeting in Toronto in 1915 that the Canadian situation mirrored that found in the United States, where the proportion of the foreign-born feeble-minded was four times as high as that of the native-born.[28]

A variety of experts claimed that these foreign degenerates were swamping the existing charity institutions. A.P. Knight, professor of biology at Queen's University, accused the federal government in 1907 of allowing the entry of an increasing number of mental degenerates and physical weaklings from Europe:

Our asylums, jails, hospitals and other charitable institutions show an increasing percentage of men and women, emigrants from the older lands, who are handicapped by a bad heredity, and quite unfit to make their way in the new world. Their children are equally unfit. They are underfed and undersized; they inherit the unsound minds and diseased bodies of their parents and are doomed to suffering and inferiority from the very beginning of their lives.[29]

Reports in the *Canadian Practitioner and Review* and *Canada Lancet* for 1908 and 1909 asserted that the block settlement of such settlers contained the "riff-raff from Europe, colonies of immigrants spreading crime, disease, and ignorance."[30]

It was the immigrant's purported contribution to Canada's crime rate that particularly alarmed observers. In a Rhode Island workhouse, reported Dr. F. McKelvey Bell of Ottawa, over 76 per cent of the criminals were foreign-born. In Canada, according to Bell, the situation was just as bad: "we have only 13 per cent of foreigners in the Dominion, [but] 40 per cent of our convicts are of foreign birth and no doubt many others are children of foreigners."[31] Similarly, Michael Steele, MP for South Perth, resorted to American sources in quoting from Dr. Goddard when informing Parliament in 1917 that "there is no such thing as hereditary criminals, it is hereditary feeble-mindedness that accounts for the conditions. Criminals are not born, they are made, and probably fifty per cent of all criminals are mentally defective."[32] Reflecting on all the vices imported to the New World by the foreigner, James Russell, superintendent of the Hamilton Asylum, warned his colleagues in the American Medico-Psychological Association in 1908 that to welcome such degenerate hordes could only put the Anglo-Saxon race in peril. "The immense virility of the Anglo-Saxon race like the sturdy oak may resist the encroachments of the canker worm for generations," he wrote, "but unless purged and purified of disease it will at last crumble and decay."[33]

Russell, in referring to the question of the declining "virility" of native Canadians, was addressing a fear raised by Dr. Peter H. Bryce. Bryce (1853-1932), educated at Upper Canada College and the University of Toronto, served the Ontario and federal governments in a variety of capacities as a medical expert. He was, from 1882 to 1904, the first secretary of the Ontario Board of Health and, from 1904 to 1921, chief medical officer of the Department of Immigration. In the latter capacity his hereditarian views clearly influenced the way in which immigration policy was carried out.[34]

Bryce's concern that the fertility of the native Canadian was disturbingly low and that of the immigrant alarmingly high was rooted in his early findings when on the Ontario Board of Health. In 1885, sitting on a provincial committee established to determine how to deal with the distressing problems of infanticide and child abandonment, he first had forced on his attention the fact that not all births were welcomed.[35] In 1889, as deputy registrar general, he expressed his disquiet at finding that Ontario cities had a fertility rate distinctly lower than that of the countryside. According to Bryce such developments were due – not to economic pressures – but primarily to the propaganda of both male and female neo-Malthusians.

> It is natural that amongst such writers many should be women; some moved thereto, at times, doubtless, from womanly sympathy for their sisters amongst the poor, borne down with the cares of children; others have been urged to speak from the standpoint of the emancipated woman, whose ambition it is to enter the arena of public affairs and dispute the field with men, and yet a still larger number have adopted this new philosophy from the standpoint of personal selfishness, and declare that they will recognize no duty which will deprive them of the right to enjoy the fullest whatever society may bring them of pleasure, and utterly refuse to undergo, if it can be avoided, the pains and inconveniences of maternity, while accepting the social protection, privileges and joys which marriage can bring them.[36]

In returning to the issue in his 1903 report Bryce argued that Ontario's low fertility could only be taken as evidence "that natural conditions are being interfered with, or being supplanted by those of a preventative character and criminal in tendency."[37] Those intent on following such practices, according to Bryce, could count on the support of chemists, physicians, and purveyors of "every form of nostrum and mechanical appliance." The danger was that if such social degeneracy continued it could threaten the destiny of the Anglo-Saxon race in playing "the dominant part over inferior races in the march of progress."[38]

Bryce's major preoccupation was with the declining fertility of Canadians, which he attributed in part to the degenerative effects of urbanized, industrialized society. Relying on such European theorists as Max Nordau, whose *Degeneration* (1895) had quickly become the classic attack on modernization, Bryce advanced the view that urbanism produced "neurasthenia," an acquired characteristic passed on from generation to generation. But though Bryce attributed declining family size in part to sterility caused by neurotic fatigue, he also blamed it on individual egoism. "How many parents," he asked, "have such clear ideas of their duty to the state that they are prepared to be inconvenienced in their pleasure by rearing a normal number of children?"[39]

Bryce believed that the rural environment was healthier and, accordingly, so were its inhabitants, "free from the degenerative effects seen in those classes which have been for several generations factory operatives and dwellers in the congested centres of large industrial populations."[40] He sketched out in a 1914 talk to the Canadian Purity Education Association his notion of defective environments producing diseases such as alcoholism and syphilis. But his was an optimistic creed, he told his audience, inasmuch as there were "two underlying principles indissolubly mingled of *eugenics* and *eusthenics*." The careful selection of immigrants on the one hand and the improvement of the environment on the other held out "the potentialities of almost infinite improvement."[41]

One way of stopping degeneration was by returning to the land and ending the cancerous growth of cities.[42] Another, as Bryce suggested in a 1919 essay, was by the adoption of measures to prevent the multiplication of the unfit. "If we desire the eradication of the weakling from the race, our action must not be negative, allowing the unfit to die. It must be positive, preventing the unfit to marry and reproduce their kind."[43] A third measure would be to deny the fit access to the means employed to restrict fertility. And last of all Bryce supported the idea of bringing to Canada the right sort of immigrants while denying access to the degenerate.

Bryce's pronatalist sentiments were echoed by Dr. Charles Hodgetts, who replaced him as Ontario deputy registrar general. Hodgetts noted in his 1910 report that immigrants often had large families.

> In this respect they are examples to a large portion of our population with whom families are at a discount, for it can unfortunately be said that while many Canadian couples are willing to enjoy the pleasures of a matrimonial life, yet it is part of their programme to unblushingly indulge in preventive practices which result in sterility . . . . The modern plan for increasing population seems to be an encouragement by the state of the importation of foreign-born, anything but the "made in Canada."[44]

The editor of *Canadian Practitioner and Review* was appalled by such findings. It was, he declared in an 1908 article, "a question of who are to be the fathers of the future children of Canada."[45]

The historian W.S. Wallace added a sociological gloss to Bryce's account of the fertility differential between native and new Canadians. "The native-born population, in the face of the increasing competition, fails to propagate itself, commits race suicide in short; whereas the immigrant population, being inferior, and having no appearances to keep up, propagates itself like the fish of the sea."[46] Professor Ross of Wisconsin was quoted in *Maclean's* magazine of December, 1914, making much the same argument: "The very decency of the native is a handicap to success and fecundity."[47]

What Bryce and his colleagues were suggesting was that immigrants were posing a double threat. They and their large families not only encumbered Canada with massive social problems; they also perversely lowered the fertility of Anglo-Saxons who had to limit their own family size if they were to pay through taxes for the support of others. The aliens were, in the words of the American eugenicist Prescott F. Hall, sterilizing their hosts![48]

By 1914 the basic line of the eugenicist anti-immigration argument was laid out. Beginning with the premise that certain inherited traits could not be attenuated by a changed environment, eugenicists proceeded to attribute all social problems associated with the immigrant experience to the innate characteristics of the individual, not to the problems posed by a strange, new homeland. Doctors, in equating intelligence to competency in dealing with an Anglo-Saxon culture, not surprisingly found high levels of feeble-mindedness in the immigrant population. Feeble-mindedness they then posited as the root cause of most of the stresses and strains experienced by their young nation. And such problems threatened to worsen over time because, the eugenicists warned, the fertility of inferior immigrant families was not only distressingly high, it appeared to have the effect of forcing down the fertility of superior native Canadians.

To judge by the continual barrage of complaints, one might have assumed that Canada had placed no restrictions whatsoever on the entry of immigrants. In fact, as early as 1869 the nation's first Immigration Act contained provisions against the entry of lunatics and idiots.[49] In 1901 the United States began medical inspections at the Canadian border and Canada soon followed suit by beginning its own medical inspections. By 1902 amendments added to the list of undesirables those who suffered from any loathsome, dangerous, or infectious disease. Orders-in-council in 1902 stipulated that spot medical inspections would take place at Quebec, Halifax, Saint John, Montreal, and Winnipeg. Their purpose was to prohibit the entry into Canada of persons with a specified physical disability or disease, persons diseased, crippled, or deformed or with a mental disorder, and persons suffering from a physical disease of a curable nature. Bryce oversaw these regulations from the time of his appointment as chief medical officer of the Department of Immigration in 1904.[50]

By 1906 the feeble-minded, idiots, epileptics, insane, deaf, dumb, blind, infirm, and those afflicted with a loathsome, contagious, or infectious disease were specified as belonging to the prohibited groups. The Immigration Act of 1910 divided the prohibited classes into three broad categories, which were in turn subdivided.[51] The mentally defective included idiots, imbeciles, feeble-minded, epileptics, and insane; the diseased included those afflicted with any loathsome disease or a contagious or infectious disease that might become dangerous to the public health; and the physically defective included the dumb, blind, or otherwise handicapped. Dr. Charles A. Bailey described to the readers of *Public Health Journal* in 1912 how the rapid "sizing up" of new arrivals by the medical inspector at the port of entry played its part in the conservation of the race.[52]

The ineffectiveness of such cursory inspections carried out in Canada by a handful of doctors was constantly harped on by the hereditarians.[53] In the first place, they charged, the railway and steamship lines were hostile to and failed to facilitate any measures that threatened to jeopardize their operations. Second, as *Canadian Practitioner and Review* noted in 1908, the fact that first-class cabin passengers were not subjected to medical inspection revealed that the importance of scientific investigation still paled before the power of social status.[54] Third, the few doctors available to make inspections simply did not have the time to provide adequate diagnoses. Finally, the co-operation of the mass of immigrants – understandably enough – could not be counted on. Lieutenant Colonel C.N. Laurie, the medical officer of health at Port Arthur, naively wondered why it was that foreigners (whom the doctor could exclude from the country) "look upon health officials as their natural enemies, whose aim and desire is to interfere and make life unpleasant for them."[55] All of these reasons could help explain why, as Dr. J.D. Pagé pointed out, the 222 feeble-minded immigrants treated in 1915 at the Toronto General Hospital represented a greater number than the total rejected for mental defectiveness out of the three million that arrived in the country during the previous eleven years.[56]

The campaign of MacMurchy and others to alert the public to the danger of the feeble-minded began to bear fruit just before the outbreak of World War One. In the spring of 1914 C.K. Clarke, superintendent of the Toronto General Hospital and professor of psychiatry at the

University of Toronto, established the Social Service Clinic in Toronto for the mentally defective. Commissioner Boyd of the Juvenile Court sent troubling cases to Clarke for examination – many of them involving immigrant juveniles.[57] In Quebec Dr. Pagé, medical superintendent of the Immigration Hospital at Sans Bruit, was authorized by the Minister of the Interior to hire a psychologist provided by Goddard's Vineland clinic. Pagé reported that thanks to Miss Mateer's help two mental defectives per 1,000 immigrants were detected as opposed to the usual five per 100,000 found when close examination was not possible.[58] What the eugenicists wanted, however, was a thorough medical inspection along the lines adopted by the American government to take place in the immigrant's country of origin. If defectives were to be prevented entry, what MacMurchy referred to as the "loopholes" in the immigration law had to be closed.

The first generation of Canadian eugenicists was very much pro-British and tended on many questions to take their lead from British hereditarians. But with the immigration issue Canadians found that Americans, having had earlier but similar experiences with a massive influx of settlers, had more pertinent points to make. In England opposition to alien immigration was voiced by eugenicists, but as the number of migrants coming *to* England was relatively small the issue did not receive a great deal of attention.[59] British eugenicists were more preoccupied by the fear that Britain was losing its most innovative and adventurous young people, who were migrating out to such countries as Canada; Canadian eugenicists tended to assume the opposite, that the failed and ineffectual dregs of Britain were being dumped on the Dominion. The pessimistic portrayal of the population situation that eugenicists in both Canada and Britain liked to paint thus led them to produce completely contradictory appraisals of the British immigrant.

Canadian commentators tended to draw much of their information on the hereditary taints of foreigners from American authors and called on the Canadian government to follow the U.S. lead in restricting immigration. Thus, J.S. Woodsworth concluded *Strangers Within Our Gates* (1909) with the suggestion that Canada should seriously observe the workings of the American Restriction League.[60] MacMurchy, likewise, described in envious fashion the facilities at Ellis Island where American physicians had the power of rejecting thousands of unfit immigrants each year.[61]

World War One abruptly ended both the massive flow of immigrants and the protests that their arrival engendered. The post-war slump of 1918-22 further impeded the resumption of new arrivals; indeed, the federal government actively employed its powers of deportation in 1919 to crush labour unrest.[62] But by 1925 business was again buoyant and a second major wave of immigration to Canada began. Largely as a result of the influence of eugenicists, the United States put into place in 1921 and 1924 restrictions on the entry of central and southern Europeans. Evidence that such immigrants were therefore choosing Canada as a destination led to calls that it should likewise adopt a quota system. Restrictions were imposed but only in the sense that illiterates were excluded and categories of "preferred" northern and "non-preferred" southern and eastern European immigrants were drawn up. Some journalists commented that it was strange that having just fought Germany, Canada should employ immigration laws that would allow the entry of the Kaiser but exclude the Pope. No one protested the fact that Asian immigration was all but ended and that the government – by determining after 1923 that only citizens of predominantly white Commonwealth countries could be deemed British subjects – effectively excluded blacks.[63]

Eugenicists were also pleased that the war, in forcing on the public's attention the importance of national health, was instrumental in leading the federal government to establish in 1919 the Department of Health.[64] Its mandate was to suppress a number of afflictions that endangered the efficiency of the population – venereal disease, infant mortality, tuberculosis, and feeble-mindedness. Many also presumed that the new department would strike at the root of a number of these problems by helping to police immigration. Speaking in favour of the creation of such a department, Charles Sheard reminded his colleagues in the House of Commons, "We have had in the past, rushing into this country, without restraint, inspection or restriction, the diseased, the mentally defective, the criminal, the unhappy, the uncertain, the infamous."[65] Dr. Michael Steele, a long-time proponent in Parliament of public health measures, stated that in his estimation the main reason for the establishment of the Department of Health was to prevent the arrival in Canada of feeble-minded immigrants, whom he likened to a "social virus."[66] The department included in its roster of experts several key personalities sympathetic to eugenic arguments – Peter H. Bryce, medical officer of the Department of Immigration; John Andrew Amyot, deputy minister of health; J.D. Pagé, chief of quarantine; Helen MacMurchy, head of the Child Welfare Bureau; and J.J. Heagerty, head of the Venereal Disease Control Branch.

In revealing the traumas suffered by shell-shocked troops, the war had also provided doctors with arguments that innovative preventive measures were needed to protect the nation's mental health. One such measure was the use of mental testing on troops, which was employed in the United States but, to the disappointment of Canadian psychiatrists, not employed in Canada.[67] In this context the Canadian National Committee for Mental Hygiene was established in 1918 by C.K. Clarke and Clarence Hincks to draw attention to the fact that both the native and immigrant populations would have to be tested if their true potential was going to be determined. The CNCMH set as its agenda a campaign against crime, prostitution, and unemployment, which it asserted were all related in one way or another with feeble-mindedness. The underlying argument of the Committee was that the old methods of dealing with such problems by institutionalization were expensive and ineffective; preventive methods, beginning with examination and testing, were necessary.[68] The Committee provided anti-immigrationists with added ammunition by asserting that its surveys proved that there was a direct correlation between immigration and insanity, criminality, and unemployment.

Even before the establishment of the Committee, C.K. Clarke had written in 1916 a violent denunciation of "The Defective Immigrant." In his opinion Canada had become a dumping ground of the riffraff of the world. He noted that as far back as 1861 Dr. Workman had found that British immigrants were overrepresented at the Toronto Asylum.[69] Clarke was backed up in the same issue of *Public Health Journal* by Peter H. Bryce's report that the rate of feeble-mindedness of British immigrant schoolchildren was twice that of their Canadian fellows.[70]

The fullest mental hygienists' account of the immigration problem was provided by W.G. Smith in *A Study in Canadian Immigration* (1920). In an inflammatory introduction C.K. Clarke typified the country's immigration policy as a tragic story of ignorant mismanagement. Politicians' "craze for numbers" and the shipping companies' greed had, according to Clarke, encumbered Canada with thousands of criminals and mental degenerates. Humanitarians held out the false hope that the newcomers could be improved, but Clarke asserted that a healthy environment could not make the insane sane or the incompetent competent. Canada needed immigrants but faced the prospect of the vicious and antisocial flooding the country unless the government followed the American example of instituting a rigid system of examination and testing.[71]

Following such a vitriolic introduction, Smith's account could not help but appear moderate and objective. In fact, he differed from Clarke mainly in style. He attacked the bonus system and the charity-sponsored schemes that had stimulated immigration, defended anti-Asian discrimination in British Columbia, and attributed to immigrants excessive rates of crime, illiteracy, and feeble-mindedness. Smith did point out, however, that many of the attacks on foreigners were based on little more than prejudice. Smith's solution included more inspection in Europe and the establishment in Canada of an Ellis Island-style immigration station where new arrivals could be thoroughly examined.[72] He presented the fact that the Americans' rate of rejection of mental defectives was one to every 1,590 immigrants while Canada's was only one to every 10,127 as evidence of the leniency of the latter country's screening process.[73] Smith called, also, for the training of a new generation of "soldiers" who would wage a "battle" for the assimilation of new Canadians. Smith concluded his study with the unlikely story of a heroic young leader of a settlement house in Yorkton, Saskatchewan, who, dying of influenza, deliriously repeated, "the foreign problem can be solved."[74]

The CNCMH's mouthpiece, the *Canadian Journal of Mental Hygiene*, carried a steady stream of articles reiterating the necessity of restricting immigration.[75] Evidence was drawn from the provincial surveys of feeble-mindedness the Committee was carrying out. It reported, for example, in 1920 that its survey of Manitoba revealed:

> that the feeble-minded, insane and psychopathic of that province were recruited out of all reasonable proportions from the immigrant class, and it was found that these individuals were playing a major role in such conditions as crime, juvenile delinquency, prostitution, pauperism, certain phases of industrial unrest, and primary school inefficiency.[76]

Similar studies with similar findings were carried out in the early 1920's by the CNCMH in British Columbia, Alberta, Saskatchewan, New Brunswick, Nova Scotia, and Prince Edward Island.

In 1920 the federal government asked the CNCMH to train three medical inspectors in psychiatry for the purposes of screening immigrants. Their training included a trip to Ellis Island, which typified to Canadian reformers the way screening should be carried out.[77] The mental hygienists repeatedly cited their American counterparts, such as Prescott Hall and H.H. Laughlin, when complaining of the laxity of Canadian immigration policies. They were particularly envious of the widespread use in the United States of IQ tests.[78]

Such tests, in fact, were popularized by Carl C. Brigham, a psychiatrist whose first work was done in Canada. In the early years of World War One, Brigham was employed in Ontario by the Military Hospitals Commission. When the United States entered the war in 1917 it sent a number of experts to Canada to observe how its ally had coped with problems posed by hordes of raw recruits. One of the experts was

Robert M. Yerkes, a Harvard psychologist interested in intelligence testing. Henry H. Goddard had brought the Binet-Simon tests from France to the United States in 1908 and employed them at the Vineland School to support the pessimistic notion that intelligence was inherited. In 1917 Yerkes, Goddard, and Lewis Terman of Stanford University set out to design a series of tests for the American military.[79] Yerkes brought Brigham back to the United States to work on the massive project, which ultimately involved the testing of two million recruits. This single undertaking, despite the dubious nature of its culturally biased results, dramatically raised the status of the psychology profession.[80]

Brigham's account of the army tests, *A Study of American Intelligence*, appeared in 1923 and played a major role in popularizing the notion of racial differences in intelligence. In 1917 Goddard had reported that two out of every five immigrants tested at Ellis Island proved to be feeble-minded. Brigham asserted that the army tests provided further evidence of the need to restrict immigration. They revealed the existence of three major European racial groupings – the Nordic, Alpine, and Mediterranean. As one moved from one to another, a corresponding decline in intelligence was noted. American racists were delighted to be informed by Brigham that the test results of blacks were the lowest of all, the average black having the mentality of a ten-year-old.[81]

Appearing when it did, just before the 1923 meeting of the House Committee on Immigration and Naturalization, Brigham's book served as an invaluable arsenal of arguments for American exclusionists. It clearly served its purpose when a new Immigration Act was passed in April of 1924 by the conservative Republican Congress that restricted European arrivals to small percentages of the same national origin recorded in the census of 1890.[82]

In Canada Peter Sandiford, professor of education at the University of Toronto, was among the foremost proponents of intelligence testing. "Intelligence," he stated in a 1927 article that summed up his views, "is a trait that is passed on by heredity."[83] He attempted to prove the superiority of nature over nurture in some of the earliest studies of twins and in the employment of data drawn from observations of the Dionne quintuplets.[84] The fact that some nationalities did better at the American army tests than others (the English and Scots had the highest grades and the Belgians and Poles the lowest) he attributed to Darwinian selection, not to the cultural blinders of the testers. Similarly, by ignoring the fact that *Who's Who* measured professional success rather than intelligence, he could conclude that "Obviously if America wants to restrict her immigration by means of the 'Quota' she should aim to keep out as far as possible Russians (Poles), Italians, and Greeks and encourage in their stead Canadians, Britishers, Germans and Danes."[85] The lesson Sandiford drew from such work was that Canada, too, had to prevent itself from being made a "dumping ground for misfits and defectives."[86]

In 1924 Sandiford carried out his own testing of British Columbia school students and was pleased to find, as predicted, that among whites those of British and German stock did best and those of Slavic and Latin stock did most poorly. He advanced as proof of the hereditary nature of intelligence the fact the parents of the brightest students were from the professional classes and the slowest from the unskilled. Sandiford, like so many hereditarians, revealed his basic conservatism in equating financial success with intelligence.

But Sandiford's tests also produced results that he found "profoundly disturbing" – they appeared to indicate that the Japanese were the most intelligent racial group and the Chinese the second. Further tests proved "more encouraging" in that white scores were higher than the Chinese, but the Japanese still came in first. Sandiford concluded that the evidence had to be taken to mean that only those few exceptionally clever Asians immigrated to Canada; it was clearly unthinkable that they were racially superior to Anglo-Saxons. Nevertheless, the ability of the Japanese and Chinese to compete successfully with whites posed, in Sandiford's words, "a problem which calls for the highest quality of statesmanship if it can be solved satisfactorily."[87] Like so many of the intelligence testers, Sandiford knew in advance what results his surveys were supposed to produce. When such tests did not confirm the superiority of the white race a "problem" was said to exist that required the intervention of government. Sandiford, the self-proclaimed social Darwinist, was ambivalent about the struggle for survival. On the one hand he declared that quality would always win out, but on the other he called on the government to protect native Canadians from the competition of immigrants by subjecting them all to stringent mental, physical, and possibly even "moral" tests.[88]

Sandiford claimed that intelligence testing was turning psychology into a "true experimental science." An indicator that psychology was finally "put on the map" in Canada occurred in 1931 when the Department of Educational Research at the Ontario College of Education received a $30,000 grant from the Carnegie Foundation. And yet Sandiford himself, while lauding the fair and reliable nature of the intelligence tests, was led to wonder why it was only in North America that there was such enthusiasm for them. "Is it the presence of the immigrant," he mused, "that has led to this anomalous state of affairs?"[89] Sandiford managed to stifle these qualms and was joined in his enthusiasm for this kind of testing by such leading hereditarians as Helen MacMurchy, Eric Clarke, and Clarence Hincks.[90]

Medicine and psychology were not the only professions to exploit an Anglo fear of the feeble-minded immigrant. Social work, much of which had been carried out on a volunteer basis by women's groups in the early twentieth century, became increasingly professionalized in the interwar period and emphasized the need to have trained experts police new arrivals. A number of its leading proponents clearly turned to the profession's advantage the spectre of foreign degeneration.

In the pre-war period the National Council of Women, whose members were engaged in most of the significant philanthropic agencies, was torn by its conflicting desires: on the one hand it wanted to restrict immigration; on the other, its middle-class members wanted a ready supply of cheap domestics.[91] Aroused by the carnage of the First World War, which in the eyes of the NCW was killing off the fit while allowing the degenerate to breed, the Council petitioned the government in 1915 for the medical inspection of immigrants to weed out mental defectives. "Contagious diseases have long been controlled by legislation," it noted, "but this more deadly, transmittable disease of feeble-mindedness is still uncontrolled."[92] In 1919 Helen Reid, a member of the Dominion Council of Health, wrote that it was necessary to prevent the entry into Canada of those British women "who in addition to their lack of training for domestic service, bring with them only too often, serious mental and moral disabilities. These women either glut the labour market here, reducing the wages of working men, or end up, alas! too frequently, in our jails, hospitals, and asylums."[93]

In the 1920's the colourful and flamboyant Charlotte Whitton, director of the Canadian Council on Child Welfare and the leading advocate in Canada of the creation of social work as a profession, carried on the campaign against the entry into Canada of the mentally deficient.[94] She claimed that Britain sought to dump its surplus labour on the dominions and that pre-war "unregulated immigration" was responsible for Canada's post-war economic problems. What Whitton objected to in particular was the entry of the feeble-minded.

> Statistics abound to show the alarming degree to which an immigration policy that sought not quality but quantity has contributed to the social problems of this young country. Fortunately the war stemmed the human tide temporarily at least, and allowed us to take stock of the population that has flowed into this country. . . . Our

strength and resources are bent to the task of keeping this country strong, virile, healthy, and moral, and we insist that the blood that enters its veins must be equally pure and free from taint.[95]

In fact, for all her avowed professionalism, Whitton undertook her survey of immigrant children with the clear purpose of tracking down as many cases of degeneration as possible.[96]

The approach taken by Whitton was illustrated in the Social Service Council of Canada's 1924 study, *Canada's Child Immigrants*. It drew evidence from a vast range of social agencies to paint a portrayal of the failures of juvenile immigration. Among its damning evidence it cited figures from C.K. Clarke's psychiatric clinic in Toronto, which showed that out of 125 immigrant girls examined, seventy-seven were mentally deficient, thirty-six were prostitutes, thirty-one suffered from venereal disease, and eighteen had illegitimate children.[97] Such a sample, of course, was in no way representative, but it was all grist for the mill of those complaining of the lack of "scientific selection" of immigrants. With similarly sifted evidence the Canadian Council on Child Welfare, of which Whitton was director, reported in 1929 that immigrant feeble-mindedness, spreading with "cancerous tenacity," was responsible for "filth, disease, criminality, immorality and vice."[98] It was with such fears in mind that in 1924 the United Farm Women of Alberta's convention struck a committee to seek to have debarred from entry into Canada the feeble-minded, epileptic, tubercular, dumb, blind, illiterate, criminal, and anarchistic. The same organization claimed in 1927 that 75 per cent of the mental patients in the province were migrants.[99]

By the mid-1920's potential British immigrants were being medically examined in the United Kingdom. Ultimately, nearly 1,500 doctors overseas co-operated in providing inspections, and by 1928 twenty-eight medical officers of the Department of Immigration were at work in Britain and Europe. Over 10,000 persons were forbidden entry to Canada in the 1920's, but this did not silence the critics.[100] The *Canadian Medical Association Journal* complained that low-grade immigrants with high fertility continued to flood Canada. Preliminary medical inspection was only compulsory for specific categories of immigrants – unaccompanied women, children on private immigration schemes, and those on government-assisted passage.[101]

In the 1920's the Canadian government employed neither intelligence testing nor a quota system to limit immigration. The country's policy was less restrictive than that of the United States – not because of greater humanitarianism but because money was to be made from

new arrivals. In the mid-twenties powerful interest groups – in particular the railway companies that stood to benefit from having immigrants on their ships, on their trains, and on their land – pressured the
Mackenzie King government to reopen Canada's doors to the central
and eastern Europeans needed to farm the Prairies. Although the
federal government launched a variety of schemes to encourage "preferred" British immigration, it also entered into the Railways Agreement with CPR and CNR in 1925 that eventually brought to Canada
165,000 central and eastern Europeans and 20,000 Mennonites.[102]

The shipping companies had their own inspections of immigrants
and were fined by the federal government for each deportee. But even
the government's own examination system at ports of entry was mainly
a matter of form and, in any event, frequently avoided by ministerial
permits. The western provinces continued to point out the inadequacy
of the inspection system; they were, of course, going to pay for the
mistakes made by either the railways or the federal government.[103]
Concerns were also expressed by westerners that many of the new
immigrants were not fulfilling their appointed task of taming the land
but, because the wheat boom had passed and the best farmlands were
already occupied, were turning to the cities. This second wave of
immigration raised the ire of the eugenicists and precipitated a backlash from a variety of nativist groups, including the Ku Klux Klan, the
Native Sons of Canada, and the Orange Order.

Obligatory inspection overseas along American lines only came in
1928 as part of an attempt by the Mackenzie King government to stem
the tide of anti-immigration sentiment. The Railways Agreement was
the focus of the attack of a motley collection of restrictionists, including leaders of the Trades and Labour Congress, members of the United
Farmers of Alberta, Anglo-Canadian bigots led by George Lloyd,
Anglican bishop of Saskatoon, nativists of the National Association of
Canada, and the Ku Klux Klan. R.B. Bennett, the new Conservative
leader, also threw his party's support behind what was obviously a
popular issue.[104]

Between February and May of 1928 a Select Committee on Agriculture and Colonization heard representatives of the railway companies, the churches, the social services, and other interested parties give
their views on immigration policy.[105] There was no official eugenicist
presence; the Committee's time was mainly divided between the
representatives of the shipping companies, who wanted a free hand to
bring in eastern Europeans, and the representatives of British interests,
who fought to ensure that Anglo-Saxon settlers received preferential
treatment.

But eugenic preoccupations clearly coloured the discussions. In Parliament a few MPs, such as J.S. Woodsworth (who had turned away from eugenics once he recognized that it was being used as a stick with which to beat the working class), Samuel Jacobs, and Michael Luchkovich, made spirited attacks on the arguments of the hereditarians. "I challenge any member of this House or any scientist," asserted Luchkovich, "to prove biologically that one race of people could not do as well as another race under similar circumstances."[106] Outside of the House Robert England, whose credentials as an objective commentator on immigration matters were somewhat compromised by the fact that he had worked for the CPR, kept up a barrage of criticisms of what he described as "the scientific determinist, geographer or eugenist" and "the violent rantings and fantastic claims of Gobineau, Stoddard, or McDougal in their well-known books."[107]

The immigration committee's final report, submitted on June 6, 1928, called for the implementation of stricter controls; the Conservative government elected in 1930 erected the barriers that put an end to Canada's interwar wave of immigration. The CNCMH hailed the closing of Canada's borders as a victory, but in fact it was the depression that terminated large-scale immigration to Canada.

Had the hereditarians been successful in imposing their views on others? For one thing, it was not always clear what those views were. Some eugenicists wanted certain ethnic groups given preference, others wanted all to be subjected to standardized examinations. Nevertheless, the general assumption was widespread that the hereditarians had popularized the idea that some immigrants demonstrated by their social incompetency the presence of a hereditary taint. Such arguments against immigration were employed by a vast range of organizations – the Church of England Council for Social Service, the Canadian National Committee on Mental Hygiene, the National Council of Women, the Social Service Council of Canada, the National Child Welfare Association. Knowing what they were looking for, each easily dredged up from the files of asylums, orphanages, rescue homes, penitentiaries, industrial schools, and psychiatric clinics sensational accounts of the social cost of admitting immigrants to Canada. Opposition to immigration in the late nineteenth century had been raised by nativists, nationalists, and labour leaders opposed primarily to the quantity of incoming foreigners; the opposition of the interwar period was increasingly led by professional groups – doctors, social workers, and psychiatrists – employing eugenic arguments to attack the quality of the new arrivals. Such onslaughts were clearly self-serving in that they allowed professions to be established and careers to be made by those who presented themselves as vital agents dedicated to the definition and defence of the race.

Canadian eugenicists were not as successful in 1928 as their American counterparts had been in 1924. This was because the self-proclaimed defenders of "intelligence" found in the Canadian shipping companies redoubtable opponents. The forces of "materialism" were so strong that as late as 1925 the Railways Agreement gave the CNR and the CPR in effect a free hand in the importation of "non-preferred" immigrants. And the closing of Canada's doors, so desperately sought by the hereditarians, was brought about, not as a result of scientific argument, but because of the economic constraints of the 1930's.

The chief "success" of the hereditarians (if one wishes to so qualify it) did not consist of seriously impeding the entry of immigrants to Canada. The hereditarians' success lay in popularizing biological arguments to perpetuate the argument – so beloved by the anxious – that the nation's problems were largely the product of the outsider. The dividing line separating the old racist from the new eugenicist was rarely as clear as the latter claimed. The message of the eugenicist was far more radical in style than in content; new intelligence tests, medical examinations, questionnaires, and surveys might be brandished, but the purpose was the old one – defence of Anglo-Saxon dominance. This was not, however, quite the same thing as defence of the social status quo. The immigration debate revealed cleavages within the middle classes and pitted professionals against business interests. Some members of the helping professions consciously employed eugenic fears as a means of forcing their way into the establishment. The more cautious were aware that such a strategy could be pushed too far. Conservative Canadians would always view with suspicion those who constantly harped on such unseemly subjects as race and sex.

4

Sex, Science, and Race Betterment

Like moths to a flame, eugenicists were inexorably drawn to the issue of sexuality. The reproduction of the degenerate, the irrational breeding of the feeble-minded, the swamping of Canada by prolific aliens were all subjected by hereditarians to morbid analysis. But they were not content to draw up negative policies to curb the fertility of the unfit; they also sought to assist in the breeding of the fit. To generations of Canadians worried that the increase in the numbers of women working outside the home, the decline in fertility, and the rise in divorces signalled the death of the traditional family, the eugenicists brought the comforting news that such threats could be countered. In moving from the discussion of the sexuality of the "abnormal" to the sexuality of the "normal," they took leading positions as the sex educators of early twentieth-century Canada.

The eugenically minded, in broaching what had theretofore remained taboo subjects – sex education, venereal disease, and birth control – presented themselves as progressive reformers, if not revolutionaries. They clearly did violate the sensibilities of many conservatives who opposed the public discussion of such private matters. It is also obvious that many ordinary Canadians – in being provided contraceptives to limit their fertility or prophylactics to protect them from disease – benefited in a practical way from such undertakings. But the intent of the eugenicists, in bringing sexual questions into the open, was not to give individuals the means by which they could freely gratify their passions. On the contrary, the eugenicists sought by investigation, categorization, and education to subject sexuality to greater control than had ever existed in the past. If the reformers had their way, the most private acts would become subject to the social management of experts.[1]

Eugenicists sought to control and direct sexuality in the first instance by bringing sexual life under public scrutiny. They were among the first to argue that sexual education of children could no longer be left to chance. If ideas and attitudes might eventually affect the well-being of the race it was imperative, they reasoned, that the young be exposed only to those judged healthy and wholesome. The reformers positively exulted in their own intrusiveness. It was their boast that they would ultimately purge youth of their secrets, morbid curiosities, and hidden desires.[2] In an early age ministers could only brandish moral injunctions in their attempts to control the sexual impulses of the young; the eugenicists' message was that if the new generation had revealed to it the dangers posed by a perverse pleasure, a venereal infection, or a thoughtless marriage, then a far more efficient form of self-discipline could be instilled.

The fact that parents were in effect being usurped as the sex educators of the young was in part masked by women eugenicists assuming the maternal role of instructing children in sexuality. The National Council of Women, although it did have its conservative members and sensed the opposition of "ignorant and ashamed parents," was adamant in its call for the rational enlightenment of young people. The Council was of the opinion that one could never start too early to teach the facts of life properly in all their "purity and beauty" and so make youth understand their responsibilities to the race.[3] The same concern for "race improvement" surfaced in 1910 at the fourth annual meeting of the superintendents of training schools for nurses in a discussion centred on a paper of Dr. Jennie Gray. Such advances could only be expected, Gray argued, if children were rationally instructed in biology. She recommended as texts for such "birds and bees" pedagogy *Child Confidence Rewarded* and *What a Young Girl Ought to Know*.[4] In Manitoba, Beatrice Brigden, a member of the Woman's Christian Temperance Union, the Women's Labor League, and the Political Equality League, was employed in 1913 by the Methodist Department of Social Service and Evangelism to provide such lectures on sex hygiene. Much of her information was drawn from Scott Nearing's *Women and Social Progress*, a compendium of progressive American eugenic thought.[5]

Doctors were also quick to enter the discussion of sex education. In 1911 the Sex Hygiene Council of the Vancouver branch of the British Columbia Medical Association recommended giving lectures on sexuality in the schools. In a 1916 report the Council congratulated itself on having instituted the first such program in Canada, though admitting that the terms "sex hygiene" and "social hygiene" were not employed because they might have aroused the prudish. A few special lectures on human biology simply followed a regular science course and even those appeared to have been very discreet.[6]

Psychologists also offered their counsels. Peter Sandiford, in a 1922 article in *Public Health Journal* calling for a more rational approach to reproduction, provided as a model extracts from a text on sex education produced by the Teachers' College of Columbia University. He argued that the home was not an effective forum for such instruction and called on experts imbued with a "dignified frankness" to take up the challenge. Assuming it himself, Sandiford produced *Tell Your Children the Truth* (1926), which was distributed by the Canadian Social Hygiene Council.[7]

A host of groups and individuals in the interwar period – doctors, nurses, Protestant ministers, social workers, the National Council of Women, the Canadian Social Hygiene Council, the Canadian Girls in Training, the YMCA, the YWCA – imbued to a greater or lesser extent with the eugenic preoccupation of "race betterment," were raising the cry that parents were not providing their children with adequate information on sexuality.[8] But though some parents might have been cowed into believing that the experts were better qualified to instruct children in sex matters, the fact was that the eugenicists were usually parroting old moralistic maxims simply dressed up in scientific garb.

In Ontario the most active of the sex lecturers was Arthur W. Beall, whose *The Living Temple: A Manual on Eugenics for Parents and Teachers* (1933) provides a fascinating account of the sort of ideas to which several generations of schoolchildren were exposed. Between 1905 and 1911 Beall, a former teacher and missionary, lectured across the province as a "purity agent" of the Ontario Woman's Christian Temperance Union. From 1911 until the 1930's he continued his work as a special lecturer for the Ontario Department of Education.[9] The gist of Beall's talks was that for the child to harm his or her own body was foolish, wicked, and "unpatriotic." Healthy children, he informed his fascinated classes, were worth about $50,000 each and so rated as "Canada's most valuable products."[10] It followed that the child had a duty to exercise, eat well, and shun filthy habits such as smoking, swearing, and telling smutty stories.

But having dismissed the girls, Beall proceeded to tell the boys that the greatest danger to life was posed by masturbation. If the "LIFE FLUID" was lost from the "LIFE GLANDS" the result was "mental bankruptcy." A boy from Perth County, Beall warned his listeners, ended up in an insane asylum because of this evil habit.

He couldn't keep his hands off the MALE PART of his body – a half dozen times a day he was playing with it, and bleeding away the precious LIFE FLUID, until one day the doctors came along and cut off the two LIFE GLANDS, just to keep the miserable dregs of a miserable existence from all being frittered away. And there [in the asylum], after all these years, useless to God or man, he still exists as a bit of mental punk, a scrap of rotting refuse on life's highway.[11]

Following such a harrowing account it can be assumed that Beall gained the compliance of his terrified pupils when he concluded his lesson with the injunction: "Please repeat after me: 'The more you use the penis muscle, the weaker it becomes; but the less you use the penis muscle, the stronger it becomes!'"[12]

What did all of this have to do with the science of eugenics? The answer has to be, very little. It is true that Beall sprinkled his stories with references to the importance of breeding. Sound fatherhood, he informed the boys, consisted of the "raising of A.1 thoroughbred live-stock." But the essential arguments against self-abuse were the old ones found in nineteenth-century texts meant for men, such as the Reverend W.J. Hunter's *Manhood: Wrecked and Rescued* (1894).[13] What was essentially different in twentieth-century works like Beall's was that children were now being provided with mystifying accounts of sexual matters by purported experts who implicitly or explicitly attacked the competency of parents and friends to deal with such subjects. The term "eugenics" in the title of a book such as Beall's signified little more than the claim that sexuality was to be discussed in a modern, scientific manner.

Young Canadian men and women of marriageable age were also instructed in sex matters by the eugenicists. Between 1905 and 1916 the Canadian Purity-Education Association, led by Dr. Peter H. Bryce, sponsored lectures and distributed literature on the horrors of mastur- bation and venereal disease.[14] In Ontario, Dr. J.E. Hett of Kitchener devoted a series of columns in the *Industrial Banner* of 1920 to the need for sex education. In Hett's grandiose scheme a government department would be created to deal with sex along eugenic lines. "The laws of sex should be studied," he asserted, "and virtue should be aimed at with the greatest ideals of life." It was ignorance, he implied, that led to the thousands of masturbators he had come across whose "sexual onanism" filled the asylums with lunatics and caused more ill health than syphilis and tuberculosis.[15] Hett also called for a "Ministry of Motherhood" that would establish maternity homes, financially compensate fit women for the expense of their pregnancies, and popularize the "science of eugenics" and the knowledge of sexuality it offered. That there was a demand in Canada for such information seems apparent. Dr. J.J. Heagerty reported in 1924 that his lectures on sex education and the accompanying film he showed (produced by the American Social Hygiene Association) at times drew crowds so large that the police were required to control them.[16]

Such crowds were not simply a result of the reformers' particular success in supplying information on the workings of the body. Two major preoccupations created a demand in the early twentieth century for any material that dealt with sexual practices. The first concern was the desire of countless Canadians to limit family size safely and effectively; the second was to obtain protection from the ravages of venereal disease. To deal with the second issue first, it has to be recalled that at the turn of the century the full impact of syphilis in causing sterility, miscarriages, neonatal blindness, insanity, and paralysis was beginning to be understood by physicians and made known to the public.[17] But the fact that syphilis could be congenitally – though not genetically – transmitted was not fully comprehended by most men and women. Eugenicists saw the value of playing up the idea of the hereditary nature of immorality and prostitution. By exploiting the fear of venereal disease they had yet another way in which to establish the argument that sexuality, if not understood and rationally controlled, could pose dangers to the nation.[18]

Eugenicists claimed that syphilis and its conduit – prostitution – imperilled the race. Dr. Charles Hastings, Toronto's medical health officer, informed the 1914 Social Service Congress that venereal disease led to degeneration and depopulation, high infant mortality, and low national efficiency. It was spread by prostitutes who turned to their trade, he asserted, not out of a need for money but as a result of a natural penchant. Citing the findings of the American eugenicist Charles Davenport, Hastings reported that "Evidence is accumulating to show that the primary factor is an inherited predisposition towards an exceptionally active sexual life."[19] The Alberta suffragist and police magistrate Emily Murphy similarly associated disease and deviant behaviour in noting that a third of Alberta's prisoners had to be treated for gonorrhea or syphilis.[20]

Since the eugenicists associated venereal disease more with specific types of behaviour rather than with specific types of bacteria, the solutions they called for to combat it tended to be more socially than medically targeted. Their concerns were inextricably tied to social and cultural values relating to sexuality, gender, ethnicity, and class. They used fear of disease as a means of social control, attacking as carriers of VD those they viewed as threats – the immigrants, the feeble-minded, and the women who violated appropriate gender roles. They argued, for example, that prostitutes not be jailed for short sentences but locked up in colonies for long periods during which they could be taught the housewifely chores of "normal" women.

Feeble-mindedness was posited by Helen MacMurchy and others as a root cause of prostitution.[21] C.K. Clarke claimed that 60 per cent of prostitutes were mentally deficient.[22] The feeble-minded became prostitutes, it was asserted, and spread syphilis, which in turn created another generation of the feeble-minded. To break this vicious cycle, the argument went, it would be necessary to prevent the reproduction of the feeble-minded and thus eventually the spread of venereal disease. It was in this context that Dr. Margaret Patterson argued in 1914 that,

> Cases of natural viciousness in either sex should be given surgical treatment. It is the only kind or safe method. When we have thus treated our cases we are in a position to help them back to a moral life and send them out as did our Master when he said: "Neither do I condemn thee, go and sin no more."[23]

It says something of the eerie self-righteousness of Patterson that in the very midst of a plea for the forcible sterilization of the unfit she could congratulate herself on not being judgemental.

When the First World War broke out large numbers of prostitutes were summarily rounded up and jailed under the Defence of Canada Order. Their illness was their crime. In France, where eventually over 66,000 cases of venereal disease were detected, the army finally accepted the necessity of providing the troops with prophylactic packs.[24] Worried by the prospect of the return of the expeditionary force, the Conservation Commission of Canada published in 1917 a report on *The Prevalence of Venereal Disease in Canada*. The coercive views of the experts, led by C.K. Clarke of the University of Toronto, were reflected in its recommending the public registration and isolation of the diseased and the segregation of the mentally deficient. The latter, the report concluded, were "unfit to understand their responsibilities and it is from this class that the majority of prostitutes and moral perverts are recruited. This class should either become wards of the state, or be rendered innocuous by reverting to the logical but extreme measure of unsexing."[25] The government of the day was not prepared to go so far, but it did follow up one of the recommendations of the Committee in establishing the federal Department of Health as a policing instrument.

At the war's end a National Council for Combatting Venereal Disease, later known as the Canadian Social Hygiene Council, was established in Toronto under the leadership of Dr. Gordon Bates. Its activities were mainly educational, including bringing English suffragist Mrs. Emmeline Pankhurst to Canada in 1923 for a nation-wide lecture tour. As Bates made clear, the goal of his Council was that set by Havelock Ellis in his classic text, *The Task of Social Hygiene* – the building up of the race. If only eugenic marriages were allowed and all citizens subjected to annual checkups, it was possible, argued Bates, to foresee the end of most diseases.[26]

What the social hygienists said very little about was the fact that Paul Ehrlich's discovery of Salvarsan in 1909 had produced a fairly effective treatment for syphilis and that the condom provided a good measure of safety against most venereal infections. Their silence on these matters was due to their concern not to appear to countenance promiscuity. It was characteristic of this approach that A.C. Jost, provincial health officer of Nova Scotia, lumped together as causes of race extinction venereal disease, drink, divorce, and birth control.[27] The eugenicists wanted to control more effectively individual behaviour, not provide greater licence. Preoccupied by the need to regulate public and private conduct, they viewed venereal disease as a *symptom* of more dangerous evils – irrationality, promiscuity, perversity. Eugenicists were making the old argument in favour of restraint but dressing it up in modern biological language.

Most of the discussion of venereal disease centred on the sexual practices of the unmarried, but physicians used the public preoccupation with this menace to argue that even those contemplating marriage should consult a doctor.[28] In 1899 the state of Michigan made venereal disease a bar to marriage, and by 1913 six other states had followed with similar laws. In Canada progress was slower, but the attempt was made to subject a broader segment of the community to surveillance. In 1909 *Canada Lancet* demanded that degenerates, criminals, epileptics, and alcoholics be denied marriage.[29] In 1919 Dr. A.H. Desloges wrote in the *Canadian Medical Association Journal* on the necessity of requiring prospective couples to produce "sanitary testimonials" in order to end all presumably heredity-linked diseases.[30] The same argument was made in a report introduced by Charlotte Whitton to the 1921 Social Service Congress:

... many unhappy and nationally undesirable homes exist because of the lack of provision preventing those, physically or mentally incapable of leading the normal family life, and procreating a normal, healthy family group.[31]

Despite warnings that such laws would not be enforceable or, as had been the case in Australia, simply would lead to a surge in the illegitimacy rate, Whitton's Canadian Council on Child Welfare continued to press for such legislation through the 1920's. Not surprisingly, in the West, where sterilization was enforced, eugenic measures were first applied to marriage. In Alberta in 1935, in Saskatchewan in 1936, and in British Columbia in 1938 evidence was required that prospective mates were free of syphilis.[32] The limited success enjoyed elsewhere in Canada by those who hoped to police marriage could be attributed to Catholic opposition, legislators' recognition of the obvious difficulties of enforcing such statutes, and the legal profession's reluctance to include the medical profession in the controlling of marriage contracts.[33]

Youths tempted by masturbation and young people tainted by venereal disease were the eugenicists' first concerns; only later did they turn their attention to the sex lives of "normal" couples. Married Canadians in search of reproductive knowledge but leery of quack pamphlets on self-abuse and nervous debility had to rely on American sex manuals in the pre-World War One period, particularly the eight volumes of the "Self and Sex Series" distributed in Canada by William Briggs, official publisher of the Methodist Church. Along with their warnings against masturbation and sexual excesses, they informed their readers that due to the "Law of Heredity" a host of physical and psychological taints were passed on from parent to child.[34] The authors of these volumes argued, however, that self-improvement was possible and could also be transmitted to future generations. In embracing the notion of "acquired characteristics" they were defending a position that most eugenicists came to regard by 1914 as very much out of date.[35]

In the interwar period Canadians in search of sex instruction still relied to a great extent on foreign authors. The Canadian Social Hygiene Council continued to recommend the works of such British authors as Maude Royden, Edward Carpenter, and Havelock Ellis. American influence was also unavoidable. In 1925 W.F. Harrison of the Canadian Publishers Association bewailed the fact that American magazines on sexy subjects with such alluring titles as *Spicy Stories*, *Snappy Stories*, and *The Pepper Pot* were penetrating Canada.[36] But they were accompanied by more wholesome treatments of sexuality, including Dr. M.J. Exner's *The Rational Sex Life of Man* and *The*

Question of Petting. The high tone of the latter work – distributed by the YMCA and the American Social Hygiene Council – was captured by a passage in which the young reader was warned that the degenerative effects of promiscuity blighted the possibility of a happy marriage in the same way that an early addiction to jazz rendered a person incapable of enjoying a symphony.[37]

In the 1930's the two most thorough marriage manuals produced in Canada were both heavily weighted by eugenic concerns: Dr. Morris Siegel's *Constructive Eugenics and Rational Marriage* (1934) and A.H. Tyrer's *Sex, Marriage, and Birth Control (Lifting the Blinds on Marriage)* (1936). Siegel, a Hamilton physician, called for the restriction of the marriage of the alcoholic, the feeble-minded, the epileptic, and the tubercular, but acknowledged the dangers of overly repressive measures.[38] His main concern was with "constructive" as opposed to "restrictive" eugenic methods. With the breaking of the old system of arranged marriages and the pursuit of individual sexual pleasure, marriage had become "reckless, nonselective, and irrational."[39] But doctors had brought down the rate of infant mortality and if given the power, he argued, they could similarly lower the level of degeneration: "What the paediatrician has done for babies, the eugenist may do for the young adults contemplating marriage."[40] The creation of a Federal Eugenic Department policing marriages would, he believed, radically improve the health of the nation.

The Jewish race, according to Siegel, provided an example of how a tradition of arranged marriages permitted the maintenance over countless generations of high levels of intellectual success and morality.[41] He did not suggest that this was due to innate superiority. Indeed, he argued that most eugenicists were unduly pessimistic in assuming that only the established class and ethnic elite had good germ plasm. Civilization benefited, according to Siegel, as the aggressive lower orders fought their way to the top.

With hindsight, it might seem surprising that a Jewish doctor – no matter how critical he was of the extravagances of the eugenicists – should range himself alongside those in favour of "improving the race." Siegel was not unaware, as he noted in *Population, Race, and Eugenics* (1939), that many eugenicists were in fact anti-Semites.[42] His hope, nevertheless, was that eugenics could purge itself of its racism and concentrate on the main issue of advancing the concept of "rational marriage." This hope was shared by Rabbi Maurice N. Eisendrath, who also was active in pushing for the sterilization of the feeble-minded and in calling – as he did in a 1936 talk at the Holy Blossom Temple in Toronto – for happier marriages made possible by greater access to birth control. The fact that Jews in Canada and elsewhere were actively involved in eugenics was one more indication of the success with which the movement presented itself as an objective science, not as a racist cause.[43]

Maurice Eisendrath contributed a blurb recommending Tyrer's *Sex, Marriage, and Birth Control*, which provided a far more practical discussion of married love than Siegel's book. Chapters dealt with the issues of monogamy, repression, male and female sex organs, the art and frequency of intercourse, pregnancy, the dangers of abortion, and birth control. Tyrer's depiction of sexuality, including as it did an emphasis on love play and the importance of clitoral stimulation, seemed worlds away from the moralistic messages produced by eugenicists earlier in the century. But if the style was new the message was familiar. Tyrer began his study by citing sources that asserted that the "generally irresponsible classes," "the lower fourth" of the population, produced more than half of the next generation.[44] The population problem, he claimed, could only be solved if the birth rate of the unfit was curbed; if birth control to save the family from such evils as "sexual disharmony," divorce, and abortion was provided; and if government benefits to encourage the breeding of the professional classes were made available. "As soon as a social system is evolved that will remedy all this and take away from parents the fear that more children may mean more distress and poverty," wrote Tyrer, "we shall find the birth-rate among the best citizens increasing."[45]

Tyrer had retired from the Anglican ministry in 1929 and in his sixties turned his attention to the issues of sex education and birth control.[46] In the winter of 1931-32 he was contacted by another eugenicist interested in contraception, the Kitchener businessman A.R. Kaufman. Kaufman supported Tyrer's efforts and ultimately established in 1933 his own Parent's Information Bureau to distribute contraceptives across Canada. By 1942 he had over fifty nurses working for him across the nation and had sent out more than 120,000 contraceptive packages. More importantly, he had in 1936-37 successfully defended in court his right to do so.[47]

Birth control had found its first few defenders in the nineteenth and early twentieth centuries among either the socially conservative Malthusians on the right or the sex radicals on the libertarian left. The real breakthrough in the popularization of the idea of the legitimacy of contraception occurred in the 1920's when Marie Stopes in England and Margaret Sanger in America exploited the emotional notion that only freedom from fear of unwanted pregnancies would permit the happy sex life essential for domestic stability. Both Sanger and Stopes had their followers in Canada, but a native, nation-wide birth control movement only began to emerge in the 1930's as a result of the efforts of Tyrer and Kaufman.[48] The significance of their activities was that they defended birth control on eugenic grounds. In doing so they were reversing the argument advanced by earlier Canadian eugenicists, who opposed contraception on the grounds that it was employed by the very families who should have been encouraged to reproduce. It thus contributed directly to the differential birth rate – the unfit having large families and the fit having small families – which was the very menace that forced the eugenicists to broach the sex question in the first place.

The venom with which eugenicists attacked the spectre of the fertility differential was perhaps best manifested in Watson Kirkconnell's writings of the early 1920's. Kirkconnell, a professor of literature at Wesley College (later to become the University of Winnipeg), an active Baptist, and a rabid anti-Communist, is worth reappraising. Because of his work with Maurice Eisendrath and Claris Silcox on the Board of Jewish-Gentile Relationships and his defence of eastern European immigrants, he has been presented as a benign pioneer of multiculturalism.[49] It comes therefore as somewhat of a shock to find in his *International Aspects of Unemployment* (1923) Canada described as a country afflicted with:

> an ever-increasing plague of useless and inefficient citizens doomed to worthlessness even before their unconsidered births. . . . In the severe competition of primitive life they would have been speedily eliminated by their very unfitness; but in the modern State they have been preserved, often in greater comfort than the hard-working unskilled labourer, and given every chance to increase after their kind.[50]

To end "the physical engendering of undesirables" Kirckconnell called for their segregation in forced labour colonies where they could be "made available for scientific treatment" and "special disposal and care on the part of the State."[51] Some might be "regenerated," but Kirkconnell envisaged that most would be:

> maintained in life-long segregation, not as a matter of punishment but for the preservation of society; and for the same profound and fundamental reasons they should be prevented, through surgical sterilization, from reproducing their worthless kind. The blessing which would be thus bestowed on a nation, by draining off from its germ-plasm those elements through which dishonesty, intemper-

ance of conduct, violence, laziness, perversion, and all of the most darkly antisocial qualities are inevitably perpetrated in its inheritance, is beyond computation.[52]

Birth control, which Kirkconnell defined as the "social program whereby the fitter elements of a community forgo normal parenthood and leave the future of the race to the teeming progeny of the unfit and improvident," had to be necessarily condemned as a "dysgenic gospel."[53]

The *Dalhousie Review* carried an article in 1925 that echoed these concerns.

The licence society allows at present to the criminal, the insane and the feeble-minded to multiply at pleasure, and to have their worse than worthless offspring cared for at the public expense, or rather at the expense of those who feel too heavily taxed to produce children that would yield better returns to the community – that is, after all, something of a social oversight.[54]

The problem was that though the eugenicists could suggest a variety of ways to curb the fertility of the unfit, they found it difficult to envisage ways to encourage the breeding of the fit. They certainly could not hope to coerce the middle class into having larger families.

Beginning on an emotional level, eugenicists' first response was to attack the patriotism of the healthy members of the middle class who, in refusing to bear more than one or two children, were in effect "sterilizing" themselves. Thus in 1918 Dr. W.A. Lincoln of Calgary upbraided middle-class women because, in his words, "the shifting of their maternal duty to the weary shoulders and the work-racked bodies of their less 'well-placed' sisters; or to the too carelessly prolific immigrant lays these women open to the charge of national disregard."[55] Helen MacMurchy chimed in with the argument that "Those who marry but voluntarily refuse parenthood are robbing themselves of their greatest joy, and are failing to serve the highest interests of their country and their generation."[56]

Feminism was singled out by a number of commentators as exacerbating the situation inasmuch as it lured healthy women away from their natural duties as wives and mothers and toward the professional world of men. University women, the readers of *Dalhousie Review* were informed in 1930, were generally "infertile."[57] In a different essay in the same journal William D. Tait, professor of psychology at McGill University, asserted that it was necessary to veto the "feminist cry of birth control":

Nature makes it plain . . . that to produce great variations we must have large numbers from which to select. To insure the greatest possible number of great minds, there must be the possibility of selection from a great number. Birth control would forbid this possibility.[58]

Tait accused the women who employed birth control – a leisured, selfish, effete elite – of attacking "the source of all our racial existence."[59] An editorial in *Social Welfare* for September, 1923, agreed that those who supported birth control were, "so far as we can learn . . . mainly mistaken faddists and selfish, unnatural women who put world pleasures before the joys of motherhood."[60]

Eugenics-minded doctors also waded into the debate with assertions that birth control was both a threat to the race and a danger to the individual. In 1924 Dr. J.J. Heagerty, director of the Social Hygiene Division of the Department of Health, lashed out at contraception as being a consequence of cowardice and the cause of immorality, prostitution, illegitimacy, and crime.[61] His colleague, Dr. Helen Mac-Murchy, opposed birth control throughout her long career. Her last major statement on the subject in *Sterilization? Birth Control? A Book for Family Welfare and Safety* was that "It is unnatural. It is contrary to one's higher instincts. It is repugnant to a member of the medical profession whose work and whose desire is to promote health and happiness . . . . It should not be undertaken or carried on except for clear, definite and grave reasons of a medical nature and under medical advice."[62] Doctors, having declared that they should decide who could marry, were now proceeding to assert that they should also monitor how the married carried out their sexual relations.

Mere moral injunctions being recognized as futile in eliciting larger families of the fit, the eugenicists' second response was to argue that the fit had to be rewarded for reproducing. Nellie McClung, although writing in the midst of the First World War, was of the opinion that Germany, with its Repopulation Society, League for the Protection of Motherhood, and League for Infant Protection, provided a model for Canada in the ways the reproduction of the healthy could be sponsored. "Our whole attitude towards the bringing of children into the world," she wrote, "has been vague and dreamy. We have left everything to all-wise Providence, shirking our responsibilities in that way."[63]

Manitoba led the western provinces by beginning in 1916 to provide mothers' pensions for the poor. The extension of the provision of such support for fit women, argued Watson Kirkconnell in 1923, would be a way of removing them from the masculine world of labour and returning them to "their more important work" of breeding.[64] J.J. Heagerty suggested prolific families be given pensions, scholarships, and tax support.[65] The popular journalist Hilda Ridley, in a 1929 article entitled "A Revaluation of Motherhood," asserted that the new "race consciousness" would eventually manifest itself in three policies: the education of the public on the "vital importance of good stock" in breeding; the teaching in high schools of heredity and eugenics; and the endowment of mothers who "could show 'clean bills' in the matter of their family histories, of which of course, they would have made a special study."[66] The fact that by 1930 all the provinces from Ontario to British Columbia had some form of mothers' allowance scheme was, of course, not simply due to the effectiveness of the eugenic campaign. A recognition of the burden of female labour in the home and a real concern for the alleviation of poverty motivated many who campaigned for such state support of parenting. Nevertheless, the fact that almost every participant in the discussion of such schemes spoke in terms of race betterment revealed the success eugenicists enjoyed in setting the terms of the debate.[67]

The conservative eugenicists remained true to the notion that birth control was a danger to the race. The more progressive began in the 1920's to face up to the fact that there was no hope of turning the middle classes away from the pursuit of fertility control as popularized in Britain by Marie Stopes and in the United States by Margaret Sanger.[68] Once that was conceded it followed that the fertility differential could only be overcome if birth control devices employed by the elite were also made available to the masses. This was an argument that Stopes and Sanger increasingly employed and one to which the eugenicists were slowly drawn.

Charles J. Hastings, medical officer of health in Toronto, was the first well-known hereditarian to concede the importance of contraception. In a 1924 article he cited a bevy of experts, including William Beveridge, H.G. Wells, and Dean Inge, to back up the argument that birth control was not contrary to, but an essential part of, eugenics.[69] On the occasion of the American anarchist Emma Goldman's talk on birth control in Toronto in 1927, Hastings again declared that although the reproduction of the "subnormal type" was his main concern he had no objections to birth control as long as it was provided under medical supervision and not by "promiscuous dispensations." "The sane solution of the problem," he declared, "is not a wholesale birth control, but an intelligent birth control which should be under the control of the medical profession, the legal profession, and the clergy."[70] In 1927 few shared his opinion. A reporter for the *Toronto Star* found that the representatives of the churches, the Ontario Medical Association, and the Social Hygiene Council would not even discuss the subject.

The *Star* reporter was unaware – as were most Canadians – that two attempts had already been made by eugenicists at launching birth control movements in Canada. In Vancouver a Canadian Birth Control League resulted from the interest engendered by Margaret Sanger's visit to the city in July, 1923. The League, though led by the socialist A.M. Stephens and composed largely of left-leaning men and women, advocated during the few years of its shadowy existence both the establishment of birth control clinics and the sterilization of the unfit.[71]

The fact that Stephens's small West Coast group was dominated by socialist feminists deprived it from the very start of the support of the respectable. Moreover, Dr. Lyle Telford, like Stephens an advocate of birth control and a member of the Socialist Party, in speaking in 1928 to University of British Columbia students on "companionate marriage" – which entailed legalized birth control and divorce by mutual consent – brought down on the radicals a rain of abuse. University president L.S. Klinck deplored the talk and the UBC senate called for the vetting of all future campus speakers. The Vancouver *Sun*'s editorial entitled "Companionate Hokum" asserted that "companionate marriage" as originally formulated by Judge Ben Lindsey of Colorado was no more than "legalized harlotry" and "sex madness." Sigmund Freud must have had a part in such a perverse concept, the editor continued, because "bolshevism is the philosophy of the socially unfit. And Freudianism is the philosophy of the oversexed." Emily Murphy concurred, warning the readers of *Chatelaine* that contraceptives could kill and in any event a marriage in which there were no children was no more than "an agreement between a flirt and a philanderer."[72]

In the East the Ontario Birth Control League was established in March, 1925, and, like its Vancouver counterpart, linked neo-Malthusian and eugenic concerns. The Ontario group was led by Dr. O.C.J. Withrow, who during his long and eventful life was constantly embroiled in what he perceived as the key struggle of the century – the improvement of the race. Graduating from the University of Toronto in 1902 he had initially practised medicine in Thunder Bay, but in 1912 he returned to Toronto where he began to work with Clarence Hincks and C.K. Clarke at the Social Services Clinic. The concern for hereditary complaints that he shared with Hincks and Clarke was complemented by a preoccupation with venereal diseases, which he studied when overseas with the Canadian army in 1916. In 1918 he was appointed secretary for sex education by the National Council of the YMCA, lecturing coast to coast and distributing a reported 750,000 pamphlets. Upon returning to civilian life Withrow pursued his new obstetric and gynecological interests. He was thus well qualified to chair the organizational meeting of the Ontario Birth Control League that met at the Foresters' Hall on March 5, 1925.[73]

Aside from Withrow the only other notable at the meeting was Robert MacIver, professor of political economy at the University of Toronto. "I support birth control," he later explained, "from the point of view of political economy, to prevent over-population and the recruitment of the population from its feeble-minded elements. It is not a matter of doing anything. It is just that the knowledge, which the upper classes already possess, should be made available for the less educated and poorer. Under present conditions population is recruited most largely from the poorest classes."[74] It was the view of MacIver and Withrow that improved health would result if all groups controlled their fertility, but social degeneration was threatened if only the elite limited family size.

The Ontario League seems to have accomplished very little and, in any event, Withrow's activities came to an abrupt end in May, 1927, when he was found guilty of performing an abortion that resulted in the death of a young woman.[75] He served close to three years in Kingston penitentiary and was only readmitted to the medical profession in 1933.[76] By that time the depression had hit and the fear of the unemployed had driven many who had previously spurned the ideology of birth control into embracing it.

In 1931 Tyrer, along with Maurice Eisendrath, Florence Huestis, vice-president of the Social Hygiene Council, and Dr. D.M. Lebourdais of the National Committee on Mental Hygiene, established what became know as the Birth Control League of Canada.[77] Support was quickly offered the movement by Protestant church leaders. Already in 1930 the Reverend Lawrence Skey of Toronto's St. Anne's Anglican Church had echoed Dr. Charles Hastings's defence of the social necessity of birth control clinics. In 1931 he and Tyrer established the Marriage Welfare Bureau, which began to send out birth control information.[78] The Bureau's avowed purpose was to improve marriages and thereby strengthen a society racked by economic tensions. Skey's colleague, the Reverend W.G. Nicholson of St. Clement's, explained that "intelligent control" was necessary to counter the "rapid growth in the number of the inefficient and unemployable; in the increase in the numbers of insane and in the perpetuation of human suffering from disease."[79] The fact that contraception could prevent the reproduction of "a stunted humanity" was likewise cited in its favour by the Board of Evangelism and Social Service of the United Church of Canada in its 1932 tract, *The Meaning and Responsibilities of Christian Marriage*.[80] At the beginning of the century, ministers had declared it a sin for a woman to limit her fertility; in the depths of the depression, pastors interested in eugenics were saying it was a sin if some did not.

> Science has come to her aid [wrote the Reverend Morris Zeidman] and if she does not avail herself of the opportunities offered by science and eugenics, she sins against her own body and against her own children who are entitled to all the love, care and upbringing which are a child's birthright; and she sins against the nation, which expects quality rather than quantity.[81]

Similar eugenic arguments were offered by a number of women's groups to explain why they were now rallying to the birth control movement. Emily Murphy, the Alberta magistrate who had condemned contraception in the 1920's, swung to its defence in the early 1930's. Quoting the Reverend Nicholson, Murphy argued that the country's social problems could only be successfully dealt with if contraception was employed thoughtfully.[82] The notion that birth control might be part of a radical, pluralistic approach to sexuality was what underlay the hostility of social conservatives to the earlier activities of Stephens and Telford. Once convinced that fertility control could be a force for stability rather than change, the respectable came out in its support.

The symbolic breakthrough of the birth control movement in Canada came in 1937 when the prosecution of one of A.R. Kaufman's workers was successfully defended and the legitimacy of such activities thereby established.[83] The trial, which took place in the small Ottawa Valley town of Eastview, has been presented by some as an important milestone in the struggle by Canadians for reproductive freedom. That might well have been one of its results, but an analysis of the trial transcripts reveals that it certainly was not the *intent* of the eugenicist A.R. Kaufman. He was drawn to birth control because he saw it as the only means by which the social elite could hope to shape Canada's population profile. Only the provision of cheap contraceptives to the masses would, in his words, limit "the unintelligent and penniless who unfortunately constitute an increasing percentage of the total population."[84]

In discussing his activities with Clarence Gamble, an American philanthropist also involved in birth control work, Kaufman made it clear that the bogey of the fertility differential was his chief preoccupation.

I think one of the reasons the self-supporting classes are limiting their families is because they have to pay for rearing other people's children and . . . cannot afford to raise more than two of their own and give them a decent education. You know as well as I do that if we breed from the bottom instead of the top we are courting disaster. Any farmer has more sense when it comes to breeding animals. We cannot be as arbitrary with human beings in controlling reproduction, but I know from experience that the inefficient and underprivileged will have small families if they know how to accomplish it and have the brains to exercise contraceptive methods. However, our observation is that about five to ten percent of the cases we contact lack the calibre to practice contraception and should be sterilized.[85]

Kaufman was no libertarian. He accepted the necessity of using any and all means to improve the race.[86]

Kaufman, treasurer of the Eugenics Society of Canada, chose as his defence attorney in the Eastview trial a fellow member of the Society, F.W. Wegenast. The main arguments in Wegenast's defence of the social value of birth control were drawn from the testimony of fellow believers in hereditary taint.[87] Claris E. Silcox – ex-minister of the United Church, general secretary of the Social Service Council of Canada, and marriage expert – testified that it was "futile to talk about equality when certain strains, economically, if not mentally and physically inferior, were breeding with utter irresponsibility."[88] Dr. William Hutton, the Brantford, Ontario, medical officer and president of the Eugenics Society of Canada, was called as a public health expert. In addition to campaigning for the sterilization of the feeble-minded, Hutton was Canada's best-known medical defender of contraception. His main contribution to the trial consisted of the assertion that there was a tendency for the unintelligent to be overly fertile, a situation, he stated, that was found in Brantford where fifty "socially inadequate" families had over 250 living children.[89] Dr. George Brock Chisolm, a psychiatrist working at the University of Toronto, appeared for the defence as an expert on intelligence testing. He argued, as did Hutton, that a biological crisis was posed by the excessive fertility of the less intelligent. Effective methods of birth control had to be made available, stated Chisolm, both to curb the fertility of the unfit and to free the fit of fear and frustration.[90] A number of liberal arguments were also marshalled by Wegenast – the immorality of depriving individuals of contraceptive information, the right of women to control their reproduction, the legitimacy of non-procreative sexual pleasure – but they were all subsumed under the broader argument that birth control would serve eugenic goals in subjecting reproduction to rational controls. When Magistrate Clayton found in favour of the defence a victory was won for both birth control and eugenics.[91]

Although eugenic notions pervaded the campaigns in favour of sex education and birth control, not all supporters of sex education and birth control were necessarily eugenicists. A practical concern for stemming the spread of venereal disease and providing couples with safe methods of family limitation was what clearly drew mass support. Some of Kaufman's own field workers were more motivated by a genuine appreciation of the plight of working-class mothers than by any hereditarian ideology.

It was also the case that, although in Canada hereditarian thinking was very much dominated by social conservatives, a few daring individuals on the political left argued that eugenics could be turned to sexually subversive ends. The most interesting forays in the field were made by Robert Bird Kerr and Dora Forster, an English, Fabian-Socialist couple who lived in British Columbia between 1893 and 1922. In articles submitted to English neo-Malthusian journals, American libertarian publications, and Canadian socialist papers, they argued that those seriously in favour of race improvement would have to accept the necessity of women's rights, divorce, and birth control.[92] Few Canadians were aware that such arguments were being penned in British Columbia at the turn of the century. Kerr and Forster did not go out of their way to make themselves known. Their attacks on existing moral standards were so daring that they only found friendly responses to their proposals in that small, cosmopolitan coterie of sex radicals scattered throughout the world.[93]

Though they felt isolated in Canada Kerr and Forster were not alone in believing that aspects of eugenics could be incorporated in a socialist program. Echoes of such concerns were heard in the left-wing press. During World War One the *B.C. Federationist* carried letters from readers calling for "eugenic babies" rather than sickly ones and reported J.S. Woodsworth's support of sex education and companionate marriage. In Winnipeg Ada Muir wrote in *The Voice* of her admiration of the American libertarian eugenicist Lillian Harman, while Florence Rowe provided the *One Big Union Bulletin* with articles on "Better and Fewer Babies." Violet McNaughton's opening of her column in the *Western Producer* in 1927 to the discussion of family limitation elicited a flurry of letters from prairie progressives interested in eugenics. "I hold," wrote Carl Axelson of Bingville, Alberta, "that it is essential for every person to study physiology to the extent of securing correct knowledge of our bodies and the relation and interdependence of sex and especially information regarding reproduction." Another writer upbraided those who were fearful that "the effort to improve the human family by using more commonsense and knowledge in the choosing of a life-mate would eliminate sentiment and love." Sophia H. Dixon, who in 1933 was to be instrumental in the founding of the CCF, cited Russia as an example of a society in which such improvements of the race were being pursued.[94]

What these progressives imagined was a better world in which a rational, scientific, but non-coercive approach would be taken to the sex question. Access to sex education, contraceptives, divorce, and the endowment of motherhood would, they hoped, free women from the trap of loveless marriages and mindless breeding. These reformers' understanding of the laws of heredity were, of course, slim to say the least. But their better-qualified opponents who supported conservative Galtonian eugenics turned their "science" to even more transparently self-serving purposes.[95]

The Eastview trial capped a thirty-year campaign by Canadian eugenicists to make sexual practices the subject of national concern and debate. While this new openness did have its liberating aspects, the intentions of the conservative hereditarians were in fact repressive. They sought to turn sex education, marriage counselling, the campaign against venereal disease, and birth control to the purposes of improved social management.[96] Their ideas seemed so rational (who could be opposed to "race betterment"?) and were so pervasive that it is difficult to think of any sex reformer in the interwar period who did not employ them. Even the final step in the disciplining of reproduction – test-tube babies – was envisaged by some Canadians in the 1930's. In 1935 Ernest M. Best, the general secretary of the YMCA, conjured up just such a vision of the creation of an "International Burbank Society for Humaniculture." "Through our knowledge of the techniques of contraception, sterilization and artificial fertilization we have the means," he exalted, "of controlling the forces of heredity."[97] He admitted that it would require courage to put into force the sorts of "biologically salutary laws" required, but he was at least able to point to an existing society in which such pioneering work had begun. "Already the Nazi state has taken active steps to direct heredity, and while we do not need to accept their absurd premises of Nordicism we can see the beginnings of intelligent social action toward racial improvement."[98]

Indeed, Nazi Germany was the society toward which those seeking confirmation of the practical benefits of eugenic measures increasingly turned. The most dramatic of these in the mid-1930's were the mass sterilizations of mental defectives. There were many in Canada who, while lamenting the brutalities of the Nazis, could not help applauding the boldness with which they grappled with the threat of racial degeneration.

5

Creating a Haven for Human Thoroughbreds

In 1933 the *Canadian Medical Association Journal* reprinted an address that Dr. H.A. Bruce, Lieutenant-Governor of Ontario, had given to the Hamilton Canadian Club. In it, Bruce, a respected surgeon, wandered far from his own area of professional expertise into the nightmare world of eugenic speculation. Between 1871 and 1931, he informed his audience, the general population had doubled but that of the mentally ill had increased sixfold. Fifty per cent of the latter were produced by feeble-minded parents who were far more prolific than the normal. Bruce warned that if some steps were not taken to stem this tide, in seventy-five years one-half of the population would be condemned to labour to support the other half, which would be institutionalized. Since the segregation of the subnormal had clearly not restricted their multiplication the only answer was to embark on a policy of sterilization.[1]

Bruce's comments did not go unanswered. Dr. W.D. Cornwall of Port Dalhousie, Ontario, retorted that Bruce was patently apologizing for the faults of capitalism inasmuch as he attributed mental illness solely to innate genetic faults and glossed over the impact of social deprivation. It was, asserted Cornwall, obvious that in a capitalist society generous, altruistic, socially minded traits were not valued; accordingly, the poor and weak were ground under while the ruthless, like Al Capone and Mussolini, flourished. If one were truly interested in eliminating the marginalized and the misfit the task would be to improve the environment rather than attempt to control breeding.[2]

Both sides of the sterilization debate were aired in the *Canadian Medical Association Journal* but those of Cornwall's opinion were very much in the minority. The pro-sterilization camp was led by such well-known medical figures as *CMAJ* editor A.G. Nichols, its assistant editor H.E. MacDermott, Dr. C.M. Hincks of the National Committee on Mental Hygiene, Dr. C.B. Farrar of the Toronto Psychiatric Hospital, Dr. W.L. Hutton, president of the Canadian Eugenics Society, and Professor Madge Thurlow Macklin of the University of Western Ontario. The general thrust of their argument was that the struggle for survival had been reversed by the advances of medicine. A resulting problem was that the unfit, who once would have perished, were now able to survive and reproduce.[3] Indeed, Dr. Hutton asserted that figures drawn from the asylum at Orillia suggested that the families of the feeble-minded had on average eight children while the normal had only three. Society was thus caught in the quandary of the feeble-minded having excessively large families while the intelligent employed birth control to limit the reproduction of fit stock. The question, said Hutton, was how "sound stock" could prevent "its dilution and pollution with the blood of the feeble-minded and the sufferers from the hereditary diseases."[4] The answer offered by his colleagues was that since doctors had helped to create the problem they had a responsibility to solve it. Medical intervention in the form of sterilization was needed to counter the surge of mental deficiency created by earlier forms of intervention. To the objection that individual freedoms might be violated as a result, A.G. Nichols responded that to spread disease purposely was considered by all a crime. Surely it followed, he argued, that "to bring into the world another individual grievously handicapped for the struggle of life, one who may in addition prove a menace to his fellows, is as much to be depreciated as murder."[5] If such "crimes" could not be punished they could at least be prevented. A "police state" already existed inasmuch as vaccinations and quarantines were enforced by law to deal with infectious diseases. A similarly aggressive attack on the roots of mental illness was justified by the same concerns for the well-being of the community.

It comes as somewhat of a surprise to find in a medical journal an impassioned debate over the merits of capitalism and socialism and the police state. The discussion of sterilization of the feeble-minded, however, was an issue that inextricably entangled medical, moral, and political issues. Many doctors were naturally enough attracted to the notion of a biologically based program of reform. Such a program would have to draw on their expertise and highlight the social importance of the profession. Convinced that the same objectivity they employed in the medical lab could be sustained when dealing with public policy, they were angered and alarmed when mavericks like Cornwall accused them of social bias and prejudice.

The year 1933 was the high-water mark of the debate over sterilization. In that year British Columbia followed Alberta in becoming the second province in Canada to pass legislation permitting the sterilization of the mentally ill and retarded.[6] The Act empowered a Eugenics Board consisting of a psychiatrist, a judge, and a social worker to order the sterilization of any inmate of a provincial institution who "would be likely to beget or bear children who by reason of inheritance would have a tendency to serious mental disease or mental deficiency."[7] But 1933 was also the year in which Manitoba rejected similar legislation, and in the later 1930's Ontario, despite the goadings of Bruce, similarly refused to follow the lead of Alberta and British Columbia.[8]

Given the fact that 1933 was the same year in which the Nazis began their own campaign for racial hygiene in Germany,[9] it might well be asked if British Columbia's sterilization law indicates that Canada also harboured fascist sentiments and programs. An analysis of the sterilization debate in British Columbia reveals that in fact eugenically based racial concerns were all-pervasive in interwar Canadian society and the most extreme policies tended to be advanced, not by conservatives, but by progressives and medical scientists.[10] British Columbia's sexual sterilization bill was of importance, not because it reflected the concerns of radical fringe groups, but because it represented the optimistic belief of respectable members of the helping professions. They asserted that many of the apparently new and menacing social problems of the twentieth century could be contained by medical intervention. What was rarely appreciated at the time was that professionals were calling for policies, such as the sterilization of the retarded, to counter a spectre that the professionals had themselves conjured up, that of a dangerous surge in the numbers of the mentally deficient.

In British Columbia, as in the rest of Canada, the "feeble-minded" were in effect "created" as a category at the turn of the century when education was made free and compulsory.[11] There had, of course, always been some members of society who because of their mental or physical handicaps had been perceived by their neighbours as somehow deficient. With the emergence of a modern, centralized, mass form of education, however, one entered a new world. To an unprecedented extent enormous numbers of children were subjected to common tests, examinations, and medical inspections. Those who met the new norms were declared "normal"; those who did not were labelled as inadequate.

The medicalization of the British Columbia school system began in 1907 with school medical inspection instituted throughout Vancouver.[12] In 1910 a full-time nurse was hired and Dr. F.W. Brydone-Jack was appointed as Vancouver's school medical officer. Josephine Dauphinée, who became supervisor of special classes, established in 1910 the first class for the "subnormal." In 1918, Martha Lindley, who had worked with H.H. Goddard of the Vineland Training School for Feeble-Minded Girls and Boys in New Jersey, was appointed Vancouver's first full-time school psychiatrist.[13] Goddard had popularized Binet's IQ test in America; Lindley in turn employed the Goddard or Terman revision of the Binet-Simon IQ scale in British Columbia.[14]

The IQ tests to which students were subjected naturally relied on "cultural experiences and the verbal skills and practices" of the cultural elite.[15] As a social product of the middle class they necessarily confused innate intelligence with an appreciation of bourgeois norms. And if tests and examinations did not single one out as a problem child, deviant behaviour could. Teachers, by attributing behaviour problems to retardation rather than to the child's environment, unwittingly participated in the creation of the idea of a growth in the numbers of the feeble-minded.

We know today that so-called mental retardation is higher between school entry and leaving age.[16] Compulsory education not only reveals cases of retardation but effectively creates them by subjecting many children to completely new and frightening demands for systematic intellectual functioning. But such apparent retardation often disappears once the individual is freed of the restraints of the institution and allowed to pursue his or her interests. The reason why the feeble-minded appeared to be increasing after the turn of the century was because the community's demands on children were increasing. Larger and larger numbers of children were labelled as incapable of being educated because they failed to respond adequately to a specific form of education they were compelled to experience.

But in the first decades of this century teachers and doctors interpreted the findings to mean that only because examinations and inspections were now being systematically carried out was the "true" extent of feeble-mindedness evident. The problem, as they saw it, was that only the school population was being surveyed; an accurate account of the ways mental retardation contributed to rending the fabric of society, and to gauge the extent to which "racial degeneration" had spread, awaited investigation of all public institutions.

In the British Empire the fear of racial degeneration was sparked during the Boer War when it was discovered that vast numbers of potential recruits were either physically or mentally unfit to serve their country overseas. In Canada there was in addition the Anglo-Saxon concern that the nation was being swamped by waves of new immigrants.[17] And finally the First World War cut a swath through the generation of young men on which the country set its hopes. Canadian authorities expressed their concerns that the post-war nation would have to shoulder the burden not only of the handicapped at home but also of the returning veterans, including over 5,000 shell-shock victims. It was in this context that Dr. J.D. Maclean, the Liberal provincial secretary of British Columbia in 1919, called on Dr. C.M. Hincks of the Canadian National Committee on Mental Hygiene to carry out a survey of the feeble-minded in the province.[18] The first such Canadian survey had been held in Ontario in 1906; between 1918 and 1922 the CNCMH carried out similar investigations in seven provinces. Hincks had already surveyed the New Westminster Hospital for the Insane in December of 1918 and in 1919 he extended his scope to include public schools, industrial schools, detention homes, and orphanages. Hincks reported not only that the extent of feeble-mindedness was high, but that it posed a serious threat to society inasmuch as it was a primary cause of poverty, crime, and prostitution.[19] What measures should the province take to protect itself from the internal and external (Hincks reported that 72 per cent of asylum inmates were foreign-born) threat of the reproduction of the feeble-minded?[20]

Until the turn of the century the feeble-minded were controlled and prevented from reproducing primarily by segregating them in asylums. The early twentieth century brought the criticism that segregation had proved both expensive and inefficient. The sterilization of the feeble-minded, it was argued, would prove to be a cheaper, more effective and humane method of restricting their breeding.[21] The stimulus for this response came first from the defenders of eugenic arguments. If, as it appeared, a policy of "positive eugenics" to encourage the fertility of the superior stock proved unworkable, at the very least one could employ a policy of "negative eugenics" to prevent the multiplication of the inferior.[22] In so doing one would eliminate not only feeble-mindedness but also the violence, vice, and misery to which it gave rise. The fact that safe, surgical methods of sterilization were now available made the suggestion eminently feasible.[23]

In North America the first bill in favour of sterilization was introduced in Michigan in 1897; the first to be enacted was in Indiana in 1907 and the second in British Columbia's neighbour to the south, Washington state, in 1910. Eventually thirty-one states would enact similar legislation.[24]

In British Columbia the earliest and most vigorous proponents of sterilization were the members of the various women's movements. It would appear that the first public declaration in support of sterilization was carried in a 1914 edition of the British Columbia suffragist paper, *The Champion*.[25] To understand why the same women who were campaigning for political freedoms should have given support to a policy that limited the rights of the handicapped requires that one recall the ethos of the early women's movement. It was very much marked by what has been called an ideology of "maternal feminism."[26] Women demanded the vote so that they could more adequately defend their homes and children. The war helped focus even greater attention on health and population issues. Consequently, after the vote was attained, a good deal of the attention of the various women's groups in the 1920's was devoted to developing programs to protect their children. Baby welfare centres, better baby contests, and well-baby clinics proliferated. Maternal feminists rallied support for a series of campaigns in favour of preventive medical attacks on tuberculosis, venereal disease, and influenza.[27] Mothers' pensions and juvenile courts were similarly fought for in the effort to shore up the family. Unfortunately, the defence of these progressive measures was often accompanied by statements that revealed the siege mentality of many of their proponents. If Canada were to be healthy and happy it was necessary to prevent the entry of immigrants who, they asserted, were over-represented by the feeble-minded, the epileptic, the idiotic, the tubercular, the dumb, the blind, the illiterate, the criminal, and the anarchistic.[28] And if normal Canadian children were to receive a healthy upbringing and a decent education they would have to be protected from disruptive and potentially degrading associations with the abnormal. In 1915 the National Council of Women asked Prime Minister Borden to appoint a royal commission on mental defectives; in 1925 the NCW came out in favour of sterilization.[29] The strongest support in the provinces came from Alberta and British Columbia, with such luminaries as Nellie McClung, Emily Murphy, Henrietta Edwards, and Helen Gregory MacGill providing public backing.[30]

The *Western Women's Weekly*, which served as a mouthpiece for the main women's groups, and the Child Welfare Association of B.C. led the campaign for sterilization in British Columbia. It informed its readers that 51 per cent of the feeble-minded were new immigrants, that certificates of "normality" should have to be obtained before marriages were allowed, that mentally defective girls in particular presented a "social and moral menace."[31] The most authoritative statements were made by Josephine Dauphinée, the supervisor of special classes in Vancouver. Eighty per cent of feeble-mindedness, she wrote, was due to hereditary causes; the portion of feeble-minded in the community had doubled in the past two decades because of their prolific nature; and the feeble-minded in turn formed the core of "the poverty stricken, criminal and degenerate classes."[32] Sterilization was the only way society could protect itself from such scourges at home. But what of threats from abroad? Dauphinée conjured up the following lurid portrayal of new immigrants: "Here we see two brothers from sunny Italy, lazy, degenerate, dissolute and mentally deficient; no challenge halts them; the port of entry is not barred – Canada is theirs for the taking."[33] To counter such threats the women's groups sought more stringent screening of immigrants.

The women's movement in British Columbia had direct access to the legislative assembly as Mary Ellen Smith, a contributor to the *Western Women's Weekly*, was MLA for South Vancouver. Smith, who had sat as the first woman cabinet member in the British Empire in John Oliver's 1921 Liberal government, was a vigorous supporter of several programs aimed at protecting women and children. It was in light of just these concerns that she rose in the Legislative Assembly in December, 1925, to call for both more restrictive legislation on immigration and a sterilization bill similar to that of Washington state. The press reported her stating that "if this were done, the English speaking peoples would maintain their position of supremacy on which the peace and prosperity of the world depend."[34]

In fact, the previous month the provincial secretary, William Sloan, had received the unanimous support of the Legislative Assembly to establish a select committee to investigate mental retardation in the province. In introducing his motion Sloan had given three reasons for such an inquiry. The first was the alarming growth of mental illness and mental retardation. In 1872 there were only two mental cases for every 2,265 citizens; in 1924 there was one for every 293.[35] This growth was in part due to the "fact" that, as Dr. H.C. Steeves, superintendent of Essondale, had indicated, in 70 per cent of cases of manic depression, dementia praecox, epilepsy, idiocy, and imbecility the hereditary factor predominated. Only in 30 per cent of cases, such as those relating to syphilis, senility, and psychosis following illness, could the physical factor be found to predominate.[36] Sloan's second reason for alarm was that British Columbia was becoming a dumping ground for foreign misfits. He reported that an analysis of the inmate population found that a bare 10 per cent were from British Columbia and only 30 per cent from the rest of Canada; a full 60 per cent were foreigners. And this in turn led to Sloan's third preoccupation, the cost of supporting the existing system of segregation, which amounted to $750,000 per year.[37] Speaking in support of the inquiry, Drs. Wrinch and Rothwell agreed that new policies were required, but that years of education were needed before the public would see the wisdom of sterilizing the feeble-minded and placing restrictions on marriage and immigration.[38]

The Royal Commission on Mental Hygiene of 1925 consisted of its chairman, Dr. E.J. Rothwell, Brigadier-General V.W. Odlum, Reginald Hayward, W.A. Mackenzie, and Paul Harrison. It held open sessions in Victoria and Vancouver, where it received briefs and evidence. It also received material from experts from eastern Canada and the United States. The Commission was mandated to investigate the reason for the growth in the numbers of the mentally deficient, examine the causes and prevention of lunacy, gauge the extent of entry into the province of the deficient, and determine the level of care currently available for the subnormal.[39]

In their 1927 first report the commissioners responded to the first issue by noting that the growth of mental problems was not as alarming as first thought; the extent was simply more accurately reported because of the larger number of facilities available for the care of the subnormal. British Columbia's rate of increase was about on a par with the rest of Canada.[40] Overcrowding did exist in the available institutions, however, so that concerns about added growth did have some foundation. The entry of defective immigrants into British Columbia was the special concern of Dr. Henry Young, secretary of the Provincial Board of Health, and Dr. A.G. Price, Victoria's city medical officer. The Commission agreed that a disproportionate percentage of asylum inmates were foreign born and called for some form of screening process to be instituted.[41]

The evidence received by the Commission on the causes of mental deficiency was conflicting. Dr. J.G. McKay, founder of the Hollywood Sanitarium at New Westminster and one of the most active participants in the Commission's hearings, asserted that 60 to 70 per cent of all mental problems were inherited. He was supported in the main by the evidence of Herbert W. Collier, superintendent of the detention home and chief probation officer of Victoria, Dr. George Hall of the Victoria Medical Society, Vancouver Police Magistrate J.S. Jamieson, Dr. Mackintosh, the Burnaby medical officer, and Mr. J. Williams of the Child Welfare Association.[42] Doctors such as K.D. Panton and W.A. Dobson, who were attracted to a psychodynamic approach to mental health problems, were sceptical of the claims of the hereditarians.[43] They were in turn supported by Dr. Helen P. Davidson of Stanford University, whose statistical analysis was included in Appendix G of the report.[44] She stated that only 11 to 30 per cent of mental defects were related to hereditary transmission. Most of the outside witnesses, however, were convinced of the primary importance of heredity and accordingly prone to support a policy of sterilization. They included Dr. C.M. Hincks of the Canadian National Committee on Mental Hygiene, Dr. C.B. Farrar of the Toronto Psychopathic Hospital, and Paul Popenhoe of the Human Betterment Foundation of Pasadena, California.[45] Moreover, even those doctors who must have been aware of the distinctions that separated feeble-mindedness from mental illness tended to lump together the problems posed by both imbeciles and psychotics.

The Commission heard a number of suggestions on how the care and prevention of mental illness could be improved. Emily May Schofield of the Victoria Local Council of Women wanted the institution of marriage certificates and special classes for the retarded. Olive Snyder of the Victoria Social Service League called, as did Schofield, for child guidance clinics.[46] Doctors Hincks and Dobson also expressed support for early treatment in preventive clinics. The preventive measure that received the most attention, however, was sterilization. The Commission reported that seven of its nine medical witnesses and the Local Councils of Women were in favour of sterilization.[47]

Among the arguments in defence of the policy of sterilization, the first was that the prevention of mental deficiency and its accompanying evils had become an economic necessity. Since there existed for the moment no cure for most forms of mental deficiency the choice was between society's carrying ever higher institutional costs or taking a preventive measure that would both limit the reproduction of the subnormal and lower the cost of their care by allowing some to be released.

The second argument in favour of sterilization was that feeble-mindedness and mental illness were hereditary complaints. Although the figures advanced to support this notion tended to vary over time, the adherents of this view were convinced that "like begat like" and that, moreover, the mental deficient exacerbated the problem by being more prolific than the normal. The Canadian National Committee on Mental Hygiene asserted that heredity was the biggest factor in mental deficiency and it and other groups could point to the purported sixteen years of success in California as reported by Popenhoe to back up the argument for sterilization. To those who argued that some feeble-minded parents could nevertheless give birth to "normal" children, the hereditarians, switching to an environmental tack, responded that such children would eventually be damaged because of inadequate parenting and so should be prevented from being born.

The third argument for sterilization was based on various moral preoccupations. Some saw sterilization as a form of "discipline" that the abnormal required for their own good and for the good of the community. To liberals who might protest against such therapeutic intervention the sponsors of sterilization responded that segregation was itself a denial of liberty. Sterilization, it was claimed, would result in greater liberty because it would permit the feeble-minded to leave their institutions and marry without running the danger of reproducing.[48] The argument that the sterilized might be even more promiscuous and degenerate because they no longer had to fear pregnancy was one to which proponents of the operation were especially sensitive. They indignantly replied, although not always with any factual backing, that sterilization resulted in greater order and self-control. It was apparent that many proponents who argued that the operation was a humane act also saw it as a sort of punishment. Indeed, some confused sterilization with castration and wanted sex offenders and habitual criminals[49] to be sterilized.

Taking all these arguments into account, the Commission supported in its *Report*:

> Sterilization of such individuals in mental institutions as, following treatment or training, or both, might safely be recommended for parole from the institution and trial return to community life, if the danger of procreation with its attendant risk of multiplication of the evil by transmission of the disability to progeny were eliminated.[50]

Written consent was to be given by the patient or spouse, or parent or guardian, or Minister of the department, and only after recommendation by the superintendent of the institution and approval of the Board of Control.

It says something of the seriousness with which mental deficiency was viewed in the interwar period that the British Columbia Legislative Assembly was specially adjourned on March 6, 1928, to allow the MLAs to hear Dr. D.M. Lebourdais give a lecture on mental defectives.[51] The *Final Report of the Royal Commission on Mental Hygiene* was submitted on March 14. No immediate action was taken because Dr. John Maclean, who had commissioned the Hincks survey in 1919 and led the government when the Commission was carrying out its investigations, was replaced as Premier by the Conservative Simon Fraser Tolmie in August, 1928.

Between 1928, when the commission's *Final Report* was filed, and 1933, when the sterilization bill was introduced, public and private pressure in favour of the policy slowly built. To an extent there was a simple continuation of the sort of lobbying that a federal commission had noted in 1926. Sterilization in British Columbia was gaining support, it reported, because:

> . . . the Women's Council of Vancouver is endeavouring to create public opinion for the establishment of this measure. The department of neglected and dependent children is strongly in favour of such a measure, and is bringing the question before the public whenever possible through various organizations.

In September, 1926, the New Westminster Local Council of Women sponsored a resolution in favour of sterilization. Some individuals, including Dr. Irene Bastow Hudson and Emily May Schofield of Victoria, voiced opposition but the Local Councils of Women, at their provincial gathering in the fall, passed the resolution.[52]

In Alberta events moved much faster. Although the concerns of the Alberta proponents of sterilization were the same as those of their British Columbian counterparts, the fervour of the former – no doubt sparked by the higher percentage of immigrants on the Prairies – was more intense. In 1928, when lobbying on the West Coast in favour of sterilization was still building, Alberta passed its own Sexual Sterilization Act. Timothy J. Christian of the University of Alberta has provided a detailed analysis of the Act; for the purposes of this study it is only necessary to provide a brief account of its passage.

Hincks and the CNCMH carried out a survey of Alberta in 1919 that was published in 1921. As they had done in British Columbia the authors of the Alberta survey attributed much of the frightening social inefficiency and immorality they encountered to mental deficiency. In particular they asserted that the recent wave of Slavic immigrants suffered from high levels of feeble-mindedness, a finding enthusiastically hailed by Anglo-Saxons. Hincks and his associates, finding it impossible to empathize with the plight of strangers in a strange land, put down as evidence of mental slowness the confusion of the new arrivals.

Such evidence was seized upon by the anxious defenders of the social status quo. In 1922 the United Farmers of Alberta convention called on the government to draft legislation providing for the segregation for life of the feeble-minded and to study the feasibility of implementing a sterilization program. In 1924 the United Farm Women of Alberta launched an all-out campaign in support of such a program. Its president, Mrs. Gunn, countered the opposition of civil libertarians with the statement that "democracy was never intended for degenerates."[53]

Progressive Alberta women such as Emily Murphy, first woman magistrate in the British Empire, and Nellie McClung, suffragist and future Canadian delegate to the League of Nations, were in the forefront of the movement. That they had little idea of what sterilization actually entailed is made clear by a reading of their works. McClung made the ridiculous claim in *The Stream Runs Fast: My Own Story* (1945) that such an operation revitalized an entire family. Whereas before the father had worried about his retarded daughter's promiscuity, now peace was restored. "Katie was well and neatly dressed. Her mother told me that she was taking full charge of the chickens now, and in the evenings was doing Norwegian knitting which had a ready sale in the neighbourhood. The home was happy again."[54] How, one has to ask, was a physical mutilation supposed to improve morality? Sterilization, of course, could be guaranteed only to end an individual's ability to reproduce, but its backers were convinced that this operation could remove at one stroke almost every social ill. In their desperate search for simple solutions Albertans chose to overlook such obvious illogicalities in the pro-sterilization arguments.

More and more Albertans harboured these views. As early as 1922 R.G. Reid, the provincial Minister of Health, declared that the government was in favour of sterilization and only waiting for public opinion to catch up. By 1928 it apparently had when George Hoadley, the new Health Minister in Premier John E. Brownlee's United Farmers of Alberta government, brought before the legislature the Sexual Sterilization Bill. Opposition was voiced by the Conservatives and Liberals but the government, assured of the grassroots support of the UFA, the UFWA, the Local Council of Women, the Imperial Order of Daughters of the Empire, and the Woman's Christian Temperance Union, pushed the bill through on March 7, 1928.

The Sexual Sterilization Act provided that mental defectives could, on the recommendation of a Eugenics Board and with the consent of the patient or guardian, be subjected to sterilization. About 400 operations were carried out by 1937 when the new Social Credit government, convinced that even more draconian measures were required, introduced amendments that removed the consent provision from the 1928 Act.[55]

Emily Murphy, having assisted in the sterilization campaign in Alberta, proclaimed to British Columbians the benefits of the operation in a series of articles she wrote as "Janey Canuck" in the Vancouver

Sun. In "Sterilization of the Insane" she argued that to protect women and children from sexual attack, to end the crippling expenses of incarceration, and to promote the mental and physical betterment of the race, sterilization of the unfit was required. "Human thorough-breds" were what Canada wanted, but at the moment the nation was burdened by 25,000 lunatics, a disproportionate number in Catholic Quebec where religious and political partisanship opposed progressive legislation.[56] In "Should the Unfit Wed" Murphy asserted that they should, but only if sterilized so that insanity, venereal disease, tuber-culosis, and epilepsy could be contained. "We protect the public against diseased and distempered cattle. We should similarly protect them against the offal of humanity."[57] And not content with having likened the abnormal to animals, Murphy proceeded to compare them to plants, asserting that sterilization was no more unnatural than pruning a tree.[58]

Murphy was in some ways a "typical" progressive inasmuch as she favoured a whole series of reforms aimed at improving the health of the family.[59] By 1932 she was as concerned with birth control and marriage health certificates as she was with sterilization. The attitude toward birth control of other eugenically minded commentators was ambivalent. The more conservative believed that the restriction of fertility by the fit was dysgenic because it deprived the community of sound stock.[60] The progressives tended to accept birth control as a fact of life among the intelligent. It did not have to be socially harmful as long as the reduction of the birth rate of superior types by contraception was balanced by the restriction of the inferior by sterilization.[61] Dr. George Hall of the Victoria Medical Society, while testifying before the Rothwell Commission in 1926, called on the one hand for "the sterilization of persons unfit for marriage," but on the other urged "that scientific methods of birth control should be known more widely."[62] Similarly, Dr. L.E. Borden of Victoria was quoted by the Vancouver *Sun* in 1932 as backing both policies. "'Birth control is the most important issue in Canada,' he said, emphasizing not only the eco-nomic cost imposed upon governments, but the wastage of human life involved in perpetuating the unfit."[63]

Murphy's defence of sterilization was perhaps the most outlandish in its extravagant claims, but almost every discussion of sterilization carried by the British Columbia press was equally one-sided. The Vancouver *Sun* in 1926 quoted a noted Viennese surgeon:

In saving the weak of mind from the hazards of a hard and selfish world, by prolonging the lives of the constitutionally weak persons with hereditary tendencies towards mental and physical disease, we are allowing more and more of the poorer human stock to survive and reproduce.[64]

In 1927 the *Sun* heralded Oliver Wendell Holmes's judgement in the American Supreme Court that sterilization was not unconstitutional since it was "the only reasonable way of protecting the strains from which the world must draw its leaders." The *Sun*'s editorialist concluded that Canada should follow the Americans, "the sooner the better."[65] In November of the same year the *Sun* returned to the subject, making the following wild claim:

It is an admitted fact in every civilized country of the world today that the unfit are multiplying at a rate something like double of the fit. Thus, for every child born with mental, physical and moral ability to maintain and promote civilization, two are born with the instincts to flout the essential discipline of civilization and tear civilization down.[66]

Readers of the British Columbia press were informed that there were "millions" of unfit stock whose reproduction was "a crime against humanity" in that it represented "the greatest burden" on civilization.[67]

On April 1, 1933, the Conservative Provincial Secretary, S.L. Howe, asked the Legislative Assembly if it were prepared to consider a sexual sterilization bill. The house unanimously agreed. Reginald Hayward, who sat on the Rothwell Commission, declared that many members had long been in favour of such a policy but remained silent because of concerns that an uneducated public would be hostile to such a measure.[68] Hayward's statement was somewhat curious; what impresses one most in the literature on sterilization in the 1920's and 1930's is the scarcity of views hostile to the program. Prior to 1933 the only vocal opponents of sterilization in British Columbia appeared to be Alan and Ada Muir. This couple had been active in left-wing political circles in Winnipeg until the First World War. In the post-war period they moved to Vancouver and established a Peoples League for Health and an Anti-Vaccination and Medical League.[69] They were interested in herbal medicine, astrology, Rosicrucianism, and mental telepathy; regular medicine they viewed with suspicion. When a Vancouver *Sun* editorial lauded the sterilization laws of America, Alan Muir replied that no one had the right to judge the fit or unfit. Going further, he claimed that doctors in their ravenous pursuit of power were doing the dirty work of the capitalists in exterminating labour leaders in prisons and asylums.[70] In March of 1929, Muir cast his net wider in claiming that operations on tonsils, adenoids, and appendixes were all evidence of "medical sadism," that the giving of iodine to schoolchildren was a way of creating drug dependency, and that sterilization was equivalent to murder.[71] All of these policies were manifestations, in Muir's mind, of the extent to which doctors were controlling government.

The fact that the only vocal opposition to sterilization in British Columbia came from health cultists like the Muirs highlights the extent to which the policy had the support of the professional classes. But though sterilization had been called for in the early 1920's, it was only introduced to the legislature in 1933. Clearly the "advanced" members of the middle class were initially concerned that the mass of the population would be hostile to the idea and would have to be slowly enlightened as to the benefits of the policy. By 1933 the politicians assumed that this education was complete.

The bill, introduced on April 1 and passed on April 7, received only cursory debate in the Legislative Assembly.[72] Tolmie's government was in the process of falling apart. The sexual sterilization bill, along with a motley collection of other measures, was rushed through three readings in the last week of the government's life. At first it appeared that there would be no debate whatsoever. The leader of the opposition, T.D. Pattullo, agreed that since segregation had resulted in "whole colonies of the mentally unfit" being created, some radical therapeutic measure was required. Pattullo mysteriously boasted that he himself had long supported sterilization despite the fact that his life had been threatened three times for taking such a stand.[73] Even Tom Uphill, the independent member from Fernie who had in the past been critical of the medical profession, fell into line; it was reported he "apologized for his opposition of the past five years and would support such a bill."[74]

At second reading, however, opposition emerged on the Liberal side of the House. Dr. W.H. Sutherland asserted that the bill was meaningless because doctors were already providing sterilizations for the mentally ill who provided their consent. Dr. J.J. Gillis, an active Catholic, opposed the bill on the grounds that mental problems should not be responded to with surgical solutions.[75] He argued that tuberculosis once had been thought to be hereditary; mental deficiency would also likely prove to be a far more complex problem than the eugenicists imagined. Though twenty-three American states introduced sterilization, he pointed out, only four continued to employ it.[76] To the anger and surprise of the government, even Pattullo did a *volte face* and now claimed that because of religious and moral objections he was opposed to the legislation. The support that he had expressed only a few days previously had, he brazenly claimed, been misinterpreted.[77]

Pattullo was obviously responding to the belated protests of the Catholic Church in British Columbia. Why the Church had kept its silence for so long is unclear. Only after the bill was actually introduced did Catholics begin to organize any opposition.[78] And only after the bill was actually passed did Archbishop W.M. Duke formally condemn it. Speaking for the province's 90,000 Catholics, the Archbishop declared the bill malicious in intent:

> The bill savours of that unfortunate country where the state tries to control everything, even the conscience of its citizens, and where man's private property and inherent rights and religious convictions are confiscated in the name of social progress and economy and hygiene. . . . It will work an injustice especially on the poor and unfortunate whom we are bound in charity, before God, not to injure permanently, but to protect effectively even at legitimate expense.[79]

Politics makes strange bedfellows. In addition to the Catholics, the only public protesters of the bill were the indefatigable Muirs. Once the legislation was in place, Alan Muir warned that with such processes the Nazi could turn on the Jew or the capitalist on the labourer.[80]

British Columbia was, of all the provinces in Canada, the one in which Catholics formed the smallest percentage of the population. The weakness of the Church in the West clearly simplified the passage of the sterilization bill. Professionals and progressives right across the country were interested in enacting similar statutes, but only in British Columbia and Alberta, with a large immigrant presence that raised hereditarian concerns and little effective Catholic opposition, could eugenic measures be confidently advanced. In those regions of the country where Catholics predominated such measures would not be broached; in Ontario and Manitoba the Catholic minority was large enough to ensure that they would be beaten back.

Despite the beginnings of some opposition, the Sexual Sterilization Act passed without a formal division in the Legislative Assembly. The Act called for a Board of Eugenics made up of a judge, a psychiatrist, and a social worker. Section 4, subsection (1) provided that:

> Where it appears to the Superintendent of any institution within the scope of this Act (i.e. any public hospital for the insane, the Industrial Home for Girls or the Industrial Home for Boys) that any

inmate of that institution, if discharged therefrom without being subjected to an operation for sexual sterilization would be likely to beget or bear children who by reason of inheritance would have a tendency to serious mental disease or mental deficiency, the Superintendent may submit to the Board of Eugenics a recommendation that a surgical operation be performed upon the inmate for sexual sterilization.[81]

The consent of the subject was required if capable of being given or that of spouse, parent, guardian, or provincial secretary.

It has been noted that the sterilization issue indicated the extent to which biologically based programs of reform gained credibility in the twentieth century. It should be further stressed that doctors not only assisted in the formulation of such programs; they also helped legislate them into being. In the 1926 Legislative Assembly five of the forty-eight MLAs were doctors, including J.D. Maclean, who called for the first survey of the feeble-minded, and E.J. Rothwell, who chaired the Royal Commission on Mental Hygiene. The 1928 assembly included six doctors and a druggist. Tolmie, as a stock-breeder, could also be considered an expert in matters of heredity. The North American eugenics movement in fact began as an offshoot of the American Breeders Association and so it was altogether fitting that it was with Tolmie as premier and in a legislature that included a pharmacist and seven doctors (the highest number of medical men ever to occupy seats in the Legislative Assembly) that the province's Board of Eugenics was established.[82] In the press, Drs. J.G. McKay, R.E. McKechnie, Edwin Carter, and Frederic Brodie all expressed support for the bill and W.B. Burnett asserted that every doctor in the province was of the same opinion.[83] Opposing views were certainly scarce, but it should be recalled that in the legislature such opposition as there was had been voiced by Drs. Gillis and Sutherland.

The Sexual Sterilization Act came into force in July, 1933, but only in November was a Board of Eugenics established. It was made up of a social worker, Laura Holland, Judge H.B. Robertson, and Dr. J.G. McKay, who had campaigned so long for just such a board.[84] In January of 1934 the press began to complain that the Board had as yet done nothing, in part because its powers were limited by the consent requirement.[85] Indeed, during the debate over the bill Drs. Burnett and Borden had wanted the legislation extended along the lines of the California legislation, which sanctioned compulsory sterilization. Such demands were taken up in 1934 by the Nanaimo Local Council of Women, which wanted criminals forcibly sterilized.[86]

The fact was that neither Alberta nor British Columbia experienced the sort of dramatic improvement that eugenicists had promised. What, then, did the sexual sterilization acts accomplish? This is a question to which we will return in Chapter Nine. Here it is only necessary to note that, despite the lack of any evidence of the effectiveness of such eugenic measures, the cry soon went up that eastern Canada would have to follow the lead of the western provinces.

6

The Eugenics Society of Canada

British Columbia and Alberta, in passing legislation for the sterilization of the feeble-minded and its supervision by boards of eugenics,
went the furthest in putting into action the hereditarian program. The
backers of such legislation, as we have seen, came from the progressive, middle-class professionals who were interested in a variety of
social reforms; there was no organized single-issue "eugenic movement" *per se.* In Ontario the campaign to have the province follow B.C.
and Alberta in passing such acts played a part in the coming together
of Canada's only formally organized group of eugenicists. This society
warrants particular attention. Hereditarian concerns were so much in
the air in the interwar period that it is often difficult to determine who
was and who was not seriously preoccupied by them. With the creation
in 1930 of the Eugenics Society of Canada, however, one could finally
point to a group of individuals who unambiguously declared that
biological taint was the single most important cause of the nation's
social problems.

The tardiness of Ontario in employing eugenic measures to deal
with the problem of feeble-mindedness is at first glance surprising. The
campaign in Canada for the control and surveillance of mental defectives was originally launched in Ontario in the decade before World
War One. Helen MacMurchy carried out the census of Ontario's
feeble-minded in 1905 that first raised the spectre of the country being
threatened by defectives. Though presenting her study in the context
of the most advanced work being done by health-care professionals,
MacMurchy did not disguise the fact that her investigations had been
elicited more by social than medical concerns. She openly conceded
that though feeble-mindedness was difficult to define, it was easy to
recognize. MacMurchy used the term "feeble-minded" to refer to the
higher-class mentally retarded who could be mistaken for the normal.

They did not have the physical stigmata of the moron or imbecile and so could even fool the ordinary physician. How did the expert spot them? Obviously, asserted MacMurchy, social failure was the clearest indication of mental deficiency. The solution to a host of social problems lay, she concluded, in rounding up such incompetents and subjecting them to custodial care.

As seen in Chapter Two, MacMurchy did achieve some success in having Ontario school children inspected and categorized. The Ontario government established in 1911 special classes and in 1914 auxiliary classes for the purposes of removing mental defectives from the normal school system. Both MacMurchy, as inspector of auxiliary classes, and Professor C.K. Clarke of the University of Toronto expressed their frustration, however, at the slow pace of change.[1]

In an attempt to force the provincial government to act on MacMurchy's recommendations a conference on the feeble-minded was held at the Toronto City Hall in 1912. MacMurchy and Dr. J.F. Conboy of the Toronto Board of Education called for a register on which would be inscribed the names of all the city's mental defectives.[2] Support for such policies was provided by E.R. Johnstone, the Canadian-born principal of the training school for the feeble-minded at Vineland, New Jersey. In Toronto he spoke in favour of stepped-up inspections and institutionalization of defective children.[3] Political clout was provided on November 8, 1912, when a hundred delegates from the Ontario municipalities met to discuss the issue. Prominent among the participants were Toronto Mayor H.C. Hocken and Controller J.O. McCarthy, Kingston Mayor F.J. Hoag, and National Council of Women representatives Florence Huestis and Mrs. F.H. Torrington. Supporting the lobbying tactics proposed by MacMurchy in her opening address, the conference participants founded the Provincial Association for the Care of the Feeble-Minded.[4] The Association had the support of the leading medical authorities. Professor C.K. Clarke of the University of Toronto and Dr. Gordon Bates (later head of the Social Hygiene Council) were, respectively, president and secretary of the Toronto branch.[5] But medical concerns were frequently overshadowed by the PACFM's concern for "vice"; the feeble-minded had to be viewed, in the words of the Association's president, T.H. Wills, as a "moral cancer."[6]

Despite the prodding of MacMurchy and her followers, the provincial government was loath to invest money in building separate institutions for the feeble-minded. Hopes were temporarily raised when the province instructed Justice Frank Egerton Hodgins to head a Royal Commission on the Care and Control of the Mentally Defective and

Feeble-Minded. The Commission began its work in November, 1917, and reported back in 1919. Hodgins painted a bleak picture of the mental health of the province and concluded by calling for youths to be subjected to further surveys, tests, and categorizations and for new asylums, mental testing of immigrants, and restriction of marriage.[7] To the reformers' disappointment the government, largely because of economic constraints, refused to implement the recommended changes. The failure of the province to respond to the Hodgins report, coming as it did just after the end of World War One, marked the end of an era. Helen MacMurchy left Toronto for Ottawa in 1920 and the Provincial Association for the Care of the Feeble-Minded collapsed.

The failure of the PACFM stemmed in part from the fact that, though it had the support of many physicians, it was to all intents and purposes not that much different from a host of other lay charitable organizations. In the 1920's a more successful campaign to alert the public to the dangers of inherited mental deficiency was launched by the Canadian National Committee for Mental Hygiene, much of the success of which was due to the organization's purported professional expertise.[8] A sense of the new organization's exalting of the expert was captured in William Tait's article on "Democracy and Mental Hygiene" that appeared in the *Canadian Journal of Mental Hygiene* in 1920. Tait, professor of psychology at McGill, blamed much of society's ills on the maternal coddling of misfits carried out by misguided philanthropists. What was required, he asserted, was a replacement of the rule of mediocrities by experts who could introduce a sterner and more "virile" society.[9]

The CNCMH was created in 1918 by Clarence Hincks, who, after having read Clifford Beer's *A Mind that Found Itself*, set out to organize a movement in Canada like Beers's American National Committee for Mental Hygiene.[10] Ironically, both men were drawn to the issue of mental health because of their own personality problems. Beers had attempted suicide, Hincks had a nervous breakdown, and both suffered throughout their lives "from cycles of depression and apathy which alternated with their periods of hypomanic, sometimes frenzied activity."[11] Hincks first saw some practical application for psychology when introduced to intelligence testing at the International Congress of School Hygiene held in Buffalo, New York, in 1913. He began to calculate the social costs of psychiatric problems in 1914 while at Professor C.K. Clarke's Social Service Clinic attached to the Toronto General Hospital.[12] The feeble-minded were, in Hincks's view, at best a drain on the community and at worst "potential criminals."[13]

By the end of World War One both business and the state were swinging round to the view that experts in mental hygiene were necessary to provide for the smooth running of large organizations. The problems posed by shell-shocked veterans, new immigrants, unruly labourers, and delinquent youths clearly seemed to indicate the need for new forms of sophisticated social control. This was what Hincks claimed the CNCMH could deliver. Indeed, his real gifts were not so much those of psychologist as those of a huckster and promoter.

Hincks, in his 1918 public appeals first in Montreal and then in Ottawa, was amazingly successful in garnering for the fledgling mental hygiene movement the support of the wealthy and influential. Clearly the evidence of the ravages caused by "shell shock" had sensitized many to the reality of psychological complaints.[14] Hincks was patronized by Lady Eaton and the Governor General, the Duke of Devonshire; he recruited to the board of the CNCMH Lord Shaughnessy, president of the CPR; E.W. Beatty, vice-president of the CPR; Sir Vincent Meredith, president of the Bank of Montreal; and F.W. Molson, of Molson's Brewery. The board in turn elected Dr. Charles Martin of McGill as president of the CNCMH, E.W. Beatty as chairman, C.K. Clarke as medical director, and Marjorie Keyes as social worker, but the moving force of the committee was Hincks, who sat as associate medical director and secretary. The CNCMH also included as members Helen MacMurchy, Charles Hastings, Florence Huestis, Gordon Bates, Peter Sandiford, Vincent Massey, and many members of the PACFM.[15] Hincks was equally successful at winning the support of local elites. The CNCMH's British Columbia branch, for example, was headed by Mary Ellen Smith, Vancouver member of the Legislative Assembly; F.L. Klinck, president of the University of British Columbia; George Kidd, president of BC Electric; and Dr. Henry E. Young, provincial medical officer of health.[16]

The CNCMH presented itself as a self-appointed body of experts prepared to advise business and government on mental health problems. Its message was that mental defectiveness did not strike by chance but followed natural laws of heredity. C.A. Porteous, assistant superintendent of the Protestant Hospital for the Insane at Verdun, asserted that only about one-third of his patients were free of hereditary taint.[17] And outside institutions, the CNCMH asserted, the vast majority of criminals, delinquents, and prostitutes were driven to their evil deeds by their mental illness.[18] It was pleased to announce that even the most up-to-date investigations of criminality, for example, found it to be "due only in a trifling extent, if any, to social inequality, adverse environment, or other manifestations of what may be comprehensively termed the 'forces of circumstances.' "[19]

The Committee's first successes were the winning of the commissions to survey the extent of feeble-mindedness in the western provinces preoccupied by the millions of dollars a year spent on asylums. These surveys were extremely important in providing some credence to the claim that the country was threatened by inherited defectiveness and were used to justify the sterilization programs of British Columbia and Alberta. In addition, the CNCMH was active in working for the increased testing and classifying of students, in calling for the building of training schools for the mentally defective, and in campaigning for the inspection and restriction of immigration.[20]

Through its activities the CNCMH served as a launching pad for both the psychiatric and psychology professions in Canada. Each won increased social status by demonstrating to the public through the various investigative activities of the CNCMH the social importance of their respective sciences. Through the influence of the CNCMH, Rockefeller money was obtained in 1926 to set up a psychiatric hospital in Toronto; likewise, via the Committee, Rockefeller money was channelled for the creation in 1925 of child study programs at the University of Toronto and McGill University.[21]

As psychiatry and psychology professionalized in the late 1920's they tended to turn away from the crude eugenics espoused in the early years by the CNCMH.[22] The strict hereditarianism of some of the first investigators never totally disappeared, but for those in the newly emerging helping professions eugenics appeared to offer too pessimistic a prospect. If mental powers were simply innate, what role could the professional play beyond testing and labelling? The pioneering Canadian child psychologists W.E. Blatz and E.A. Bott, for example, though continuing as members of the CNCMH, were attracted to behaviourist theories that held that the child's early environment played the crucial role in determining future mental health and economic productivity. Whereas the old-fashioned eugenicists were concerned with the incarceration and sterilization of the defective, the new generation of environmentalists were preoccupied with devising preventive programs that would pre-empt the very emergence of "abnormality."[23] Delinquency would be increasingly attributed by such child-care experts to poor parenting rather than to poor genes. The question posed in 1930 by Charles Martin, dean of medicine at McGill, "How often does the hand that rocks the cradle unwittingly plant the seeds of permanent ill-health!" was echoed by Alan Brown, professor of pediatrics at Toronto: "How often do we see the young infant stop crying at two weeks of age when it is picked up by either parent? Herein lies the potential Juvenile Court case."[24]

It is important not to exaggerate the gap that separated the eugenicists and the environmentalists. Although their methods differed, their goals of efficient social management were similar. Hincks's own views on inherited defectiveness did evolve. In 1919 he estimated that 80 per cent of the feeble-minded came from tainted stock but by 1925 admitted that the figure was closer to 50 per cent and that the majority, if spotted early enough, were "redeemable." He continued to defend the utility of sterilization, however, arguing that it was worth sterilizing all those who were identified as possible of passing on their mental defectiveness. In the 1940's he was still pessimistically pointing out that more children entered mental hospitals than graduated from university.[25]

It was not the CNCMH's surveys but the depression that provided the real impetus in Ontario for the implementation of eugenic measures. In 1929 a Royal Commission on Public Welfare chaired by P.D. Ross investigated provincial hospitals, asylums, and other institutions. Concluding that feeble-mindedness was mainly inherited and led to crime and prostitution, Ross recommended a provincial policy of compulsory sterilization: "Your commission recommends that some endeavour be made by legislation to lessen the amount of evil which is certainly promoted by unchecked sexual freedom of criminals or defectives who have a record of immorality."[26] It was in this climate that the Eugenics Society of Canada was created.

Various discussions had taken place since the mid-1920's concerning the creation of a Canadian eugenics society. In August, 1924, Charles Hastings wrote the British Eugenics Society to report that a Eugenics Education Society of Toronto had met on July 27, 1924.[27] Hastings had succeeded in having a eugenic discussion added to the program of the British Association meeting in Toronto that same year, but his projected Canadian organization did not flourish. That Hastings's eugenic concerns were shared by other health professionals was, however, apparent. In the August, 1924, meeting of the Ontario Health Officers Association a proposal for the sterilization of the feeble-minded won the enthusiastic support of those convinced that misfits were kept alive and allowed to propagate because of misdirected charity. In the Toronto press it was reported that,

Dr. Laurie [of Port Arthur] told *The Star* that if the method of the survival of the fittest could be started he would not be surprised if every beggar in the world would soon be exterminated. "It would be an ideal age," he remarked hopefully.[28]

A second attempt to create a Canadian eugenics society, but this time linked to the American rather than the British movement, took place in the late 1920's. C.C. Little of the American Eugenics Society approached Charles C. Macklin, professor of anatomy at the University of Western Ontario, with the idea of establishing a sister organization in Canada. In March, 1930, Macklin reported back that his efforts in this regard had come to naught. The responses he had received from Professors Ralph Shaner at the University of Alberta, C. Maclean Fraser at the University of British Columbia, W.P. Thompson at the University of Saskatchewan, and J.C. Boileau Grant at the University of Toronto had not been enthusiastic. Macklin resigned his position as president of the Canadian Eugenics Committee avowing that "I feel that I am not the proper man for this post. . . . I should very much like to see a well qualified man in the chair, but regret that I cannot suggest anyone at the present time."[29] Ironically, it was not a man but a woman, Macklin's wife – Madge Thurlow Macklin – who emerged as one of Canada's most prominent defenders of eugenics.

In December, 1930, David B. Harkness wrote to inform the British Eugenics Society that a Eugenics Society of Canada had met for the first time on November 6, 1930.[30] Its avowed object was to carry out an educational program of race betterment that would result in the passage of legislation discouraging defective reproduction while encouraging fit parenthood. The British were obviously a bit leery of accepting the affiliation of the Canadian organization and wrote to Professor E.J. Urwick at the University of Toronto to ask confidentially about the new organization.[31] Urwick, professor of political science and economics, had devoted a chapter of *The Social Good* (1927) to "The Problem of the Unfit" in which, while wholeheartedly agreeing with the eugenicists about the dangers of degeneration, he cast doubt on their proposed remedies. In contrast to their penchant for equating biological and social worth, Urwick asserted that he "would very cheerfully entrust the future of our civilization to the care of most of our working men and women I know and their children. They might even improve it."[32] Despite such criticisms, it was to Urwick that the British eugenicists turned when they sought information on Canada. He could assure them that the members of the Eugenics Society of Canada were indeed a respectable lot.

The executive of the Eugenics Society of Canada was composed of Dr. William Hutton, medical health officer of Brantford, A.R. Kaufman, the Kitchener industrialist, and D.B. Harkness, welfare expert and magistrate.[33] The society appears never to have had more than a hundred members but many occupied positions of some importance. A breakdown of the membership reveals it was not the narrowly academic group C.C. Macklin had envisaged but rather a society dominated by the members of the medical and welfare professions, with a sprinkling of representatives from the religious, business, political, and academic worlds.[34] Doctors and welfare workers were over-represented not simply because they thought they knew something about inherited disabilities; eugenics was an ideology that exalted both professions as playing potentially crucial roles in protecting social stability.[35]

The doctors the ESC attracted were not (with the notable exception of Madge Thurlow Macklin) located in genetic research labs but, in the tradition of Helen MacMurchy and Charles Hastings, came mainly from the field of public health. The most active was the ESC's sometime president, William Hutton, a model progressive medical reformer. Hutton had graduated from the University of Toronto in 1911, served as a major in the medical corps from 1914 to 1919, and was Brantford's medical officer of health from 1919 to 1959. He was involved in a number of innovative public health measures – supporting small pox vaccinations, the pasteurization of milk, and the provision of diphtheria toxoid – but is perhaps best remembered today as the "Canadian father of fluoridation" for making Brantford the first Canadian city with a treated water supply.[36]

In the 1930's Hutton was keenly preoccupied by the population question. He never shied away from contentious issues and was, for example, one of the first Canadian doctors to express his support for euthanasia.[37] Hutton contended that doctors had to break many of the old false taboos. For a start they had to admit that preventive medicine was actually saving the weakest strains in the population. The task, therefore, was to encourage the reproduction of the fittest germ plasm, on the one hand, and, on the other, to reduce that of the least fit by immigration restriction, sterilization, and birth control.

Hutton's support of birth control was based on his belief, as he expressed it in a letter to Marie Stopes, that it could bring down the birth rate of those who "lacked initiative."[38] He was proud to inform the Toronto *Globe and Mail* in 1932 that "The subject of birth control has engaged and is engaging some of the greatest minds in medicine and sociology. Moreover, the giving of such information under strict conditions is the official and authorized policy of the health department of the City of Brantford."[39] It was as the leading medical defender of birth control in Canada that Hutton was called to testify for the defence in the 1937 Eastview trial.

As a director of the Eugenics Society of Canada, Hutton saw his main task as campaigning to build up support for sterilization. In 1934 he informed the readers of the *Canadian Medical Association Journal* that Canada's fertility differential was frightening. He advanced figures indicating that whereas Canada's best families as listed in *Who's Who* had on average 2.42 children, the parents of the inmates of the Toronto Psychiatric Hospital had 3.42, those of the Belleville School for the Deaf had 4.37, those of the Brantford School for the Blind had 5.1, and those of the Orillia Asylum for the Feeble-Minded had 8.7. In fact, Hutton was not comparing like to like, but his juggling of figures served his purpose of raising the spectre of the "normal" being threatened with the "dilution and pollution with the blood of the feeble-minded and the sufferers from the hereditary diseases."[40] Only state intervention in the form of sterilization could ward off disaster.

It was clear from Hutton's writings that he envisaged sterilization as a panacea. Poverty would disappear with the poor. "Who are the feeble-minded?" he asked, "They are people with the mental capacities and abilities of children. In the cities they tend to drift towards the slums. Indeed the slums are largely the product of the segregating of the subnormals. . . . For their benefit as well as for our own we should control their reproduction."[41]

In the same way that Hutton represented the medical and welfare interests of the Eugenics Society of Canada, A.R. Kaufman, the Society's financial secretary, represented its business concerns.[42] By his own account Kaufman was drawn to the population issue as a result of his experiences as owner of the Kaufman Rubber company, manufacturer of Life Buoy rubber footwear. In the winter of 1929, when discharging employees, he was informed by his factory nurse that the poorest had the largest families. Upon investigation Kaufman concluded that "the less the intelligence the larger the families, and the more hopeless their condition."[43] His response was to have the nurse suggest sterilization, which he asserts was accepted by a number of employees. About half of the cases were first declared mentally deficient by the local mental health clinic; the other half suffered from physical complaints. Kaufman believed that anyone suffering from "tuberculosis, epilepsy, syphilis, nerve diseases, heart conditions, kidney conditions, congenital deafness, congenital blindness, etc." should be operated on.[44] His workers were dealt with in the first years, thanks to the medical co-operation of another member of the ESC, Dr. R.G. Ratz. By 1937 Kaufman claimed responsibility for arranging for 435 sterilizations.[45]

Kaufman moved on from supplying sterilizations to create the Parents' Information Bureau to provide the poor with cheap contraceptives. Kaufman's birth control activities are fairly well known, but his eugenic interests, which underlay them, are not. He was, however, quite clear about his motives. The segregation of the defective only burdened the "normal" with crushing taxes.[46] Such social services could be pruned by recourse to a simple operation. It could not be judged a violation of the feeble-minded's personal liberty because their lack of intelligence already denied them the freedom of making rational decisions. All that was required was for the state to have the courage to act forcefully. "Voluntary eugenic sterilization is not illegal," Kaufman wrote, "but there is a need for a voluntary sterilization law to not only encourage social workers and reassure doctors in this work, but also to provide the necessary funds for work that I do not think should be gratuitous. Ontario grants for public welfare exceed appropriations for education, and care of mental defectives costs more than universities."[47] Even with the provision of cheap, effective birth control, Kaufman believed that 5 to 10 per cent of the population would lack the incentive to employ it and would therefore need to be sterilized.

Kaufman summed up his thoughts on sterilization in a pamphlet entitled *Sterilization Notes*, which was little more than a potpourri of citations on the costs of caring for the feeble-minded and the arguments of the eminent in favour of the operation.[48] He declared that 10 per cent of this "menace" were in turn the offspring of deficient parents. The "successes" of sterilization programs in Alberta, British Columbia, California, and Germany he cited, while castigating the opposition of reactionaries. An aggressive anti-Catholic, he enjoyed asserting that 44.5 per cent of first admissions to mental hospitals were Roman Catholic and responded to papal attacks on sterilization by claiming that "Roman Catholics continued the practice [of castration] even into the Twentieth Century to provide male soprano voices for their cathedral choirs."[49]

Kaufman drew his arguments from a number of American and British sources, but he was particularly impressed by the savage attacks made on the feeble-minded by the American humorist H.L. Mencken. Kaufman sent copies of Mencken's articles to many of his own correspondents and attempted some levity in describing his own activities to the humorist.

I agree that it might be more merciful and cheaper to "have at them [the poor] with machine guns", but the law has an inconvenient way of insisting on prolonging people's agony. My first reaction when I took some interest in the deplorable state of affairs of some people was to "dump them in the lake", which is even cheaper than your method. Since my idea was also impractical from a legal standpoint, I decided to do the next best, and up to date have through my nurses and cooperative doctors accomplished over 400 sterilizations. . . . My hope is that ultimately such work will be taken over by public authorities. In the meantime I feel that a demonstration is the best argument and I think if you manage to sterilize a few thousand liabilities the work may eventually get public recognition.[50]

Summing up his reasons for his sterilization and birth control work, Kaufman concluded:

I have said, and still think, we must choose between birth control and revolution. We are raising too large a percentage of the dependent class and I do not blame them if they steal and fight before they starve. I fear that their opportunity to starve will not be so long deferred as some day the Governments are going to lack the cash and perhaps also the patience to keep so many people on relief. Many of these people are not willing to work but I do not criticize them harshly for their lack of ambition when they are the offspring of people no better than themselves.[51]

The eugenicists were quite open in admitting that the strength of their argument in favour of sterilization was based as much on the economic fears engendered by the depression as on the "logic" of their genetic argument. As the economic situation deteriorated, support for such policies grew. In 1931 C.F. Neelands of the Ontario Reformatory at Guelph called for the sterilization of the unfit and anti-social and at the 1932 annual ESC meeting in Hamilton, Judge Harkness read a proposed sterilization bill that would be presented to the Ontario legislature.[52] In March of 1932 Hutton addressed various Rotary, Lions, and Kiwanis meetings and succeeded in having the Ontario service clubs pass a resolution in favour of such a law.[53] C.H. Carlisle, president of Goodyear Tire and Rubber, similarly defended sterilization in public talks. It should, he told the Toronto Gyro Club, "be made available so that those sections of society which are most prone to submit to their passions through ignorance should not be responsible for increasing the misery of the world."[54]

The highlight of the 1933 annual meeting of the Eugenics Society, held in London, Ontario, was a paper by Miss Grace Jackson of the London emergency relief committee. She informed her audience that "Dependency, due to mental deficiency, is a chief cause of the need for social services."[55] One "low grade" family, she asserted, had in a little over a decade cost the community more than $25,000. Sterilization would prevent the reproduction of such paupers. The same argument was made by Professor Roy Fraser of Mount Allison College. "Let us strike the word democracy from our lips," he pleaded, "until we have earned it by giving a fair deal physically and spiritually to every child in the land." His notion of a "fair deal" was the prevention by sterilization of the birth of children who, scientists determined, should not be born. For the good of the nation, he asserted, experts in eugenics and genetics had to elbow aside the "would-be improver of human life" and their "educational panaceas, social cure-alls, and Utopian recipes."[56]

By January, 1933, the *Toronto Star* reported that the Eugenics Society's sterilization policy was being endorsed by many: Toronto surgeon James Cotton asserted that it would cut taxes and reduce disease; Frank Sharp of the Big Brothers Association saw it as a way of preventing the tragic consequences of the marriages of mental defectives; Professor C.B. Farrar of the Toronto Psychiatric Hospital viewed it as a way of ending the fertility differential since only the "better classes" employed birth control; and Frank Stapleford of the Neighbourhood Workers' Association called for its application to "low grade families."[57] In the fall of 1933 resolutions in favour of sterilization circulated by the Industrial School Association of Toronto received the support of the executives of both the Infants Home and the West End Creche.[58]

Probably the single most widely reported defence of sterilization was made on April 28, 1933, by Dr. H.A. Bruce, Lieutenant-Governor of Ontario, in a talk before the Hamilton Canadian Club.[59] Bruce had nothing new to contribute to the discussion, but his likening of the operation to "damming up the foul streams of degeneracy and demoralization which are pouring pollution into the nation's life blood" revealed a striking gift for hyperbole.[60] The importance of Bruce's talk was that it provided the eugenicists with an eminently respectable public champion. Bruce had also addressed the issue of the "propagation of the unfit" in a March speech to the Toronto Academy of Medicine that won the support of other medical notables, including F.W. Marlow, past president of the Toronto Academy of Medicine, and H.B. Anderson, president of the Ontario Medical Association.[61]

The Ontario Medical Association at its May, 1933, Hamilton convention formally endorsed sterilization both for institutional inmates about to be discharged and for mental defectives requesting such an operation. The OMA declared that "mentally defective persons are increasing out of proportion to the rest of the population."[62] In the same month the Ontario branch of the Canadian Manufacturers' Association, clearly impressed by Bruce's advocacy, supported a motion, moved by its treasurer, T.F. Moneypenny, in favour of the same measure.[63]

Doctors formed the single largest group within the Eugenics Society of Canada and could count on the support of many of their colleagues. The nation's leading psychiatrist, C.B. Farrar, head of the Toronto Psychiatric Hospital and editor of the *American Journal of Psychiatry*, was a member of the ESC and an active proponent of sterilization.[64] Social problems, to Farrar, were medical problems. Crime, for example, he viewed as an illness. "The average criminal," he wrote in an article attacking the parole system and arguing in favour of permanent custody, "being also a mental invalid, gravitates most naturally into a life of habitual crime. It is not only somewhat absurd, but often specifically dangerous to allow such individuals to be at large at all."[65]

Incarceration was expensive, however, and Farrar turned to sterilization as a cheap way of attacking some specific social problems. He acknowledged in a 1926 article that the religious, the sentimental, and the hypocritical opposed such measures but declared himself heartened by the interest shown in such policies in western Canada.[66] Although Tredgold, the leading British authority, had evidence that only a small percentage of feeble-mindedness was inherited, Farrar continued to argue in the 1930's that the real figure was between 33 and 65 per cent. He declared himself willing to lose one potential genius if ninety-nine defectives were also eliminated. "In other instances," he wrote, "it [sterilization] may recommend itself on economic grounds, for example, that of impoverished parents of an already considerable family, particularly if of inferior stock, who must constantly depend upon charity, and with whom birth control technique is impracticable."[67]

Such medical support for eugenics was maintained through the 1930's. *The Canadian Doctor* carried an article in January, 1936, defending Germany's sterilization policy. The Nazis, it declared, had merely "erased" the reproductive powers of 200,000 people and in so doing saved immense amounts of money. "Increasing taxation of every kind imposed on the average citizen," the article concluded, "has impelled him to examine every avenue offering possibility of relief and sterilization is one of them to receive [the] greatest attention and support."[68] In 1939 H.E. MacDermott, the assistant editor of the

Canadian Medical Association Journal, was still maintaining that California's experience with sterilization proved that "it must be included as indispensable in the struggle against mental disease, deficiency, and dependency."[69]

The ESC's medical backers were not all as eminent as Bruce and Farrar. At the 1935 annual ESC meeting a keynote paper was presented by Dr. Frank N. Walker, who claimed that racial intermarriage led to mental and physical defects. Even among the eugenicists Walker stood out as distinctly odd. In a 1926 article he seriously argued that the marriage of the blue- and brown-eyed resulted in sterile offspring, and that blonde women had difficulty in giving birth to brown-eyed children.[70] In a slightly less sensational talk, A.M. Harley informed the 1935 ESC meeting that since the 1870's the number of feeble-minded had increased six and a half times while the normal had only doubled. In a gauche attempt at humour, he quipped that "the law of Ontario is almost as sterile as we hope to make some of our citizens."[71] William Hutton's contribution to the discussion was the declaration that the Nazis had already put into place an admirable sterilization law.[72] It was an indication of the seriousness with which such ideas were taken in the 1930's that on February 4, 1935, Ontario Premier Mitchell Hepburn received an ESC delegation including Rabbi Maurice Eisendrath, F.N. Walker, and William Hutton. At the conclusion of the meeting the Premier, while giving the delegation the impression of his support, temporized by declaring that his government was still gathering information on the success of Alberta's and British Columbia's eugenic experiments.[73]

Some believed such information was already available. Constance Templeton in a 1934 *Chatelaine* article described the feeble-minded as "Canada's Lost Generation." The sterilization laws of Alberta and British Columbia were intended, she wrote, to "protect" the defective from their own dangerous fertility and the results were encouraging.[74] The June, 1935, issue of *Social Welfare* carried a similar essay by Ernest M. Best, general secretary of the National Council of the YMCA, in which he asserted that given Canada's current predicament, "the real solution can only be found in those eugenic measures which will tend to reduce the percentage of the physically and mentally handicapped in succeeding generations. To be brutally frank, every step we take to protect, preserve, educate, and adjust the subnormal to existing society is a biological disadvantage to the race."[75] The fullest discussion of the pros and cons appeared in Helen MacMurchy's *Sterilization? Birth Control? A Book for Family Welfare and Safety* (1934). After reviewing sympathetically the evidence provided by eugenicists and commending the policies of the western provinces, she concluded, "We are beginning to see that our troubles and burdens are caused by a very small proportion of our people. Out of every thousand of us there are about ten who are the chief cause of our present enormous expenditures for institutions and other forms of relief and care." Good citizens, she protested, were paying through their taxes for the "lawlessness, dependency, ill-health and incapacity" of the bad.[76]

In the depths of the depression, local Ontario politicians began to respond to such arguments. In November, 1935, Dr. L.W. Dale, reeve of Newmarket, called for the sterilization of the children in the York County shelters. "If we are forced to keep such children in our shelters instead of having them admitted to Orillia," he protested, "we should at least have the right to sterilize them and protect our social order."[77] In December Agnes MacPhail, Canada's first woman Member of Parliament, affirmed before a meeting of the United Farm Women that it was immoral to allow defectives to breed. "I just wonder how much longer we're going to allow sub-normal people to produce their kind. It is a blasphemy of the worst kind. You farmers – would you want the worse type of your cattle to be seed-bearers?"[78] MacPhail's assertion was countered by Margaret Gould, secretary of the Child Welfare Council, and Robert E. Mills of the Toronto Children's Aid Society, but supported by Miss Jessie V. Moberly, secretary of the Toronto Infants' Home.[79]

The Newmarket town council and the Simcoe County council passed resolutions in favour of sterilization in February, 1936.[80] The Barrie-Simcoe council also used the claim that defectives reproduced "with great carelessness" in its call for their sterilization before being discharged.[81] Although some writers of letters to the editor attacked sterilization as "something to give doctors a job" and "a far fetched fad of doctors and fanatics," the city councils of Belleville, Brantford, Chatham, Galt, Kitchener, North Bay, Oshawa, Port Arthur, Sault Ste. Marie, Toronto, and thirty-three other town and township councils had by 1937 endorsed the program.[82]

At the 1936 annual meeting of the ESC held in Toronto a resolution was passed calling for all provinces to follow Alberta's lead in enacting sterilization laws "to prevent parenthood among those obvious cases whose presence in our community constitutes such a social menace and such an economic burden upon taxpayers."[83] Support was expressed in February, 1936, by Dr. Harvey Clare, director of Guelph's Homewood Sanitarium, who warned: "Heredity is responsible for practically all feeble-mindedness, yet in a great band across Northern Ontario feeble-minded people are breeding, and no attempt is being made to restrict their ever-increasing numbers."[84] In the same month Dr. Clarence G. Campbell, president of the American-based Eugenics Research Association, spoke to the Toronto Canadian Club. He informed his listeners that eugenics had to be "of first concern to every patriotic Canadian." The *Toronto Star* quoted him as stating, "It was 'encouraging' to see that Germany had been 'intelligent enough' to undertake a program to improve the race."[85]

In his 1935 presidential address to the Eugenics Society of Canada, Hutton similarly hailed Germany's introduction of compulsory sterilization. He conceded that the German law was severe, but in the long run he was confident it would eliminate those who "clutter up our social institutions."[86] Praise for Germany's sterilization of "50,000 misfits" also figured centrally in H.A. Bruce's speech to the Toronto Conference on Social Welfare on April 24, 1936.[87] The fact that the Lieutenant-Governor continued to defend eugenics could only lend an aura of respectability to such theories.

In June the annual convention of the Association of Ontario Mayors was provided by William Hutton with a full explanation of the eugenics program in *A Brief for Sterilization of the Feeble-Minded*. All the familiar themes were there: since the struggle for survival no longer took place the feeble-minded flourished, were extraordinarily fertile, and spawned vice, crime, illegitimacy, and disease that burdened the community with crippling taxes.[88] Accepting the argument that sterilization would allow the province to avoid paying the millions of dollars in care required for an adequate system of segregation, the Association swung its support behind sterilization.[89] Going even further, the mayor of Fort Erie called for the sterilization of *all* fathers on relief, even those not clinically categorized as mentally defective.[90]

The provincial political leadership remained cautiously sympathetic. Premier Hepburn declared in Sudbury on July 23, 1936: "Sterilization of the mentally unfit is one of the major problems now engaging the attention of the Ontario Government. There are some 14,000 defectives in Ontario Institutions, and the Province could build four more institutions. While the Government is not considering immediate legislation, it is being seriously considered."[91] Despite such hedging, Monsignor M. Cline branded Hepburn's argument that economic reasons might justify sterilization a symptom of "class tyranny." The Reverend Basil Doyle agreed and noted that one would not attempt to make everyone tall by eliminating the short.[92] The fact that Ontario Catholics, led by Bishop McNally of Hamilton, had from the early 1930's been vociferously attacking both birth control and sterilization obviously played a role in holding the provincial political leadership back from fully endorsing either.[93]

Less fearful was the Toronto Board of Control, which sent a delegation on September 14, 1936, to Queen's Park to ask the provincial government to sterilize imbeciles. Mr. A.W. Laver, Toronto city relief commissioner, claimed that:

> . . . out of 30,500 social case families in Toronto, 2,277 are clear cases calling for sterilization – lack of sterilization law is yearly increasing the relief burden in Toronto – this was partly because women of low mentality, giving birth to illegitimate children, usually come to the city to lose themselves – 63% of the whole social case load is caused by illegitimacy and immorality of all types – that means not only relief but hospitalization, the care of defectives in mental hospitals, infants' homes, children's aid societies and all that sort of thing. I must point out that the whole thing is running us into a tremendous sum of money – our costs in 1925 were $27,000; in 1936 they were $314,000 and over 14% of the increase is due to this sort of thing. . . . I think the laws should be so drafted that any person asking state aid could be compelled to be sterilized if a fully qualified board were of the opinion that he should be.[94]

Dr. J.A. Faulkner responded cautiously that the government was convinced of the seriousness of the situation and was weighing its options.[95] Further pressure was applied in November, when the Ontario Provincial Council of Women presented the government with a resolution calling for "legislation to check the reproduction in selected cases of the mentally defective."[96]

In 1937 the ESC tried another tactic to flush out political support. A delegation led by Hutton approached Harold Kirby, the Ontario Minister of Health, with a proposed amendment to the Medical Act that would simply make sterilization legal and leave the question of the applicability of the operation to the individual surgeon.[97] But as benign as such legislation might appear, its true intent was indicated when the ESC cited developments in Nazi Germany as worthy of emulation: "Germany is seeking to purify the German people of defective inherited characteristics by widespread compulsory sterilization and over 300,000 persons have been sterilized. In our country under the democratic form of government, we believe in trusting the good sense of our professional people and depending upon public education to achieve the same ends."[98] In short, the argument was that Canada, too, had to be "purified," but in its own particular way.

To make an even more effective presentation of its case the ESC attempted in the late 1930's to gain access to the airwaves. The leadership of the CBC dreaded such touchy issues. In February of 1937 the CBC banned a pro-sterilization address that Hutton proposed to give, which included the line, "it must be obvious to all reasonable people that a fool is entirely unfit to serve as parent and educator of children whether he has inherited his foolishness or not."[99] This ban followed that of the Reverend Morris Zeidman's planned January talk on birth control. In September, birth control talks on the CBC were again prevented.[100] But early in 1938 Major Gladstone Murray, general manager of the CBC, in a clear reversal of policy, asked the ESC to put on a series of radio broadcasts and left the choice of subjects up to the Society.[101] In an obvious attempt to appear as moderate and respectable as possible, the Society had talks given by C.W.M. Hart, professor of anthropology at the University of Toronto, on evolution; W. Burton Hurd, professor of political economy at McMaster University, on population; Dr. Herbert Bruce, on German population policy; A.M. Harley, on the California sterilization law; and Dr. William Hutton on the future of the race.

Hutton's and Harley's contributions contained the now familiar defences of eugenics. Bruce's two talks were the most daring, larded as they were with praise for the Nazi's sterilization of "300,000 useless, harmful, and hopeless people." Such an action he presented as merciful and in harmony with nature inasmuch as it "reinforces in the human species that selective urge which prevails throughout the rest of nature." What Canada required was a similar "biological housecleaning."[102]

The contributions of the two academics, Hart and Hurd, were more circumspect. Hart was an intellectual nonentity, but the fact that someone like Hurd would share a platform with eugenics zealots like Bruce and Hutton deserves attention.[103] A Rhodes scholar, Liberal, Freemason, and member of the Order of the British Empire, Hurd was a distinguished scholar. As the leading authority on Canadian demography, he had been commissioned to prepare analyses of the 1921 and 1931 federal censuses. His early contributions to the discussion of Canada's population problems were more than academic exercises, however, revealing as they did a number of deap-seated anxieties. He found that Anglo-Saxon fertility was low and that of the French and new immigrants was high. The West, Hurd fretted, was "isolating" itself as it was submerged by waves of Slavic farmers.[104] Their rates of criminality were high, their rates of literacy low. "This country," he sourly noted, "is also paying for its immigrants through increased insanity and crime."[105] Assimilation was not occurring. Hurd shared A.R.M. Lower's "displacement theory" that these new arrivals were forcing the best Canadians to migrate to the United States. He predicted in 1929 that twenty more years of such developments would "transform this population cleavage into a cultural problem of the first magnitude."[106]

The immigration "problem" had, of course, been largely solved when the depression cut off the flow of new arrivals. Hurd now saw the threat to the population being posed by the mentally and morally defective.[107] Although not a declared eugenicist, he was willing to concede that unless some solution was found the costs of caring for the subnormal would bankrupt the nation. Hurd's participation in the ESC's series of radio addresses signified the extent to which eugenicists could draw on the support of those alarmed by the changing nature of Canadian society, including those advising the government on population policy.[108]

The ESC's hopes that its propaganda was about to bear some fruit seemed to be justified when in 1938 the Ontario government appointed a Royal Commission on the Operation of the Mental Health Act. Horrified at the numbers of women incarcerated at the Ontario Hospital in Cobourg simply because they were poor and pregnant, the Commission concluded that sterilization was called for. With cold-hearted candour the Commission pointed out that "if sterilization was permitted a comparatively large number of young women patients could be liberated and that while they would still be a sex problem in the community they would not be the same problem."[109] But once more the government refused to act.

Despite a rising tide of criticism, by 1939 the ESC could congratulate itself on having rallied a good deal of public support in Ontario in favour of sterilization. No doubt the majority of the population had no clear opinion on the subject, but the domination of the discussion by the proponents of such measures was obvious. What galled the ESC was its inability to convert this rhetorical support of sterilization into law. It has been suggested that the hostility of Dr. B.T. McGhie, deputy minister of health, was crucial in blocking its implementation in Ontario.[110] This no doubt played a role, but it is easy to exaggerate the extent to which politicians take medical opinion into account when determining health policies. The caution shown by provincial politicians in dealing with the issue stemmed more directly from their fear of bringing down on their heads the wrath of Catholic constituents.

Sterilization legislation was passed in the western provinces where Catholicism was weakest; it would not be in eastern provinces where the Church was strong. Even the support given eugenics by eminent Ontario geneticists was not sufficient to tip the balance.

7

Genetics, Eugenics, and Human Pedigrees

Eugenics was thrown into disrepute by the excesses of the Nazis. How, it was to be asked after the Holocaust, could a science have been turned to such atrocious purposes? The answer advanced by a number of historians is that the question is misleading because eugenics, marked as it was by the self-serving interests of its adherents, was patently not a science. Though eugenicists claimed to be elaborating a hereditarian science, most knew little of the true workings of genetics. Indeed, by the 1930's, so the argument goes, the gulf was widening between value-free genetics and politically engaged eugenics. "These individuals," writes Kenneth M. Ludmerer in describing such medical researchers as Madge Thurlow Macklin and Laurence Snyder, "were not eugenicists of the old school; indeed, they belittled the goals and values of the earlier eugenicists."[1] Geneticists, as professional scientists, had perhaps once appreciated the eugenicists' publicizing of the importance of heredity, but now they found the extravagances of the amateurs increasingly embarrassing. If the former did not do as much as one might have wished to publicize the inaccuracies of eugenics, this could be attributed to the fact that they purposely shunned politics and resolutely remained in their labs.

Those who make such an argument are certainly correct in pointing out that as genetics became more sophisticated and technical it could no longer be so easily accessed to support the program of the eugenicists. It is wishful thinking to believe, however, that one witnessed a simple triumph of science over prejudice. Recent research has revealed that many geneticists continued to be committed to some form of eugenics. The older interpretation, in exaggerating the "divorce" of genetics and eugenics, failed to acknowledge the support eugenic policies continued to receive through the 1930's and 1940's from highly trained geneticists.

In Canada it was certainly far from apparent that the goals of "pure" science were that far removed from those of eugenics. The Canadian Eugenics Society counted as its members Roy Fraser, professor of biology at Mount Allison University, W.T. MacClement, professor of biology at Queen's University, T.R. Robinson, professor of psychology at the University of Toronto, and Madge Thurlow Macklin, professor of physiology at the University of Western Ontario. H.B. Fantham, professor of zoology at McGill, was vice-president of the New York-based Eugenics Research Association, of which fellow McGill zoologist J.K. Breitenbecher was also a member. Two of Canada's most eminent scientists – A.G. Huntsman, University of Toronto professor of biology and director of the Fisheries Board of Canada, and F.E. Lloyd, professor of botany at McGill and in 1933 president of the Royal Society of Canada – sat on the advisory council of the American Eugenics Society. C.L. Huskins, professor of genetics at McGill (in whose memory the Canadian Genetics Association established in 1954 the annual Huskins Memorial Lecture), defended the eugenicists' sterilization program in the press. Similar support was offered by A.H.R. Butler, professor of botany, and Vincent W. Jackson, professor of zoology, both of the University of Manitoba. The Canadian contingent who attended the 1932 International Congress of Eugenics in New York included, in addition to Madge Thurlow Macklin, William Hutton, and Frank Walker of the Canadian Eugenics Society, Alan Deakin of the Dominion Experimental Farm at Ottawa, Professor Henri Prat of the Université de Montréal, and Helena Shepherd of the Canadian National Committee on Mental Hygiene.[2]

No better example of this blurring of the lines between science and pseudo-science could be found than in the career of Madge Thurlow Macklin, who in the 1930's was the country's pre-eminent human geneticist and the most important scientific defender of eugenics. Macklin was representative of a number of like-minded medical scientists in Europe and North America who believed that health care, genetics, biology, and social work could only benefit from an appreciation of eugenics. This chapter accordingly presents an overview of her life for the purpose of providing, not a biographical sketch of one isolated individual, but a case study of the 1930's Canadian scientist as eugenicist.

Few Canadians today know much about Macklin, but a recapitulation of her remarkable career is warranted for a number of reasons. First, such an analysis reveals how difficult it was in the interwar period for a woman scientist in Canada to receive fair treatment, and it suggests the sorts of strengths necessary to overcome the male chauvinism of the academic medical community. Second, it demonstrates the pioneering contributions a Canadian made to the science of human genetics. Finally, and of particular pertinence to the subject of this study, such an examination indicates the manner in which eugenic and genetic preoccupations continued to be linked right up until the Second World War.

Madge Thurlow Macklin was born in Philadelphia in 1893, the fourth child (third of four daughters) of Margaret De Grofft and William Harrison Thurlow. This middle-class Methodist family soon moved to Baltimore, where Madge Thurlow attended public school.[3] Her first love was mathematics, but at Goucher College, which she entered in 1910, she was so impressed by a dissection demonstration that she swung her interests to medicine. Her instructors were taken both by her brilliance and by her reformist zeal. Medicine was a way, she declared, by which she could help improve the world. Indeed, as an undergraduate she expressed the pious hope – considered daring at the time – of ultimately using her knowledge of medicine and social work to participate in the struggle against white slavery (forced prostitution). Out of a similar concern for social justice she threw herself into suffrage work just prior to World War One. Even men who came to heckle her soapbox lectures found it difficult not to be impressed by what one of her Goucher instructors described as a "brainy, devoted, modest, refined, dauntless young woman." If she had an obvious fault it was, according to the same source, a lack of "sympathy for the erring, of being somewhat combative and intolerant."[4] The accuracy of this portrayal was to be frequently borne out in Macklin's later life.

Having won four scholarships during her years at Goucher, she graduated in 1914 as a Phi Beta Kappa and winner of a fellowship to Johns Hopkins, the finest medical school in the United States. It had attracted an excellent research staff from around the world, including a brilliant young Canadian, Charles C. Macklin. Madge Thurlow began as Macklin's research assistant; in 1918 they married. Though almost immediately pregnant, Madge Macklin received her M.D. with honours in 1919 and taught briefly as an assistant in physiology at the Johns Hopkins School of Hygiene until 1920. The following year the Macklins, who now had two daughters, moved back to Canada where Charles was appointed professor of anatomy at the University of Western Ontario. During his thirty-two-year career at Western he was to acquire an international reputation based on his investigations of the functional anatomy of the lung.[5]

Madge Macklin taught in the department of histology and embryology at the University of Western Ontario from 1921 to 1945. The university treated her shabbily throughout her long and distinguished career. As a faculty spouse she was exploited as a part-time instructor until 1930 and then only appointed to the rank of part-time assistant professor. Though she was a gifted and popular teacher, the administration never paid her more than half of what a male colleague would have earned, and during some years in the depression she worked for no pay at all. The university never allowed her to teach a course in her specialty – human genetics. Yet outside of London, Ontario, she was making a world-wide reputation with her publication of what eventually amounted to some 150 scholarly articles and the presentation of as many public addresses on genetic disorders. And all this time she was raising a family. Even the birth of a third daughter in 1927 did not slow her down. "I have," she later boasted, "lost one period of four months, one of two months, and another of three weeks from teaching and research while I had the three daughters."[6] Though a housekeeper took care of the children during working hours, Charles and Madge Macklin made a point of being at home with their girls at lunch and after school. To carry out successfully so many responsibilities this 5'2" woman, who in middle age weighed close to 200 pounds and suffered at times from migraines and phlebitis, clearly had to have immense reserves of energy.[7]

Madge Macklin finally left Western at the end of the Second World War. For over twenty years she had been limited to teaching embryology to first-year med students and assisting Charles Macklin in his histology course. In 1945 the administration informed her that even her sessional appointment would not be renewed. Clashes with her colleagues had contributed to her termination. Dr. Murray Barr, the historian of the Western medical school, while admitting that she was treated poorly, recalled: "Her situation can be explained in part by the hesitation in those days to employ a husband and wife in the same Faculty, let alone the same department. Other reasons were more personal. Dr. Macklin was frank and outspoken in expressing her views, and her espousal of the eugenics cause offended some influential citizens."[8]

In 1946 Madge Macklin was appointed cancer research associate at Ohio State University by the National Research Council. Her salary there of $5,000 a year compared favourably to the average of $700 a year she had received at Western.[9] More importantly, she was allowed to give a course in medical genetics and had as her colleague another impassioned proponent of human genetics, Laurence Snyder. Her professional success did entail personal costs. Charles Macklin, though feuding with the administration, stayed on at Western Ontario. Until her retirement in 1959 Madge Macklin could only return to London to see her husband and daughters on vacations and holidays.

If Madge Macklin was embittered by the treatment she had received at Western, she must have enjoyed all the more her subsequent honours and awards. In 1938 she was the only woman at the First International Cancer Symposium at the University of Wisconsin and the first in 1942 to give the Gibson Memorial Lecture at the University of Buffalo. In 1938 she was awarded an honorary LL.D. from Goucher and in 1957 the Elizabeth Blackwell Medal of the American Medical Women's Association. In 1959 her colleagues in the American Society for Human Genetics acknowledged her pioneering work by electing her as president. In 1959 Madge Macklin retired and returned to Canada a few months before her husband's death. Her own death in 1962 followed three quiet years in Toronto with her daughters and grand-children.

Very little work has been done on the history of women scientists in Canada, but the trials and tribulations of Macklin's career make a good deal more sense when set in the context of the findings in Margaret W. Rossiter's *Women Scientists in America: Struggles and Strategies to 1940* (1982). She tells us that between the wars United States women scientists continually met with double standards and lack of recognition in graduate school, in the pursuit of grants, and in seeking employment. Professional potential was further limited by marriage. Only 18.2 per cent of Rossiter's active women scientists were married in 1921 and only 26.4 per cent in 1938.[10] Marriage to an eminent male scientist might provide some leverage, but for most it remained a trap because many universities expected women to resign when married or enforced anti-nepotism rules that effectively barred a wife from employment at her husband's university. Married women scientists were thus commonly unemployed or under-employed, re-stricted to low-level teaching, and ghettoized in research assistant positions doing "women's work."[11] In response, women scientists developed a number of defensive strategies, including the establish-ment of their own groups, prizes, and honour societies to provide compensatory recognition.[12] But if a woman were too strident in her criticisms of the sexism of the scientific world she might well find herself condemned as "abrasive" (which also served as a code word for Jewish) and even further isolated.[13]

Macklin fits Rossiter's description almost too perfectly: she arrived in Ontario as a result of her husband's professional interests and was regarded by the administration as linked to his lab; she was restricted to first-year teaching at pitifully low wages; she received scant credit for her remarkable publishing record; and finally, she was dismissed, in part, because of her outspokenness. Much of the recognition she received came from women in the form of her appointment as Catherine Milligan Lecturer at Goucher College in 1936, her election to Sigma Delta Epsilon (the honorary science fraternity for women), and her winning in 1957 of the Elizabeth Blackwell Award.[14] Placed in the light of Rossiter's findings one has to conclude that Macklin's fate at the University of Western Ontario was structured by the gender relations operating in the world of science, not by her "outspokenness."

If the fact that she was a woman led many of Madge Macklin's colleagues to underestimate her abilities, it is also likely that her own concerns as a woman for the central importance of bearing healthy children in part led to her path-breaking work in genetics. In a 1932 review of a book on child psychology she declared that as a mother of three daughters she was not impressed by claims about the malleability of children. She was convinced that the existence of innate differences could not be denied. "I believe that it is only psychologists of a certain class that have ever believed that babies were a handful of plastic clay, waiting for the environment to mold them," she declared, and went on to assert that even personalities, like biological faculties, were "dependent upon chemical entities inherited in the germ plasm."[15] The challenge that Macklin came to regard as the central one facing scientists was to work out the ways in which such hereditary forces impacted on human health.

Until the 1930's most work in genetics had been done on fruit flies and mice. Many scientists felt that because of the inability to control human breeding and the relatively long time before the traits of one generation could be looked for in the next, work on human heredity was futile. Macklin was convinced that genetics and medicine had much to offer each other and came to be known as the founder of "medical genetics," a term she coined. Her scientific reputation was based on carrying out pioneering work on inherited diseases, elaborating sophisticated statistical methodologies to expedite her research, and pressing on her medical colleagues the importance of including in the medical curriculum courses in genetics.

Macklin, trained in histology and embryology, was drawn to the question of developmental abnormalities by reports of work done on cancer at Chicago by Dr. Maude Slye.[16] Macklin's best-known studies were also going to be on the hereditary aspects of tumours, but in the 1920's she also carried out work on abnormalities of the eye, hemophilia, and mongolism; in the 1930's she made important contributions to the study of erthroblastosis fetalis, dental anomalies, and tuberculosis.

Macklin's main contention was that heredity played a key role in a large number of diseases: diabetes, cancer, heart disease, retinal glioma, amaurotic idiocy, hemophilia, and some forms of tuberculosis. Many doctors were not convinced. In a 1931 article Macklin stated that medical students were left in virtual ignorance of the genetic basis of disease. "They have been so scornful of such an idea, so that one practitioner not so many years ago indignantly demanded to be shown a 'club-footed ovum' when inheritance of defect was being discussed."[17]

To the argument of her medical colleagues that cancer simply struck by "chance," Macklin replied that the fact that more than one member of a family developed the same tumour on the same organ at a similar age was more than mere coincidence.[18] To the response that a common environment was the cause, she asked why it was ten times more likely for a parent and child both to have gastric cancer than a husband and wife. Even more startling were her findings related to eye tumours. She informed the 1938 meeting of the American Association for Cancer Research that she had "found 163 instances in which related persons were affected; none in which husband and wife had the same tumour."[19]

In the early years Macklin was prone to downplay environmental factors and exaggerate inheritance. She was, for example, most reluctant to accept the idea that pipe-smoking contributed to cancer of the lip. By the late thirties she allowed that the role of chronic irritation and internal secretions could not be denied, but she still stressed the primary role played by inheritance in neoplastic diseases.

Macklin, in her brisk, no-nonsense fashion, was clearly attracted to the notion of inherited diseases that struck, not by whim, but according to Mendelian "laws." They were, she suggested, as irrefutable as the laws of gravitation. Many found such a deterministic portrayal unpalatable, but not Macklin. Lay readers were obviously impressed by the scientific detachment with which she, for example, surveyed the increase in cancer in Canada.[20] To those appalled by the apparent surge in cancer deaths in the twentieth century she coolly responded that they were getting what they asked for. Everyone had eventually to die of something. If improvements in public health allowed the masses to escape death from contagious disease and accident then they would inevitably fall victim to cancer and heart disease. Though the fainthearted might lament the relative rise in such complaints the rational, so Macklin argued, would necessarily recognize such an increase as an indication of the conquest of the old causes of mortality. "We purchase freedom from the infectious diseases of yesterday by the tacit promise to pay with death in another form tomorrow. We may delay the payment of the promissory note for years, but in the end, we pay."[21]

To prove that cancer or a predisposition to cancer had a hereditary basis, Macklin set about elaborating sophisticated statistical methods. It was her intention to apply to both physical and mental hereditary illnesses "the same rigid scientific yardstick of controls that the chemist, the physicist, or the biologist must use in evaluating their theories."[22] To do so she assembled a mountain of statistical material, which she sought to analyse thoroughly through the use of the statistical pedigree approach and the employment of data on twins.[23] Much of her work was done on breast cancer, which led her into the further investigation of statistical problems posed by diseases restricted to one sex. She was particularly critical of researchers who failed to make such discriminations. A 1933 study, for example, in comparing New York life insurance policy owners who died of cancer with those who did not found that the relatives of the former group did not have a higher rate of cancer than the relatives of the latter. The weakness of such a study, argued Macklin, was that the researcher, first, overlooked the fact that 90 per cent of the policy owners were male, and, second, made no provision for their inability to acquire such female forms of cancer as carcinoma of the breast and uterus.[24]

> It reminds me of a man who was once in my audience when I was lecturing on inheritance in cancer. He arose and said, "My great-grandmother died of cancer of the uterus, as did her daughter, who was my grandmother. My own mother had it, but was operated upon in time to save her life. If you are right about inheritance of cancer that is a very black outlook for me." I assured him on that score he had nothing to fear, for it was like being all dressed up and no place to go.[25]

In short, Macklin asserted that it was useless simply to talk about "cancer" as if it were a single entity; one had to look for the same types of tumours on the same organs at the same age of onset.[26] One also had to be aware that since cancer, unlike other hereditarily linked diseases, had a late age of onset, its genetic factor in a relative could be hidden by an early death due to some other cause.[27] Most important of all, one had to go to elaborate lengths to make sure that statistical biases were not built into the study. If deductions were to be of any value they had to be based on sets of data that could be meaningfully compared.[28] Clearly, Macklin's early mathematical training was of immense value to her. Although she frequently downplayed her competency in statistics, her contribution to cancer research obviously lay in her wedding of genetics and mathematics.

After completing an analysis of the data, Macklin's own conclusions regarding breast cancer were that "Grandmothers, aunts, and sisters of women with breast cancer have had breast cancer with a frequency which is significantly greater than that of women in a similar age range either in the general population or in two sets of selected control samples. . . . The fact that the presumably genetic factor responsible for the excess of breast cancer is enhanced to the greatest degree in childless women shows the interaction of genetic and intrinsic factors."[29] On the other hand, her study of cervical cancer revealed that, if it did have a genetic basis, it was aggravated by early childbearing.[30]

Macklin's findings have not fully withstood the test of subsequent research. Though she successfully correlated particular types of cancer and time of onset, she failed – like many other eugenicists – to note that correlation was not the same as causation. Karl Pearson likewise correlated the physical and mental attributes of English schoolchildren. Macklin and Pearson were so convinced of the power of heredity that they ignored the fact that the correlations they unearthed were as likely the result of environmental as of genetic causes. Today it is believed that a relatively small proportion of all cancers are due to genetic factors. Macklin is still cited, however, as a scientist whose extensive and meticulous research broached the question of how one might determine the role heredity could play in susceptibility to cancer.

To create the human "pedigrees" that would reveal hereditarily linked anomalies required an enormous amount of painstaking case collecting. Macklin's great hope in the 1930's was that eventually some central statistical bureau would be established to track all cancer operations and cancer deaths.[31] In the meantime she pointed out to insurance companies that they should assist in gathering such information since they had a financial incentive in tracking down hidden illnesses.[32] She also assumed that once people were made aware of such hereditary influences they would be prepared to undergo routine medical checkups rather than wait until illness struck. But the main question was whether or not such patients would be treated by sufficiently enlightened general practitioners.

Some doctors obviously found genetic explanations disheartening because they assumed that if a disease were inherited then they could do nothing to prevent it. Macklin's response was that, on the contrary, a knowledge of such genetic linkages in a family promised more accurate and earlier diagnoses, more effective and rational therapeutic action. For example, if doctors were made aware as a result of making a thorough clinical history that the close relatives of a patient suffered from gastric cancer, they could look for and remove such tumours even before warning symptoms appeared. Likewise, cases of early diabetes could be tracked down among the relatives of the diabetic patient. Genetic knowledge promised to make medicine not less but more preventive and interventionist than it had ever been. Macklin reminded her colleagues that in the nineteenth century the pathologist gained most of his information from autopsies on the dead whereas in the 1930's he was called in to examine specimens while the patient was on the operating table. She looked forward to the day when diagnosis was advanced "to the point at which the patient is alive and as yet without symptoms."[33]

What particularly disturbed Macklin were doctors who told parents who had already given birth to one child suffering from serious genetic defects to try again. "How unjust," she wrote, "to the parents who have already had the misfortune of bringing into the world one defective child to raise their hopes by false promises."[34] She reported the case of a specialist who intended to treat a man whose first two children had died at birth from hemorrhage into the lungs for *his* lung complaint before the next conception. "I pointed out that if the father had had a leg missing and if the two children had each been born without a leg, that he (the obstetrician) would not expect to insure the presence of two legs on the third child by the expedient of fitting a wooden leg onto the father before the beginning of the next pregnancy. Altering the father's somatic make-up would not improve the quality of the germ plasm he passed along to the next offspring."[35] Macklin's dictum was that in such cases of potential birth defect it was always better to be accurate than hopeful. By 1940 she granted, however, that modes of transmission of disease could vary from family to family and therefore demanded careful individual clinical histories.[36]

To track such inherited abnormalities Macklin was insistent that doctors revise their method of record-keeping. In the past they only asked about illness currently afflicting the patient; Macklin stressed the necessity of also inquiring into the patient's family medical history. This in turn meant that doctors would have to be trained to know what to look for. She reported that she once heard a doctor:

> . . . make the statement that he thought that some chemical in tobacco was productive of cervical cancer, because every woman

who had come to him in his practice with cervical cancer worked in a cigar factory at some time in her life. On inquiry, I found that all the women in town in which he practised worked in a cigar factory at some time in their lives, so that it could be equally well claimed that rolling tobacco leaves was the cause of fractures, babies, indigestion, and corns in the women of that community.[37]

Even those doctors concerned with intrinsic as opposed to extrinsic causes of disease were, according to Macklin, carelessly speaking of certain diseases "running in a family" and not discriminating between congenital, childhood, familial, and inherited anomalies.[38] And some, she lamented, in their ignorance of the laws of heredity continued to believe in such old wives' tales as the one that held that firstborns were most prone to congenital defects.[39]

Turning from medical practice to medical training, Macklin argued that medical schools, in failing to offer courses in genetics, were seriously handicapping their graduates in their ability to offer the best possible service to their patients. In 1936 she pointed out to her Canadian colleagues that in Britain a Human Heredity Committee had been established. Macklin insisted that Canada, which already devoted funds to the genetic study of cereals, had to follow suit with courses and an institute devoted to human genetics.[40] Macklin was perhaps best known in her profession for her long, vociferous campaign to have departments of medical genetics established in medical schools. In articles, essays, and interviews she hammered away with missionary zeal on the reiterated argument that genetics had to be incorporated in the medical curriculum.[41] Her assertions in the 1930's of the central significance of genetics were prophetic; in 1938 only one medical school in North America had a compulsory course in the subject; by 1953, 55 per cent had followed suit. The irony, of course, was that she herself was not allowed to offer a course in genetics during the twenty-four years she was at the University of Western Ontario.

In 1962 the president of the American Society of Human Genetics honoured the memory of Madge Macklin, who, he reminded his colleagues, "played a pioneer role in introducing genetics to the medical fraternity, and whom we all loved for her energy, tenacity of purpose, humor, compassion and the whimsical tirades with which she would castigate her male colleagues."[42] After having examined her life and scholarly work it is difficult to disagree with the accuracy of the description. It is only when one turns to her involvement in the eugenics movement in the 1930's that some doubts arise regarding her "compassion."

Macklin was herself quite explicit in calling on doctors to equip themselves with "emotional immunity" when it came to dealing with the question of whether or not the feeble-minded should marry and have children.[43] She regarded their reproduction as the chief source of the nation's ills. The profession had, she declared, a duty to support the creation of a healthy, normal race. Physicians and surgeons thus had an enormous responsibility to defend the child's right to be born "free" of defect. At the same time, she denied parents' "right" to have abnormal children.[44] Macklin recognized the volatility of the issue. In a 1931 article in *Science* she stated, "Because the whole subject is so closely bound up in the minds of the public with what we are pleased to term the 'inalienable right of man' the very attempts to study the problem calmly and sanely are thwarted by the reactionaries who insist upon placing emotion before fact."[45] It was thus in the guise of a progressive, professional scientist that Macklin threw her support behind the Eugenics Society of Canada and in particular its campaign for the sterilization of the feeble-minded.

Macklin was very active in both the Canadian and the international eugenic movements. She wrote on eugenics from the mid-1920's. In 1930 she was one of the original organizers of the Eugenics Society of Canada, executive secretary of the organization between 1932 and 1935, and director in 1935. She attended Canadian and international eugenics conferences throughout the thirties, sat on the editorial advisory board of the Eugenics Research Association, contributed to *Eugenics Review* and *Eugenics News*, and gave dozens of talks on the subject before women's groups and businessmen's clubs.

The central social problem of the day, as Macklin saw it, was that society was being swamped by the feeble-minded.[46] Drawing on her mathematical gifts, she calculated that in the province of Ontario the mentally ill and defective were increasing far faster than the general population. She denied that such figures were the results of either changes in diagnoses or more accurate reportage. The surge in numbers was real, she asserted, and due to the fact that the unfit were no longer weeded out by disease.

> The great increase in mental cases can be ascribed in part, I feel, to our preventive medicine and public health measures which inadvertently save the poor stock along with the good. When one reads of the terrible typhus, cholera, small-pox, diphtheria, yellow fever and

scurvy epidemics that devastated the province of Ontario, some of them less than a hundred years ago, one realizes how many persons who might have been potential mental cases were killed off before they arrived that far. If the mentally subnormal and mentally ill tended to have a lowered physical stamina, then such epidemics would have worked selectively, eliminating them in larger proportion than they weeded out the mentally capable.[47]

The problem was compounded, claimed Macklin, because the differential birth rate was very much in favour of the defective. Uncritically accepting the figures of Dr. W.L. Hutton, she asserted that normal families had on average three children, while the families whose children ended up at the Orillia Home for the Feebleminded had an average of nine.[48] Intermittent wars, according to Macklin, further exacerbated the situation. "War," she informed a meeting of the Eugenics Society of Canada, "is dysgenic – that is, it is opposed to eugenics – since it culls out the best physical and mental material to be destroyed, and leaves behind to be parents of the next generation those who were not good enough to be shot."[49] Macklin's dire prediction was that if no dramatic action were taken "complete submersion and disappearance of the normal stock" was inevitable.[50]

Macklin presented herself not simply as a foe of the defectives but rather as a defender of "that element of the race which retains not only high physical endowment but also those intellectual qualities which permit of independence, and those spiritual assets which induce us to exercise it."[51] During the depression years she regarded this class, of which she was of course part, as very much under siege. In a 1939 speech before the Canadian Life Insurance Officers Association she lauded their profession for its inculcation of the virtues of thrift and foresight. Too many in the community, in her opinion, relied on the handouts of paternalistic government and on "hard-working tax payers to pay the bill that others may enjoy the benefits."[52] These same middle-class taxpayers had to restrict the size of their own families because they had to support not just their own children but also those of the defective in the asylums. In a public talk in 1933 she stated,

> By our modern system of government, we care for the mentally deficient by means of taxes, which have to be paid for by the mentally efficient before the latter can claim any of their earnings for themselves. We rob the normal, who would be an asset to the community, to care for those who are only a liability.[53]

The consequence was "the steadily falling birth-rate, noticeable chiefly among the more intelligent classes, a situation that our politicians may deplore, but which will certainly not be remedied as long as the excessive burden of taxation is maintained."[54]

In an equally provocative address to the 1934 Ontario Education Association, Macklin warned that the public school system was also being undermined by the presence of defectives. She was convinced that the average level of intelligence was declining because more of the unfit were now in schools. For ages, Macklin told the assembled delegates, this class's "lack of enterprise, intelligence, and ambition had kept them living in the slums and hovels."[55] Now "philanthropy" was caring for them, providing them with a "veneer of normality," and encouraging them to marry and reproduce. Flooding into the schools, they were pampered by teachers drunk with the environmentalist's delusion that brains could be put into heads that lacked them at birth. A self-sustaining system was emerging, warned Macklin, because, as a result of misdirected charity:

> . . . we create a larger and larger army of persons who desire to perpetuate the existing conditions, an army composed on the one hand of the inadequate, and on the other of those paid by the community to look after them.[56]

The "inadequate" were, Macklin angrily noted, even allowed to vote and so protect the system that fostered them.

What could be done? First, Macklin argued, the "normal," those whose "industry and intelligence enabled them to acquire a higher standard of living," had to be protected. In noting anthropologist Franz Boas's critique of the eugenic program, Macklin declared:

> Those who object to the eugenic program talk about the "social rights" of the defectives. They lose sight of the social rights of the normal person. Is it not within his right to refuse support for his neighbour's physically and mentally defective children? . . . it is time that some advocate of the rights of the normal man should come forward, and demand his fair share of his own earnings to look after his own children.[57]

Likewise in schools, continued Macklin, it was time for teachers to return to their primary duty of giving special attention to the brightest. Schools had once followed the teachings set down in Jesus's parable of the talents: "To him who had intelligence and the capacity to use his talents more was given; but to him who had little, and not the capacity to use what he had, even that little was taken away."[58] It was time, insisted Macklin, to return to that system. A "new deal" in education was required that would reward the "aristocracy of intellect" with scholarships while penalizing the incompetent.[59]

> For individuals who fall below a still lower grading, the parents shall bear the entire cost of education if they desire their children to be educated. Thus the intelligent classes who have largely limited their families in order to give educational facilities to those children they already have will not find children such a great liability and can afford to have more; while those who have not found them a liability because of the social services rendered in the past will either be prohibited from having their family or will find it to their advantage to have fewer children.[60]

The educational system, Macklin concluded, had a responsibility both to the intelligent individual and to the race. Such an onerous responsibility could only be fully carried out if educators came to appreciate the laws of heredity.

Macklin's reading of these laws led her to support the positive eugenics program of attempting through various financial bribes to raise the fertility of the "efficient." But since such campaigns seemed doomed to futility, she also embraced the campaign for the sterilization of the feeble-minded. If one wanted to empty a trough of water, she reasoned, one began by first turning off the tap.[61] Correspondingly, if one really wanted to eliminate mental defectives they had to be prevented from breeding. Despite the arguments against sterilization made by leading experts in the field, such as the English researcher L.N. Penrose (who was to teach at Western during the war years), Macklin persisted in arguing that sterilization was the only sure answer.[62] She assured readers of the *Canadian Medical Association Journal* that she had "incontrovertible scientific facts" that if such limits were not placed on the defective, then the nation faced the "annihilation of the normal stock."[63]

The defectives, she argued, tended to marry thoughtlessly and have huge families. Or worse yet, their promiscuity contributed enormously to the illegitimacy rate. They either passed on their tainted genes to their children or were so incompetent as parents that they left their children psychologically scarred. In the first instance prevention of reproduction was called for on genetic grounds:

> This will not eliminate all defectives but will materially reduce their percentage in the population. This holds true no matter whether the defect is a dominant or a recessive one. This statement is not based upon impressions, but can be demonstrated by mathematical for-

mulae. Quarantining and vaccinating against small pox have not eliminated it but they have changed it from a world-wide terror to an almost forgotten disease.[64]

In the second instance prevention of reproduction was warranted on psychological grounds:

Surely no mentally defective person, whether feeble-minded or mentally ill, is capable of producing that atmosphere of normality which is to confer on the child of tomorrow that sense of balance which is to enable them to walk the mental tight rope without slipping. No one would maintain, least of all the psychiatrists, that those who have not been able to make their own Unconscious behave are capable of so instructing their children that they in turn will be led into ways of sanity and paths of mental peace.[65]

The decision to control the reproduction of the deviant could be undertaken once doctors and the general public were convinced by eugenicists of the fact of "original human inequality."[66]

Macklin's most sweeping statements concerning sterilization appeared in her 1939 discussion of schizophrenia. She supported Franz J. Kallman's call for the sterilization of not just the patients but also their children, parents, and "all relatives of schizophrenics who by virtue of their known genetic constitution are certain of their carrying a latent factor for the disease." Macklin only chided Kallman for not being a "little more enthusiastic about the eugenic program."[67]

Macklin maintained her support for sterilization despite the attacks of English authorities like Penrose and the hostile review of the practice published by a committee of the American Neurological Association in 1937. The committee reported that because the mentally ill had a short life expectancy, and low marriage and fertility rates, the idea that they were more fecund than the normal was a myth. More importantly, the report noted that the sterilization program was inherently class-biased because only working-class patients were in the sorts of institutions where such practices were carried out. Macklin's unrepentant response to the report was first to challenge its accuracy, second to argue that if the middle class at the moment escaped the law the answer was to extend its purview, and third to suggest that even epileptics, though they did not pass on their condition genetically, should be sterilized because their purported inability to be good parents violated the child's "inalienable right" of security.[68]

The fact that birth control by the mid-1930's was winning the public support of the respectable in Canada was advanced by Macklin as one more reason why sterilization should be accepted. She shared the opinions of Kallman, whom she quoted approvingly to the effect that eugenic measures should logically be accepted in a "population which already practices birth control extensively for economic and social reasons. Granted birth control, it is difficult to understand why its first object should not be the prevention of inferior children."[69] Many eugenicists were concerned that birth control was dysgenic inasmuch as it lowered the fertility of just that segment of society which should be encouraged to reproduce – the industrious and the thoughtful. Macklin was of the opinion that birth control did have a place in the eugenic program, though she believed that sterilization was a more efficient method by which to lower the fertility of a targeted population.[70]

Macklin was also alert to the danger of the foreign feeble-minded entering Canada from abroad. In 1926 she began her important series of articles in the *Canadian Medical Association Journal* on diseases of the eye with the expressed hope that they would be of some interest to "those individuals who are desirous of maintaining within Canadian borders a citizenry of high physical as well as mental endowments."[71] The United States, she noted, had already instituted a system of carefully screening immigrants. Canada was threatened with being swamped by the abnormal unless it complemented a policy of preventing the reproduction of the native mentally deficient with a selective immigration policy that denied entry to the deficient foreign-born. Canada might have no way of preventing her brighter citizens from leaving, concluded Macklin, but it could at least prevent the arrival of the unfit.

To appreciate fully the significance of Macklin's support of eugenics, it has to be recalled that in the same pages of the Ontario papers that reported her attacks on the feeble-minded, the indigent, and the immigrant appeared accounts of the victims of the depression at home and of the fascists abroad. Her call for someone to rise up to defend the propertied and the respectable against the dispossessed reads all the more chillingly today when one recalls how similar this sounds to the appeals made by the Nazis. Perhaps Macklin did not fully appreciate the ends toward which eugenics was being turned in Germany, yet such ignorance would have been remarkable, especially given the fact that she visited Nazi Germany in 1937 to acquaint herself with the programs being employed by Dr. Kurt Pohlisch to deal with the mentally ill.[72] Upon her return to Canada her avid support of the sterilization program continued unabated. Only after the Western powers went to war with Germany and subjected the scientific racial programs of the Nazis to public opprobrium did Macklin and other North American eugenicists temper their support for sterilization.

Why did such an obviously gifted woman, who was herself a victim of discrimination and prejudice, throw her support behind a movement that chose to make the weakest members of the community the scape-goats for all its ills? It would be easiest to assert that Macklin simply did not know what she was involved in. H.J. Eysenck has written, apropos of this phenomenon: "Scientists, especially when they leave the particular field in which they have specialized, are just as ordinary, pig-headed and unreasonable as anyone else and their unusually high intelligence only makes their prejudices all the more dangerous."[73] Macklin clearly knew very little of the subject of feeble-mindedness about which she willingly pontificated. Indeed, in dealing with the question of the heredity of mental illness she abandoned the sort of sophisticated and demanding analysis of data that she employed in investigating cancer. Much of her hostility to the care given the poor and the sick was based simply on her social conservatism. In a talk given to the Paris, Ontario, YWCA in 1935, for example, she lamented the fact that old age pensions "made charity respectable," that mother's allowances penalized the thrifty, that philanthropy supported "useless" families.[74] She was as much alarmed by the "heavy economic waste of caring for the hereditary defective" as she was by the purported consequences of the passing on of their traits.[75]

But there is no denying the fact that Macklin was an expert in hereditary illnesses. One wants to know how she could be so apparently objective in dealing with some hereditary complaints and so biased when dealing with others. Her ruthless condemnation of the feeble-minded appears all the more puzzling when contrasted to the great empathy with which she spoke of the cancer patients whom she believed to be equally victimized by bad genes. She called for the former's sterilization, but explicitly rejected the notion that attempts be made to breed out cancer. Her reasoning, as summed up in a 1932 article in the *Quarterly Review of Biology*, was that since neoplastic diseases had a late age of onset the cancer victim, unlike the mental patient, might well accomplish something important before being incapacitated.

> If we can live a life of usefulness, of mental and physical well being until we reach three score or three score years and ten, then we have had our day, and if cancer comes to claim us, it may give us less suffering, less anxiety than many of the diseases which are less dreaded.[76]

She repeated the argument in 1938, warning that Maude Slye's success in breeding cancer out of mice could not be extended to humans. "We might well ask, then do we want to breed cancer out of the race, if by doing so we breed out all the good qualities that frequently go with it?"[77] Macklin then conjured up a hypothetical cancer victim – a brilliant college co-ed whose grandparents had died of cancer. There could be no question of sterilizing such a productive young woman, for to do so would be to lose her "highly intellectual heritage."[78] It is not really necessary to know that Macklin herself was a brilliant undergraduate whose father and maternal aunt died of cancer to perceive her failure of imagination. The only valued life, in her estimation, was the one lived by those who shared her class and cultural values. It is sad to think that her own struggle to win intellectual recognition despite the handicap of being a woman might have made her less, rather than more, sympathetic to those attempting to overcome mental handicaps.

We began this chapter by posing the question of whether or not a wide gulf separated eugenics and genetics in the 1930's. Recent studies have shown that in America and Europe the two certainly overlapped. An analysis of Macklin's career leads to the conclusion that the same was true in Canada. One writer of a brief but laudatory biographical sketch of Macklin has suggested, however, that if she involved herself in the eugenics movement it was because "she had sufficient foresight to realize that if physicians did not assume a leading role the movement would be taken over by politicians, publicists and prejudiced extremists."[79] Such an argument would appear to be based on the premise that doctors are better qualified than anyone else to judge such questions as who should be allowed to reproduce. This was, of course, the very argument that Macklin herself strove so mightily to advance and one even shared by many colleagues who might not have called themselves eugenicists.

Eugenics was to an extent only a symptom of a more pervasive elitism that the medical profession would espouse in the twentieth century. Macklin's own support for the eugenics movement could be construed as only an episode lasting little more than a decade. It was an important episode, however, because in those years North American eugenicists and geneticists would declare their ambitions with a candour that could not be sustained once the Nazis made the world aware of the full consequences of biological politics.

8

The Death of Eugenics?

Under the headline "Two Doctors Disagree in their Own House on Eugenics Problem," the *Toronto Star* gleefully reported in January, 1933, that Charles C. Macklin did not share Madge Thurlow Macklin's enthusiasm for sterilization.

"I am not particularly interested in the study of heredity," said the ostensible head of the Macklin house, "my problems are in a different field, but I have not yet formed an opinion favourable to sterilization. The reason is that in my view there are not enough low grade people in the world. The troubles of mankind are not due to the low grade run of human kind. What we have suffered is from the brilliant men who have burdened Canada with our railway problems of today. Will anyone say that it was the section man and not the director that has been to blame?"[1]

The *Star* reported this clash of ideas in the Macklin household with the obvious expectation that its reading public, leery of the hereditarians' more extravagant claims, would be amused at the news of such a contretemps. Eugenicists clearly spoke to the needs of many who were searching for new arguments to buttress the social status quo, but they were never successful in convincing all Canadians of the overarching importance of heredity. Though the Eugenics Society of Canada managed for the most part to have its attacks on environmentalism taken seriously, large sections of the public were obviously reluctant to follow to its logical consequences the hereditarian argument.

When it was presented in its most outrageous forms it was not spared public ridicule. Dr. F.N. Walker's expressed belief in the necessity of taking into account eye colour, height, and head shape before marrying was accordingly lampooned by the editors of *Maclean's*:

Jack and Jill went up the Hill
    To get a ring and wed.
Jack came down – his eyes were brown
    And Jill's were blue instead.
Little Bo Beep, she lost her sheik
    Her life is plunged in pathos.
Her chin, they say, is retroussé
    Her fiance's – prognathous.
Maiden, though your heart should break;
    Be eugenic when you wed.
Phrenological caution take,
    Maiden though your heart should break.
A corpuscular mistake
    Means bad endocrines ahead.
Maiden though your heart should break,
    Be eugenic when you wed.

The magazine's response was:

Phooey on eugenics' dictum!
    Darling, let's just syncretize.
Shout, each endocrine victim,
    "Phooey on eugenics' dictum!"
Both our pa's went out and picked 'em
    Out a spouse like other guys.
Phooey on eugenics' dictum!
    Darling let's just syncretize.[2]

The critiques of eugenics that appeared in the Canadian popular press in the 1930's were good humoured and their targets generally presented as well-meaning if overzealous academics. But the outbreak of the war and the Nazis' shifting of the focus of their eugenic program from sterilization to euthanasia provoked a sharp reaction against eugenics everywhere in the Western world. Faced with the evidence of such barbarous policies, many who had once been tolerant of, if not impressed by, eugenic arguments rushed to condemn them. Canadian eugenicists who had openly praised the vigour with which the Nazis had set out on their program of race betterment now fell silent.[3] None rose to defend the eugenic programs when they were declared in 1940 by *Saturday Night* to be "scientific frauds" or when *Maclean's* in 1941 spelled out how Germany had moved from the sterilization to the killing of its insane and feeble-minded.[4] Indeed, most of the professionals who had dabbled in eugenic speculation followed Macklin's lead in seeking to distance themselves as much as possible from a movement whose basic principles had been plunged into disrepute. It is unlikely, however, that they so easily abandoned their cherished beliefs. "I do not like Hitler's motives or methods," A.R. Kaufman wrote to Guy Burch of the Population Reference Bureau in 1941, "but he apparently feels that the lower strata is not good for cannon fodder and is attempting to get rid of it. Judging from newspaper reports, etc., Hitler's methods of getting rid of the parasites are harsh but effective."[5]

The war destroyed the Eugenics Society of Canada, but before disintegrating it attempted, by offering to provide homes in Canada for "the finest children from the Motherland," to save both its honour and its reputation. In fact, neither end was accomplished. But this "Homes in Canada Service" scheme was, from its curious inception to its farcical conclusion, a typically eugenic undertaking and its story provides a fitting epitaph for the misguided efforts of the ESC.[6] In 1940, when London was subjected to the Blitz and the British government began the evacuation of children, W.L. Hutton telegraphed Lord Horder of the English Eugenics Society: "Send 250 children to me for location in Brantford. Will proceed to organize hospitality in other towns and cities. Will cable you specific instructions. Given some time we will provide the cream of Canadian homes for the cream of British children."[7]

But how was one going to skim off the "cream"? When D.B. Harkness wrote to the English Eugenics Society in June of 1940 he made it clear that Canadian eugenicists assumed that social standing could be taken as a rough and ready indicator of fitness. Harkness noted that one supporter of the ESC in Canada had declared: "I would hesitate to open my home to just any refugee who might be sent to me but if I knew that I was receiving a child or children of a doctor for instance, I would be delighted to make all the provisions I could."[8] In a later letter Harkness acknowledged that, given the current public hostility to eugenic notions, associated as they were with the Nazis, one would have to be discreet in describing the means used in screening potential applicants. "We are, of course, avoiding the use of any such term as 'preferred' but will simply state that our endeavour will be to suit the home in Canada to the case history."[9]

The Canadian immigration service quickly agreed to the scheme and in London the ESC had the assistance of Canada's High Commissioner, Vincent Massey, his secretary, Charles Ritchie, and Ritchie's assistant, George Ignatieff.[10] The recruitment of potential evacuees was carried out quietly by the English Eugenics Society in such a way as to complement the socio-biological preoccupations of the ESC.

Children were supposedly selected on the basis of health, heredity, intelligence, and whatever "valuable qualities" the family could boast of.[11] In fact, social status clearly mattered most of all. The professions of the fathers of the first small batch were all solidly upper middle-class: company director, professor, mining engineer, flight lieutenant, insurance official.[12] The problem was getting their children on ships to Canada. Exasperated British evacuation experts protested that there were already 190,000 children awaiting evacuation. If the ESC wanted to offer hospitality, they asked, why did it not just open its homes to the first arrivals?[13]

This was, of course, the nub of the question. The ESC was not interested in sheltering all comers; it offered protection to only the "cream" of British children. It was still stubbornly seeking in the last months of its existence to advance the cause of "race betterment." Although all too aware that such a cause was now inextricably linked in the public mind with the horrors of the Nazi regime, the ESC surreptitiously sought to hold true to the old hereditarian course.

Wracked by its inner contradictions and the growing hostility of both the British and Canadian governments to private evacuation schemes, the "Homes in Canada Service" soon sputtered to a close. By 1941 only about two dozen children and accompanying mothers had been brought to Canada.[14] Bizarrely enough, one of the first families to arrive was almost immediately evicted by its wealthy host. The English mother and her children had to be removed, the horrified businessman reported, because the woman had the audacity of praising the Communists for their opposition to the fascists.[15] This row marked the collapse of both the evacuation program and the ESC. The program was obviously not functioning and in its absence the ESC no longer had any *raison d'être*. What never seemed to dawn on the organizers of the scheme was the grotesque irony that, in rallying to oppose the horrors of Nazism, they could think of little else than falling back on their own paltry efforts of race betterment.

W.L. Hutton candidly informed a British colleague that the "Homes in Canada Service" had been seized upon as a way of providing the ESC with a reputable reason for carrying on. But though the failure of the former meant the demise of the latter, Hutton asserted that the weakness of eugenics in Canada had a more fundamental cause.

We ran up against one of the hard facts of Canadian politics – the steadily increasing dominance of the Catholic Church in Canadian affairs. Forty-eight per cent of the Canadian populace gives adherence to the Catholic faith. . . . The activities of the Canadian Eugenics Society called forth increasing opposition from Catholics. The Ontario government grew cold towards us. Teachers in our universities found pressure was exerted upon them if they dared to talk eugenics. Our membership started to dwindle.[16]

Hutton's belief in some sort of Catholic conspiracy aimed at closing off government and academia from the influence of the hereditarians appears to have been a product of his own imagination. Nevertheless, Catholic opposition was clearly important in attenuating the success of the eugenicists in Canada, and the association of the eugenics program with the atrocities committed by the Nazis finally sealed its doom. But there were other forces at work that need to be considered if one is to explain why old-style eugenics died away in the first years of World War Two. In addition to Quebec-based Catholic opposition, the rising hostility of practising geneticists to eugenics and a changing social climate that was becoming less hospitable to the hereditarian cause underlay the demise of the traditional eugenicist movement.

Prior to the Second World War much of the most vociferous opposition to eugenics was voiced, as Hutton stressed, by Catholics. But the eugenicists, revelling as they did in the role of progressive reformers, were not altogether unhappy with being the subject of Catholic attacks. Pope Pius XI's 1930 bull, *Casti Connubi*, denounced – in addition to eugenics – divorce, birth control, and companionate marriage.[17] In responding to such broadsides the eugenicists presented themselves as more than mere conservatives defending a tottering social status quo. They could with some justice claim to represent not an old elite but a new meritocracy led by the helping professions, to be freeing society from the dictates of religion and subjecting it to the teachings of science.

When Canadian eugenicists spoke of their Catholic enemies they were thinking particularly of Quebec. For the eugenic national agenda to be furthered, French Canada would have to change. A.R. Kaufman was accordingly proud of his success in penetrating the province with his birth control message. "I recently started a birth control worker in the attractive Catholic nest in Montreal," he wrote Margaret Sanger in 1935, "and while my organizer and worker have given quite a few perfectly good Catholics heart failure, the predictions that birth control work cannot be done in Montreal have not been true up to date."[18]

But some Catholics apparently fought back. In 1938 Kaufman's colleague, A.H. Tyrer, drew up a vitriolic pamphlet entitled *To the Protestant Ministers of Canada* in which he claimed that Catholics had pressured Macmillan to end its publishing of his book *Sex, Marriage, and Birth Control*. He asserted that the Church had for years attempted to cut off the "priest-ridden people" of Quebec from contraceptive knowledge in order to increase their number and thereby the province's political power. Now Catholics in Quebec were organizing behind Adrien Arcand, claimed Tyrer, for the purposes of establishing "a fascist Canada dominated by an obscurantist and reactionary hierarchy."[19] Tyrer warned his fellow Protestant ministers that a civil war in Canada was imminent and something had to be done. But caught up in his own hysterical fears of the country suffering Spain's fate, he failed to indicate just what sort of pre-emptive action he had in mind.

Even in a book such as Watson Kirkconnell's *Canada, Europe, and Hitler* (1940), purportedly written to rally all elements of the nation in its struggle with the enemy, Quebec fertility was presented as being as disquieting as Adrien Arcand's fascism.

> The Anglo-Canadian can nevertheless scarcely view with equanimity the rapid replacement of his own stock by that of alien groups. The Anglo-Saxons, who have displayed the greatest political genius of any age or people, have bequeathed to Canada the master-principle of responsible government and federalism . . . . Unless we are prepared to take parenthood as a serious duty, *la revanche du berceau* will speedily submerge us in both East and West.[20]

But as a dedicated anti-Communist, Kirkconnell swiftly swung round in 1944 to suggest in his *Seven Pillars of Freedom: An Exposure of the Soviet World Conspiracy and its Fifth Column in Canada* that the fertility differential in Canada served primarily the interests, not of the fascists, but of the Communists.[21]

There was obviously an element of paranoia in the way the eugenicists attributed their every discomfort to Catholic machinations. It is true, however, that as early as 1910, when reports on Montreal's high infant mortality rate were construed as an argument in favour of family limitation, the Catholic press raised the cry, "we do not want to see male and female professors of eugenics corrupting the morals of Catholic Canada."[22] Opposition to eugenics was voiced in *The Catholic Register, Catholic World,* and *Western Catholic*, but English-speaking Canada never produced a particularly incisive or searching critique of eugenics. Only in Quebec did a number of writers (priests for the most part) subject hereditarian theories to close analysis.

French-Canadian opponents of eugenics regarded the science as a threatening, foreign ideology propounded by Protestant Anglophones. Quebec did have its own section of the Canadian National Committee on Mental Hygiene, led by A.H. Desloges, the provincial superintendent of asylums, and S. Boucher, the city of Montreal's health director. They undertook the testing and segregating of backward pupils, but prudently refrained from broaching the question of sterilization.[23] Accordingly, when the Oblate father Ceslas Forest launched the first serious attack on eugenics in a 1930 issue of *Revue dominicaine*, he took aim at its American proponents. He attributed the growing popularity of their doctrine to misguided desires for perfection on the one hand and a selfish hostility to the weak on the other. There was no proof, Forest charged, that sterilization policies worked; even if they did they still would violate Christian notions of morality and charity.[24]

Antonio Barbeau, an expert in neuro-psychiatry, who spoke out against eugenics in the 1930's on a number of occasions both on radio and before public audiences, pointed out that in Canada the eugenics movement had influential supporters like Bruce and Hutton. Despite the little as yet known regarding human genetics they were, to Barbeau's dismay, raising the spectre of "degeneration" and asserting that they had the ability to determine who was "defective."[25]

Dr. Gaston Lapierre, professor of pediatrics at the Université de Montréal, in a 1935 article on "Les campagnes internationales actuelles d'eugénisme," placed the Canadian debate in its international context. Everywhere, he asserted, eugenic theories were based on crude economic arguments of self-interest and the perverted employment of scientific data. And responding to the defence of sterilization made by Dr. William Hutton before the Montreal Women's Club in 1933, Lapierre asked how one was going to decide who was "fit" or "unfit." Beethoven was deaf, Homer blind, and Caesar epileptic; clearly they would have been sacrificed by the eugenicists. But how much further would one go, once launched on such a campaign that totally ignored the moral value of human beings. The Germans had already sterilized 200,000; would Canada follow suit? And would not Quebec have most to suffer if such policies were ever in force? Lapierre foresaw horrific judgements being handed down: "Mère de six enfants . . . stérilisation; chomeur depuis un an . . . stérilisation: famille pauvre depuis deux générations, fréquemment à charge aux pouvoirs publics . . . stérilisation, etc. Réfléchissons bien."[26]

Less impassioned was the brief critique of eugenics in Louis-Marie Lalonde's *Hérédité; manuel de génétique* (1936). Lalonde (known as Father Louis-Marie) was particularly well placed to discuss the subject inasmuch as he was both a priest and a professor of genetics at the Agricultural Institute at La Trappe. Lalonde confined himself largely to pointing out the scientific holes in the eugenicists' argument. He was not averse, however, to envisaging genetic knowledge that respected the body and soul being employed for human betterment. He also noted that the Church accepted the rhythm method as a legitimate way to limit births.[27]

The Catholic theologian Hervé Blais produced the fullest account of the Canadian eugenic movement in his 1942 study *Les tendances eugénistes au Canada*. Blais, in addition to carefully analysing the workings of existing eugenic legislation – premarital blood tests, marriage restrictions, immigration inspections, and sterilization – reiterated that Catholics opposed any practice that in serving the needs of the state entailed the sacrifice of human dignity and individuality. But Blais, like Lalonde, pointed out that this did not mean that the Church was indifferent to potential problems posed by reproduction. After all, Church law forbade marriage between relatives up to the fourth degree, set the age of marriage at sixteen for males and fourteen for females (whereas in Quebec the state was content with the ages of fourteen and twelve), and demanded the consent of parents.[28] Priests, though they opposed the use of coercion to prevent the marriages of the unfit, did try to dissuade them from marrying and honoured such sacrifices. Similarly the Church, though it condemned the unnaturalness of birth control, counselled parents to employ "self-control" in order not to have more children than they could adequately raise. Catholics and eugenicists might agree that the threat of "degeneration" was real, but, Blais asserted, its root cause was the growing immorality and materialism of which eugenics was itself a symptom.[29]

Although the evidence suggests that federal and provincial politicians in eastern Canada and the Maritimes were dissuaded by Catholic hostility from supporting eugenic programs, it is not at all evident that Catholic theorists – who produced the fullest critique of Canadian eugenics – were successful in converting any non-believers. Certainly no eugenicist ever produced a mea culpa. Indeed, the fact that priests almost always equated birth control – which in the interwar period was employed by ever-growing numbers of Canadians – with the most distasteful forms of eugenics, such as forcible sterilization, no doubt blunted the impact of their argument among the general public. But this line of attack was maintained.

Father Henri Martin, like so many other Québécois, attributed the "miracle" of French-Canadian cultural survival to its traditionally high fertility. He warned the 1923 meeting of the Semaine Sociale de Canada that there was worrying evidence of a fall in the Quebec birth rate clearly related to the penetration of the province by new ideas. Neo-Malthusian ideas – "ces doctrines perverses et de ces pratiques infâmes" – had to be combatted.[30] The same views were advanced by

Forest in 1930, Lapierre in 1935 and 1941, and Ferland in 1938. A report entitled *Eugénisme et stérilisation* prepared for the Congrès français de la natalité, which was circulated in Quebec in 1934 by the École sociale populaire, asserted that eugenics led to contraception, which in turn led to promiscuity and abortion. The authors argued in a rather confused fashion that as humans were not animals any discussion of their "breeding" was in bad taste; a few lines later the authors expressed their hopes that humans would, in reserving sex simply for procreation, become more like animals. A similar linkage of contraception and hereditarian views was sketched out by F.-M. Drouin in a 1936 talk to the Association St. Jean Baptiste in Ottawa. Drouin warned his audience that outsiders were seeking to "emancipate" Quebecers from the Catholic faith that fueled their fertility. The Anglican and United churches had embraced birth control and now eugenicists were deluging Quebec with brochures, books, and pamphlets in hopes of winning converts. Drouin condemned sex education as immoral, birth control as an insult to women, and sterilization as a form of mutilation.[31]

In the 1940's the Jesuit journal *Relations* continued to headline discussions of contraceptive practices with such titles as "un fléau se propage!" and "Suicide nationale organisé."[32] Catholic critics, in thus giving the impression that they considered the forcible sterilization of the feeble-minded and the voluntary employment of contraceptives by married couples as equally immoral, were unlikely to have impressed the secular-minded.

The botanist Jacques Rousseau noted that, ironically enough, Catholicism itself could be accused of playing some role in Quebec's declining fertility. He asserted in *L'Hérédité et l'homme* (1945) that though the negative eugenic program of sterilization and euthanasia had to be condemned, it was legitimate to seek to improve the race by programs aimed at providing better housing, hospitalization, and standards of living. But the Church, he pointed out, though purportedly in favour of marriage, in fact taught its young in colleges and convent schools that it was a poor second compared to the religious vocation. This, he speculated, must have had the result of deterring some of the best young Québécois from marrying.[33]

The fact that botanists such as Rousseau and Lalonde attempted to combine both religious and scientific arguments in their condemnations of eugenics leads one to the question of how science, and in particular modern genetics, contributed to the decline of eugenics. It has been argued that eugenics was strong at the beginning of the century because it had the support of many within the scientific community but that it was to wither and die once geneticists abandoned it.[34] By the 1930's its critics in the scientific community included such luminaries as H.J. Muller and Raymond Pearl in the United States and J.B.S. Haldane and Lancelot Hogben in Britain.[35] The central point of their critique was that the simplistic argument of the eugenicists that "like produced like" was not true. Genetic combinations were now known to be so complex (especially as the importance of recessive characteristics was explored) that scientists could only be sceptical of the crude social engineering sought by the hereditarians. This was the line of argument followed in the 1934 Brock Report made to the British government. While defending the right of the feeble-minded to seek voluntary sterilizations, the report opposed compulsory sterilization because it could not be justified on hereditarian grounds, would not in any event displace the need for institutional care, and threatened to lower mental institutions in the public esteem.[36]

Scientists in Canada were slow to challenge the assertions of the eugenicists. Only in the late 1930's, when it appeared that the ESC might succeed in having sterilization legislation introduced in Ontario, did serious opposition begin to be voiced.[37] Although most doctors were either publicly indifferent to or supportive of the eugenic program, a few key members of the medical profession began to speak out. A.H. Sellers of the University of Toronto School of Hygiene pointed out in 1937 that American investigators had revealed that the purported surge in the numbers of the feeble-minded was a myth.[38] The assertion of Dr. C.L. Huskins, professor of genetics at McGill University, that the sterilization of the feeble-minded would result in "happiness" was attacked by his colleague in the psychology department, W.D. Tait. Declaring himself moved more by practical than humanitarian concerns, Tait declared that such operations would benefit no one.[39] W.E. Blatz, the pioneering Toronto child psychologist, was equally sceptical. Blatz sought to rescue the honour of the medical profession by asserting that most of the defenders of eugenics were in fact ignorant of genetics and came from welfare work rather than medicine.[40] A similar argument was made in an article entitled "The Doctor and Eugenics" that appeared in *The Canadian Doctor* in August, 1936. The author was alarmed that the members of the ESC, in their zeal to push through reforms, were exaggerating social concerns and downplaying medical theory. Doctors, the anonymous author concluded, had to make sure that the public was not carried away with eugenicist fervour.[41] Some doctors, already discreetly carrying out sterilizations, were concerned that the eugenicists were inadvertently making into a public issue something that the profession would prefer to deal with privately. "The radical statements emanating from this group," wrote Dr. Horne, medical superintendent of the Orillia School for the Retarded, "have done more to retard sterilization law than anything I know of."[42]

Perhaps the best-qualified opponent of the Canadian eugenicists was University of Toronto geneticist John W. MacArthur.[43] In 1930, when he first made a public statement on the population issue while defending Dr. W.E. Gallie, professor of surgery at the University of Toronto, MacArthur sounded very much like a member of the eugenicist camp. Gallie had cruelly informed the Ninth Conference of the International Society for Crippled Children that the deformed should not reproduce and indicated that he did not care whether sterilization or birth control was employed to prevent physical and mental defect.[44] In making the eugenicists' standard wild assertion that the world would be a better place if only doctors had their way, Gallie came under attack. MacArthur rose to his defence and argued that since birth control was employed by the fit it should also be made available to the deformed.[45] In subsequent public statements, however, MacArthur distanced himself from such eugenic notions. In 1935 he castigated the ESC's secretary, F.N. Walker, for his ludicrous views on the dangers of interracial marriage.[46] In 1937 MacArthur pilloried ESC president William Hutton for attempting to create a "eugenic panic."[47] In 1938 he provided *Social Welfare* with a glowing review of J.B.S. Haldane's classic attack on eugenics, *Heredity and Politics*, which contained a venomous portrayal of the sterilization activities of the ESC's financial secretary, A.R. Kaufman.[48]

In the late 1930's R.O. Earl, professor of biology at Queen's University, also entered the lists against the eugenicists. Noting with dismay that the "cult" of eugenics now enjoyed the support of such prominent Ontario public figures as the Lieutenant-Governor and the Minister of Health, Earl declared that it was time for those with genetic expertise to present the "facts." The facts were that since even the "fit" were not purebred, one could never know how they would breed, and, in any event, the interaction with the environment was crucial to subsequent development. British and American scientists now knew, for example, that the majority of the feeble-minded had "normal" parents. Sterilization thus could not produce an improved race. And even if it were possible to breed true, concluded Earl, the likelihood would be the emergence of a dreary, homogenized state like that sketched out in Huxley's *Brave New World*. Human society, in Earl's view, thrived on variety; the eugenicist program was divisive in the short run – opposed as it was by the country's Catholics – and doomed to failure in the long run.[49]

Ironically, one of the most powerful medical opponents of the ESC's sterilization program was himself a member of the ESC – the Ontario deputy minister of health, Dr. B.T. McGhie. In a 1937 review of the report of the Committee of the American Neurological Association on sterilization, which revealed that the purported growth in numbers and high fertility of the feeble-minded were in fact myths, McGhie concluded "there are no grounds for sensational alarm concerning the salvation of the race in respect of the subnormal."[50] In McGhie's opinion registration was futile, segregation expensive, and sterilization – except in a few rare cases – pointless. McGhie's hope lay in special education.

Growing Catholic and scientific hostility played a role in undermining eugenic thinking in Canada, but as was seen in the case of Madge Thurlow Macklin, eugenicists were not to be silenced by simply presenting them with the "facts." The changing social and economic climate was the crucial factor in eroding the popularity of hereditarian views. The heyday of eugenics had been the poverty-stricken depression years, when many in the propertied and the professional classes welcomed the notion that it was not the economic system but the poor and sick who were responsible for society's failings. But the same unemployed young men who were feared during the depression were to be feted in times of war. With the outbreak of the Second World War the pendulum of popular opinion swung swiftly away from the crude individualism of the eugenicists and toward the social interventionism of the welfare-minded. Between 1939 and 1944 the federal budget increased fivefold. Money, which once proved impossible to find to provide relief, was magically conjured up to pay for munitions. There were now jobs for all, and the spectre of the unemployed that had haunted the propertied disappeared. The government found itself promising that citizens who were called upon in a period of total war had rights to certain minimum services in peacetime. The inauguration of family allowances in 1945 represented the birth of the Canadian welfare state, exactly the sort of state the old-fashioned eugenicists had so long opposed.

Was eugenics dead? The war in effect put an end to people calling themselves eugenicists, but it did not put an end to eugenic speculation. Remnants of such views were evident in the salvos fired at the family allowance program. The eugenically minded, of course, had always supported progressive legislation that served the interests of race betterment but were appalled by the new social welfare policies that seemed to abandon such goals.[51] The chief argument advanced by the federal government in support of family allowances was that by redistributing wealth they would in a Keynesian fashion sustain consumer spending and so prevent a return to the sort of depression from which the country had so recently extricated itself.[52] The response made by C.E. Silcox was that such programs were a "bad thing biologically": on the one hand, they threatened to tax away the wealth of the innately superior middle classes for the benefit of the "imprudent, the inefficient, the careless, and the maleducated"; on the other, they promised to be exploited by non-Anglo-Saxons to increase their political power.[53]

In a 1945 tract entitled *The Revenge of the Cradles*, Silcox continued to hammer away at what he claimed were the harmful effects of family allowances. Such grants, he claimed, would help maintain the high fertility of Quebec ("They breed, while we bleed"), but would not raise the family size in English-speaking Canada. "The only real threat," he asserted, "is in the fact that the decline tends to be among the responsible people, while the less responsible still obey the injunction to be fruitful and multiply. It would seem as if society today were resolved that the morons shall inherit the earth."[54] Charlotte Whitton, who had opposed the concept of a family allowance when it had been first advanced in the 1920's, supported Silcox by asserting that it represented a "subsidy to the birth of defectives."[55]

Even the armed forces were not spared the eugenicists' propaganda.[56] The Canadian Legion Educational Services distributed to the military a pamphlet entitled "Marriage" by the American eugenicist Dr. Paul Popenoe. Popenoe, as the most strident defender of California's sterilization program, had played a direct role in the passage of sterilization in British Columbia and Alberta.[57] An admirer of Hitler and an apologist for the Nazi eugenic program in the 1930's, he prudently presented himself in the 1940's as an expert on family and marriage counselling. But even in such articles as "First Aid for the Family," which appeared in *Maclean's* in 1947, Popenoe made it clear that his basic ideas had not changed. "At the bottom of society there is always a rotten layer that is a source of trouble and expense," he wrote, "but the social and biological decay that is most dangerous is that which begins at the top. Among the 'social elite' and the climbers the birth rate has been falling and marriage has been deteriorating for a couple of centuries."[58]

How could the misfits be controlled in the post-war world? Clarence M. Hincks provided the answer in an article entitled "Sterilize the

Unfit," which appeared in *Maclean's* in 1946. "Modern war," he informed his readers, "is definitely not a sound eugenical experiment."[59] According to Hincks the 10 per cent of inductees who were rejected as mentally inadequate were allowed to breed while the fit were either killed or prevented from reproducing during their long years in the armed forces. Returning to the argument that he had originally made at the end of the First World War, Hincks argued that sterilization had to be used to limit the multiplication of the subnormal. He was careful, however, to avoid referring to the Nazis' use of such policies; indeed, by lauding the work done on sterilization in "pre-Hitler Germany" he sought to give the impression that such rational policies were opposed by the Nazis.[60]

The activities of Hincks, Silcox, Whitton, Kaufman, and Popenoe serve as a useful reminder that though the ESC vanished, eugenic ideas did not disappear at the end of the 1930's. Many were to resurface in the post-war world as part of what was now called "social biology." More importantly, a number of eugenic policies were maintained, the most blatant being the sterilization of the feeble-minded, which in Alberta and British Columbia remained in force until 1972. By determining the impact of these programs it is possible to gain some idea of the human cost that resulted from hereditarian speculation and reach some final estimate of the role played by eugenics in Canada.

Coming up with hard data on the sterilization policies of Alberta and British Columbia is not easy and indeed was only recently attempted. We know that in Alberta, between 1928 and 1971, 4,725 cases were proposed for sterilization and 2,822 approved. In British Columbia the total number sterilized is impossible to determine since the files of the Board of Eugenics were either lost or destroyed, but no more than a few hundred were subjected to the operation. The small numbers involved were a result of the narrower provisions of the British Columbia legislation. In Alberta sterilization was approved if a patient's reproduction involved risk of hereditary taint; in British Columbia it was only allowed if such a taint was likely to result. Moreover, in Alberta sterilization was not limited, as in British Columbia, to inmates of institutions, but was also proposed for clients of the Mental Hygiene Clinic.[61]

Timothy J. Christian has produced an excellent analysis of the administration of the Alberta Sexual Sterilization Act. It is clear from his account that the Act was almost solely employed to control the weak and marginalized. Sixty-four per cent of those sterilized were women, 60 per cent were under the age of twenty-five (20 per cent were less than sixteen), and the majority were single and unemployed

or unskilled. Once the consent provision was ended in 1937 a disproportionate number of Roman Catholic and Greek Orthodox patients
were treated. Among those both approved for and ultimately sterilized
eastern Europeans were overrepresented and Anglo-Saxons un-
derrepresented. But the clearest evidence that differential treatment
was meted out by the Alberta Board of Eugenics is provided by an
examination of its care of Indian and Métis patients. In the last years
of the Board's activities, Indians and Métis, who represented only 2.5
per cent of Alberta's population, accounted for over 25 per cent of
those sterilized.[62]

If it is difficult to determine the full extent of the use of the British
Columbia legislation, it is even more difficult to determine the "success" of sterilization. An attempt to do just this was made in 1945 by
M. Stewart in a report entitled "Some Aspects of Eugenical Sterilization in British Columbia with Special Reference to Patients Sterilized
from Essondale Provincial Hospital since 1935."[63] To determine if
sterilization of the sixty-four cases at Essondale had had the desired
results, Stewart essayed a full case history of each patient; this was not
always possible because, once discharged, many simply disappeared
from view. In the main, it was those who had awkward economic
adjustments to face and came to the attention of the social services who
could be traced. But even with its gaps the Stewart report is revealing
inasmuch as it shows that sterilization was not carried out in random
fashion. There was a marked sexual division. Of the sixty-four sterilized, seven were men (six married and one single) and fifty-seven
were women (eleven married and forty-five single). Six of the seven
men operated on were over the age of twenty-five; thirty-three of the
fifty-seven women were under twenty-five and three were under
fifteen. The one single male had no children whereas the forty-six
single women had had thirty-three illegitimate children. Even the
diagnoses differed along sex lines. Of the males, six were declared
psychotic and one an imbecile; of the females, eighteen were psychotic, eighteen imbeciles, and twenty-one morons. Six of the seven
men were discharged after the operation but only forty-one of the
fifty-seven women. In short, the picture that emerges of the "typical"
sterilized patient was of a young, unwed mother who had been diagnosed as mentally retarded.

What was the effect of the operation?[64] Of the sixty-four sterilized
only forty-seven were discharged. Fourteen remained in care, two died
while in care, and one died as a result of the operation. The fourteen
who were not discharged can certainly not be counted as "successful"
cases; in fact, since sterilization was supposed to be carried out only

to permit a return to the community, it is not clear why they were operated on in the first place. Of the remaining forty-seven, Stewart had follow-up information on twenty-seven; he optimistically assumed that a lack of subsequent reports could be taken as a sign that major problems had not ensued. The reports classed the twenty-seven as thirteen "successes," twelve "doubtfuls," and only two failures.

To reappraise the supposed success or failure of the operation it has to be recalled that sterilization was defended by those who wanted to eliminate hereditary taints, decarcerate inmates and so save the province money, improve the life of the mentally deficient, and facilitate moral improvement. The perfect case would have been one in which all four goals were attained; these were, in fact, rarities.

Although a Board of Eugenics was established with the purported purpose of supervising a policy based on the theory of hereditary taints, the Board did not include an expert in genetics and did not show any great interest in the subject. Only in sixteen of the sixty-four cases was any mention made of kin having histories of mental problems. Instead of hard data on genetically linked complaints, the Stewart report fell back on reference to incarcerated kin, siblings seen at Child Guidance Clinics, rumours of incest and suicide, and the pat phrase, the "family history is not good," as sufficient evidence of hereditary taint. The point that the issue of heredity was slighted in the Board's discussions was made by one of its own members, Isobel Harvey, who wrote in 1944 to E.W. Griffith, the assistant deputy provincial secretary. Harvey complained that another member, Judge Manson, was too busy to attend to the Board's duties. "His mind [was] never on eugenics," she stated, and he had no idea of the patient's problems.[65] Harvey wanted Manson replaced; as it turned out she was removed and the Board's lukewarm interest in eugenics continued.[66]

Those interested in the economies that would result from sterilization might have argued that by removing inmates from the asylum the province was saving money.[67] Such an argument was countered in the Stewart report itself, however, in its depiction of the mentally handicapped who had been simply abandoned to the support of the family or local community. For example, case number thirty-eight was reported a "success" despite the admission that this imbecile with an IQ of thirty-nine was now living in wretched conditions and her two illegitimate children were in care. It was not so much a question of money being saved as shifting the responsibility from the province to the local community.

The argument that sterilization actually improved the life of patients appeared to be fully borne out only in two cases.[68] In each, a manic depressive married woman was diagnosed as suffering from break-downs following pregnancies (puerperal psychosis). The operation, in removing the threat of subsequent conceptions, allowed these women to lead normal lives. In other female cases, however, "success" was assumed if the woman simply married or found employment as a domestic. These women had all been diagnosed as imbeciles or morons; the fact that they had been shunted from institutional care into an appropriate female role meant that, whatever their living conditions, they would be recorded on the credit side of the ledger. As regards those cases in which males were reported to have been successfully reintegrated back into the larger society, it is of interest that three of the six ended up in the armed forces: an imbecile and a paranoidal schizophrenic in the army and a manic depressive in the navy.[69] How sterilization contributed to their ability to serve the nation in wartime was not made clear.

Did sterilization result in moral improvement? The Stewart report makes it obvious that the operation was frequently carried out for the purposes of preventing illegitimate births. As noted earlier, forty-six of the fifty-seven women sterilized were single. In running over the reasons given for their sterilization, one reads that case thirty-six has a "sexual colouring" to her ideas, that case twelve has "sexual inclinations," that case twenty-eight is "easily led," that case thirty-one had an abortion, that case thirty-two had "sex difficulties," that case thirty-seven was "too friendly," that case forty-one's "sexual propensities are quite marked," and that case forty-nine was from a family in which incest had taken place. Sterilization obviously ended the possibility of these women having children. Indeed, the report indicates that three of the women were provided with abortions for pregnancies already under way. No doubt many of these women had been sexually exploited outside the asylum; the tragedy was that the Board of Eugenics was sterilizing the victim, not the aggressor, of such sexual attacks. Never satisfactorily explained was how sterilization was supposed to curb promiscuity, as its defenders claimed. Those hostile to the operation pointed out that it would be just as reasonable to assume that once free of the danger of pregnancy the released patient would be more promiscuous than ever.

Defenders of sterilization might still defend the morality of the operation, however, on the grounds that at least it was carried out only after the patient's consent or that of a guardian had been obtained. Dr. A.L. Crease, the superintendent of Essondale, in a letter accompanying a copy of the 1933 Act sent to an Ontario colleague, asserted:

About all our bill has accomplished is to make legal what has been done for years, that is sterilization where it was requested. . . . You and I know that sterilization and the removing of ovaries has gone on in the gynaecological services, and no particular reports with regard to the subject have been kept. People do not seem to object to this at all but when sterilization for males comes up there is quite a stir.[70]

Crease's comments on the extent of unreported sterilizations are important because they indicate that prior to legislative enactment such operations had been carried out in British Columbia; these assertions further indicate that they took place in provinces such as Ontario, where no enabling legislation ever existed. But what Crease and others failed to appreciate is that even with the law that required the patient's consent, such consent could hardly be considered freely given when it was the price that had to be paid to obtain release from an asylum.

Moreover, the doctor who performed sterilizations was placed in a curious moral position. Surgeons who sterilized the sane were liable to prosecution for having helped people "maim" themselves.[71] The 1933 Act provided legal immunity to doctors who provided the same operation for asylum inmates on the grounds of serious hereditary defect. As the records indicate, however, there were few cases in which there was convincing evidence of such defect. A reappraisal of the data available on sterilization in British Columbia leads to the conclusion that the legislation was infrequently and chaotically employed. There is little evidence that any of its eugenic, economic, humanitarian, or moral goals were achieved.

The importance of the sterilization acts in Alberta and British Columbia lay not in what they accomplished but in what they symbolized. They came into being because in the interwar years sterilization won the support of a large number of professionals who were convinced that a concern for the well-being of the community justified radical therapeutic intervention in the lives of the handicapped. Social workers played a key role in supporting such arguments, one suspects, because in attributing the most intractable social problems to hereditary taint they could thereby rationalize their own limited successes. Doctors, of course, were even more important in campaigning for sterilization, in helping to obtain its legislative passage, and in carrying out its administration. But despite the extent of medical input into the debate, sterilization was, as noted, rarely carried out for strictly medical reasons. Indeed, the Canadian sterilization acts were passed just as advanced medical opinion was turning against sterilization. As early as 1926 A.F. Tredgold, the eminent British authority on retardation, had co-authored a letter to *The Times* of London, stating that sterilization would have "very little effect on the prevention of mental deficiency, and it would certainly lead to serious social evils and it would be inimical to defectives and to the community were it adopted."[72]

Epilogue

A measure of the humanity of the inhabitants of Sir Thomas More's imagined, sixteenth-century Utopia was the degree to which they relished the companionship of the mad. "They have singular delite and pleasure in the foles," he reported. "And as it is a great reproche to do annye of them hurte or injury, so they prohibit not to take pleasure of foolyshnes."[1] In early twentieth-century Canada such an indulgence would have been regarded as distinctly odd; it was taken as a given that in the modern world any handicap that impeded "racial efficiency" was lamentable. "It is beyond question," declared a 1915 government Board of Inquiry, "that productive efficiency is essential for the average citizen if he is to be capable of maintaining his economic value to the community, and becoming and continuing [to be] socially and industrially a sustaining and helpful unit rather than a burden."[2] Few active in public life spurned the idea of striving for a perfectly rational world purged of physical and mental defect. The eugenicists differed from most of their contemporaries not so much in envisaging a radically different future, but in supporting the intrusive social policies they felt were needed to bring it into being.

Who were the Canadian eugenicists? Although they raised the spectre of society being menaced by the marginal, they saw themselves as not so much defending an old world as fighting to bring a new one into being. They believed that the problems created by urbanization, immigration, and industrialization demonstrated that the nineteenth-century faith in the ability of the marketplace to restore social equilibrium was misplaced. The "hidden hand" of the laissez-faire world had to be replaced by controls and regulations wielded by trained managers and administrators. Such a faith in the ability of science to remake society particularly reflected the aspirations of those who regarded themselves as a talented elite, but it appealed to individuals right across the political spectrum.

We began this study by noting that the pioneering socialist Tommy Douglas, having produced a Master's thesis in sociology in 1933 that was a classic hereditarian diatribe, would have to be included in the eugenic camp. As he made clear in a 1934 article entitled "Youth and the New Day," what drew him to eugenics was its promise of change.

For generations there has been no supervision of the eugenics of the race. The result has been that those least fitted to propagate have done so, and have filled our jails and mental hospitals at an alarming rate; while the so-called intelligentsia have been steadily restricting their birth rate . . . . Youth will take a different view of eugenics than did their forefathers. Superstition will be cast aside and those who are mentally or physically unsound will be prevented from rearing offspring to become a menace and a burden to society. The next generation will spend less on punishment for the criminal, and more on remedial measures to remove those factors that have produced the criminal.[3]

Douglas was, of course, to be proven completely wrong. By the 1940's the eugenic arguments had come to be viewed by the citizens of the Western democracies as old-fashioned if not reactionary. Douglas himself, always torn between a faith in experts and a belief in grassroots radicalism, was frightened by what he saw during a 1936 trip to Germany and turned away from eugenics. In 1944, as Saskatchewan's Minister of Health, he firmly rejected two reports recommending the sterilization of the feeble-minded. His boast that Saskatchewan spent a higher percentage of its budget on health and education than any other province was the sort of statement that would have rendered the eugenicists of the 1930's cataleptic.[4]

The Canadian eugenicists were not monsters or simple-minded reactionaries. Some were no doubt mean-spirited; others were compassionate and idealistic. Most saw themselves as progressives who were seeking to wed science, medicine, and social welfare. They were activists anxious to intervene in the lives of the poor and ill to prevent not just the spread but the emergence of social problems. They optimistically envisaged a future in which disease and degeneration would have no place. In their enthusiasm to change the world they plunged into the discussion of a host of issues – immigration, education, public health, intelligence testing, welfare, feeble-mindedness.

How extensive was the spread of eugenic ideas? It is a difficult question to answer and of course depends a good deal on what one means by eugenics. Even members of the Eugenics Society of Canada did not always agree on their goals. Different sorts of people were drawn to eugenics for different reasons. Certainly all believed in the need to improve the race, but some thought such a goal could be achieved by voluntarism, others saw the need for coercion. If one wishes to minimize their importance one could say that the nation's only "true" eugenicists were the hundred or so members of the Eugenics Society of Canada. If one wishes to exaggerate their importance one could claim that, since almost every middle-class reformer spoke of "improving the race," they all have to be described as eugenicists.[5]

At the most general level there were few Canadians in the 1920's and 1930's who had not heard some politician or health expert at one time or another employ eugenic arguments and vocabulary. Every up-to-date high school or college biology text awarded eugenic theories the sort of respectful attention that a creditable theory warranted. What most Canadians made of these ideas is hard to say, but given the references to "eugenic babies" in letters to the editor and the equation of "practical eugenics" with birth control it is clear that at the very least a new pseudo-scientific language had been successfully imposed on the discussion of human reproduction. Few politicians, of course, knew anything about genetics, and most no doubt employed hereditarian concepts primarily for tactical reasons. Mothers' allowances and school medical inspections, for example, were defended on eugenic grounds, but their proponents were often equally motivated by simple concerns for the health of women and children. Nevertheless, the average English Canadian was schooled to be as accepting of the notion of "race improvement" as of the idea that Canada was a Christian nation.

At a higher level of involvement in the eugenic crusade one would have to include those who, like Tommy Douglas, felt that something dramatically new had to be tried if Canada were to survive the social dislocations of the twentieth century. Science was believed to hold the key. Such activists momentarily studied and embraced eugenic theories, but they were often activated by a mix of motives and frequently moved on to more promising ideological alternatives. Apparently contradictory hereditarian and environmental beliefs could clearly be sustained by many social reformers in an untidy but all-too-human fashion.

Finally, one comes to the most dedicated eugenicists, those who not only espoused eugenic ideas but who sought to act upon them. In practice very few of those who bandied about hereditarian concepts concerning the differential birth rate or the menace of feeble-mindedness were in any position to do anything practical about such problems. But in the new professions were individuals who were attracted to eugenics for the obvious reason that the fears it raised served their career interests. Most members of the beleaguered middle class were frightened by the prospect of increased numbers of immigrants and idlers, but only a certain number plunged into campaigns for sterilization of the feeble-minded or immigration restriction. Professional affiliations largely explained the affinity of individuals to eugenics. The members of the helping professions contributed the largest contingent to the eugenics movement because, whatever else might be said about eugenics, there is no doubt that the popularization of concepts of biological determinism served to enhance the status of the new experts in social management – social workers, doctors, and psychiatrists. It is impossible to say what percentage in each profession supported the eugenics program. Most members did not involve themselves directly in such discussions. What is clear is that in none were the opponents of hereditarian theories as predominant as its supporters. For vigorous denunciations of hereditarian theories Canadians had to turn to American and British sources.

The prominent names in public health, psychiatry, genetics, and social work were all associated with eugenics. MacMurchy and Macklin were only the best-known adherents of hereditarian views. Those who regarded themselves as hard-headed found especially alluring the notion that there were situations in which experts could determine that the needs of the community required the abrogation of individual rights. Though the eugenicists claimed to be serving science it was clear that what preoccupied them were social, not medical, problems. Deviant behaviour – as defined by white, male, middle-class, Protestant professionals – and not any proof of genetic failure was what led to sterilizations. In place of medical diagnoses the eugenic boards relied on the social criteria of what represented "normal" morality, sexuality, and work habits to classify their charges. The timing of outbreaks of hereditarian hysteria was likewise determined, not by advances in medical science, but by social preoccupations. Thus, when class fears occurred – as they did during the great immigration wave prior to World War One, in the years immediately following the war, and in the depression – eugenic activities increased.

The association of eugenics with the outrages perpetrated by the Nazis ultimately brought the science into disrepute. This is not to say that the Canadian eugenicists were fascists. Most found the Aryan theories and anti-Semitism of the Nazis crude and distasteful. They were not being merely self-serving when they expressed their shock at what occurred in Germany. But they were lacking in candour when they chose to ignore the fact that the Nazis in some cases simply implemented eugenic programs. Recent studies of Nazi Germany have alerted us to the fact that the racial hygiene policies carried out after 1933 did not suddenly spring full-blown from the minds of madmen; they had been planned and discussed in Weimar Germany by respectable doctors and scientists. Under Hitler many of these same eugenicists were willing to administer these programs.[6] Germany provided a salutory lesson of what could happen to a society that embraced the dangerous notion that the social and economic challenges of the twentieth century could be solved by recourse to a biological solution.

We now understand the system of values and scientific theorizing that went into creating the eugenics movement and the social factors that led to its acceptance in Canada. It clearly had an impact on government policies relating to immigration, care of the mentally ill, and social welfare. It is important, however, not to exaggerate the eugenicists' influence. They were themselves only too aware of how little of their agenda they succeeded in implementing. They were always too frightening and too elitist to garner much mass support. As dismissive as they were of old-fashioned liberal optimism, they could not woo most Canadians away from a belief in the possibilities of self-improvement. Even policy-makers who espoused eugenic theories were held in check by fears of stirring up religious and political opposition. Nevertheless, it must not be forgotten that in campaigning for the sterilization of the feeble-minded, eugenicists were responsible for serious crimes being committed against the weakest members of the community. The tragedy is that we know so much about the eugenicists, but next to nothing of their policies' victims.

The old eugenics slowly faded from the scene but did not disappear. It was only in 1972, after the two western provincial Social Credit governments were defeated, that sterilization legislation was removed from the statute books of Alberta and British Columbia.[7] But in 1978 it was discovered that in the absence of any legislation hundreds of such operations were still being carried out each year in Ontario. A Scarborough woman informed the press that she was told by her doctor that her nine-year-old girl should be sterilized. "I was aghast," she reported. "He went on to say that we had to consider the interests of society and not run the risk that she'd produce more retarded people."[8] Although the provincial government put a stop to these operations they drew attention to the fact that many doctors felt that medical procedures could be legitimately employed to deal with social problems. A 1970 Osgoode Hall Medical-Legal Questionnaire revealed that 67 per cent of physicians agreed that "forcible sterilization" of the criminally insane, retarded, and feeble-minded was "a desirable social policy."

Evidence also surfaced that some women seeking abortions had sterilizations forced on them by therapeutic abortion committees as part of a "package deal."[9]

Nor was Canada immune to the arguments made by Arthur R. Jensen, H. J. Eysenck, and William Shockley that IQ tests could be used to locate intellectually inferior groups in the community. Indeed, in 1989 the University of Western Ontario psychology professor Philip Rushton made headlines by defending ideas on innate racial differences in intelligence that were only marginally more sophisticated than those advanced by the eugenicists of the 1930's.[10]

Of far greater significance was the fact that after World War Two, just as the crude social engineering policies campaigned for by the traditional eugenicists were being consigned to the dustbin of history, geneticists were making important breakthroughs that established the basis for a "new eugenics." A revolution in genetic research resulted from the use of karyotypes, which permitted the display of chromosomes in the cell nucleus. A karyotype produced from a tissue culture obtained from a foetus made it possible for the first time for doctors to know its genetic makeup. An important contribution in these developments was made by Murray L. Barr, a colleague of Madge Thurlow Macklin at the University of Western Ontario, who in 1949 announced the discovery that the staining of chromosomes could be employed to reveal the genetic sex of the patient. More importantly, chromosome mapping revealed by the 1970's that over fifty disorders – Downs syndrome being the best known – were due to genetic accidents. By the late 1970's, if amniocentesis suggested a birth defect, doctors could direct a prospective mother to genetic counselling, which in turn could recommend a therapeutic abortion. The increased range of methods of prenatal diagnosis – amniocentesis, fetoscopy, and ultrasound – which could detect such complaints as Downs syndrome, Tay Sach's disease, and spina bifida, made possible the avoidance of untold misery. But, asked Catholics and mental health activists, was there not the danger that this pursuit of the "perfect child" might be accomplished by an uncharitable though unconscious denigration of the handicapped? And was there the possibility that genetic counsellors would come to resemble the members of the old eugenics boards in determining who should or should not reproduce?[11]

Reproductive research not only changed expectations about what sorts of babies would be born; it also radically revised views on how they would be born. The general public was startled by the announcement in 1978 of the birth of the first "test-tube baby." Feminists expressed alarm that the feat had brought to fruition the hopes expressed by a number of pre-war eugenicists of pre-empting women's reproductive role. The current explosion in reproductive technologies – artificial insemination by donor, in vitro fertilization, sex selection, and surrogate motherhood – has raised a host of ethical and legal questions that the public is slowly coming to grips with. Enormous powers either to harm or to heal are now wielded by medical scientists. Doctors, in holding out the hopes of a "cure" for infertile women, are also implying that the childless are in some way diseased. It is a moot point whether the woman who goes to the fertility clinic is exercising a new-found "freedom" or succumbing to the old social pressure of proving her womanhood by bearing babies.[12]

The "traditional eugenicists" were preoccupied by issues of race and class; they simply did not have access to the sort of genetic knowledge required to carry out their proposed improvement of human biology. In the 1990's genetic researchers have the tools available to make a major impact on the quality of human life, but there is the danger of assuming that their greater scientific sophistication somehow renders them less susceptible to social pressures. The race, class, and sex of patients still obviously does make a difference in the way in which they are treated. White, middle-class – not poor, native – women become the happy mothers of test-tube babies.

To pursue all the ramifications of the "new eugenics" would require another book. Suffice it to say here that the ambition of medical scientists to intervene in reproduction has never been so great as it is today with the vast range of methods of genetic manipulation at hand. They might well take the time to learn the history of their own discipline. In the past many of those seeking to reward the procreation of some while reproving that of others found themselves on the slippery slope that led down toward the Nazis. The story of the hopes and aspirations of the previous generations of eugenicists provides a warning of the directions in which such sentiments can drift.

Notes

Abbreviations

CF	*Canada français*
CL	*Canada Lancet*
CJMS	*Canadian Journal of Medicine and Surgery*
CJMH	*Canadian Journal of Mental Hygiene*
CJPH	*Canadian Journal of Public Health*
CMAJ	*Canadian Medical Association Journal*
CPR	*Canadian Practitioner and Review*
CPHJ	*Canadian Public Health Journal*
DR	*Dalhousie Review*
ER	*Eugenics Review*
JH	*Journal of Heredity*
PAMPA	*Proceedings of the American Medico-Psychological Association*
PHJ	*Public Health Journal*
QQ	*Queen's Quarterly*
SN	*Saturday Night*
SW	*Social Welfare*

Preface

1. T.C. Douglas, "The Problems of the Subnormal Family" (M.A. thesis, McMaster University, 1933), Saskatchewan Archives Board, Douglas Papers, p. 34. On Douglas, see Lewis H. Thomas, *The Making of a Socialist: The Recollections of T.C. Douglas* (Edmonton: University of Alberta Press, 1982), p. 72; Thomas H. McLeod and Ian McLeod, *Tommy Douglas: The Road to Jerusalem* (Edmonton: Hurtig, 1987), pp. 12, 39-41. On Douglas's mentor at McMaster, A.L. Mc-Crimmon, and attempts to produce a "Christian sociology," see Charles M. Johnston, *McMaster University*, 2 vols. (Toronto: University of Toronto Press, 1976, 1981); Stewart Crysdale, *The Industrial Struggle and Protestant Ethics in*

Canada (Toronto: Ryerson, 1961), p. 43; Arthur J. Penty, *Towards a Christian Sociology* (London: Allen and Unwin, 1923).

Chapter 1

1. W.L. Lochhead, "Genetics – The Science of Breeding," *Canadian Bookman*, July, 1919, p. 66.
2. Ruth Schwartz Cowan, "Nature and Nurture: The Interplay of Biology and Politics in the Work of Francis Galton," *Studies in the History of Biology*, 1 (1977), pp. 133-208.
3. See Lyndsay Farrell's 1970 Indiana University Ph.D. thesis, which was recently published as *The Origins and Growth of the English Eugenics Movement, 1865-1925* (New York: Garland, 1985); for extensive bibliographical information on the Anglo-American eugenics movement, see Daniel Kevles, *In the Name of Eugenics: Genetics and the Uses of Human Heredity* (Berkeley: University of California Press, 1985).
4. Cited in C.P. Blacker, *Eugenics: Galton and After* (London: Duckworth, 1952), p. 65; and for other laudatory biographies, see Karl Pearson, *The Life of Francis Galton*, 4 vols. (London: Cambridge University Press, 1914-1930); D.W. Forrest, *Francis Galton: The Life and Work of a Victorian Genius* (London: Elek, 1974).
5. See Kevles, *In the Name of Eugenics*, pp. 3-19; Raymond E. Fancher, "Biographical Origins of Francis Galton's Psychology," *Isis*, 74 (1983), pp. 227-33; Fancher, "Francis Galton's African Ethnography and Its Role in the Development of his Psychology," *British Journal of the History of Science*, 16 (1983), pp. 67-79.
6. Francis Galton, *Inquiries Into Human Faculty and Its Development* (New York: Dutton, 1907), p. 17n.
7. Charles Booth, *Life and Labour of the People of London*, 17 vols. (London: Macmillan, 1902-1904); Seebohm Rowntree, *Poverty: A Study of Town Life* (London: Macmillan, 1901). See also Michael S. Teitelbaum and Jay M. Winter, *The Fear of Population Decline* (New York: Academic Press, 1985), pp. 45-55.
8. E.S. Pearson, "Karl Pearson: An Appreciation of Some Aspects of His Life and Work," *Biometrika*, 28 (1936), pp. 193-257; *ibid.*, 29 (1938), pp. 161-248; Donald A. Mackenzie, "Karl Pearson and the Professional Middle Class," *Annals of Science*, 36 (1979), pp. 125-43; Bernard Norton, "Karl Pearson and Statistics: The Social Origins of Scientific Innovation," *Social Studies of Science*, 8 (1978), pp. 3-34.
9. Jan Sapp, "The Struggle for Authority in the Field of Heredity, 1900-1932: New Perspectives on the Rise of Genetics," *Journal of the History of Biology*, 16 (1983), pp. 311-42; Donald A. Mackenzie, "Sociobiologies in Competition: The Biometrician-Mendelian Debate," in Charles Webster, ed., *Biology, Medicine, and Society* (Cambridge: Cambridge University Press, 1981), pp. 243-88.
10. Hamilton Cravens, *The Triumph of Evolution* (Philadelphia: University of Pennsylvania Press, 1978), pp. 34-41. See also Frederick B. Turnbull, "August

Weismann and a Break from Tradition," *Journal of the History of Biology*, 1 (1968), pp. 91-112.

11. J.D.Y. Peel, *Herbert Spencer: The Evolution of a Sociologist* (London: Heineman, 1971).

12. See Greta Jones, *Social Darwinism and English Thought: The Interaction Between Biological and Social Theory* (Brighton: Harvester, 1980); Roger C. Bannister, *Social Darwinism: Science and Myth in Anglo-American Social Thought* (Philadelphia: Temple University Press, 1979); Donald C. Bellamy, "Social Darwinism Revisited," *Perspectives in American History*, 1 (1984), pp. 1-130; and on Europe, see Loren K. Graham, "Science and Values: The Eugenics Movements in Germany and Russia in the 1920s," *American Historical Review*, 82 (1977), pp. 1133-64.

13. The idea that evolution could be leading in the wrong direction was popularized by Benjamin Kidd in *Social Evolution* (London: Grosset, 1902) and *Principles of Western Civilization* (Toronto: Mornay, 1902). Kidd saw religion serving as the necessary check; attacked on this point by Galton and Pearson he replied in *The Science of Power* (New York: Putnams, 1913). See also C.W. Saleeby, *Evolution: The Master-Key* (London: Harper, 1906); O.C. Beale, *Racial Decay: A Compilation of Evidence from World Sources* (Sydney: Angus and Robertson, 1911).

14. Bentley B. Gilbert, *The Evolution of National Insurance in Great Britain: The Origins of the Welfare State* (London: Joseph, 1966); Jose Harris, *Unemployment and Politics: A Study of English Social Policy* (Oxford: Oxford University Press, 1972).

15. Robert Owen, *Lectures on the Marriages of the Priesthood of the Old Immoral World*, 4th ed. (Leeds: Hobson, 1840), p. 32; K.M. Ludmerer, *Genetics and American Society: A Historical Appraisal* (Baltimore: Johns Hopkins University Press, 1972), p. 10.

16. Richard Soloway, "Counting the Degenerates: The Statistics of Race Deterioration in Edwardian Britain," *Journal of Contemporary History*, 17 (1982), pp. 137-64.

17. See Gareth Steadman Jones, *Outcast London* (Oxford: Clarendon Press, 1971).

18. Donald A. Mackenzie, *Statistics in Britain, 1865-1930: The Social Construction of Scientific Knowledge* (Edinburgh: Edinburgh University Press, 1981), pp. 15-50; see also G.R. Searle, *Eugenics and Politics in Britain, 1900-1914* (Leyden: Noordhof, 1976).

19. Richard Hofstadter, *Social Darwinism in American Thought* (Philadelphia: University of Pennsylvania Press, 1945).

20. Cited in Forrest, *Galton*, pp. 99-100; see also Richard Soloway, "Neo-Malthusians, Eugenists, and the Declining Birth-Rate in England, 1900-1918," *Albion*, 10 (1978), pp. 275ff; Angus McLaren, *Birth Control in Nineteenth Century England* (London: Croom Helm, 1978), pp. 141-56.

21. Pearson to Drysdale in 1894, cited in *Malthusian*, December, 1897, p. 90; see also Karl Pearson, *The Ethic of Freethought* (London: Black, 1901), p. 371.

22. Pearson, "Pearson" (1938), p. 189.

23. See also Frederic Harrison, *Realities and Ideas* (London: Macmillan, 1908); Jill Conway, "Stereotypes of Feminity in a Theory of Sexual Evolution," in Martha Vicinus, ed., *Suffer and Be Still* (Bloomington: University of Indiana Press, 1972), pp. 140-54.

24. Pearson, *Freethought*, p. 355. Similarly, Charles Darwin expressed the concern that birth control might pose the danger of "extreme profligacy amongst unmarried women." Darwin to G.A. Gaskell, 15 November 1878, in F. Darwin, ed., *More Letters of Charles Darwin* (London: Murray, 1903), II, p. 50.

25. Karl Pearson, *The Chances of Death* (London: Edward Arnold, 1897), p. 251.

26. W.C.D. Whetham, "The Extinction of the Upper Classes," *Nineteenth Century and After*, 66 (1909), pp. 105-06.

27. C.W. Saleeby, *Woman and Womanhood* (London: Heineman, 1901), pp. 6, 13, 262, 333.

28. Havelock Ellis, *Studies in the Psychology of Sex* (Philadelphia: Davis, 1910), VI, pp. 588ff. See also Phyllis Grosskurth, *Havelock Ellis: A Biography* (New York: Knopf, 1980).

29. Havelock Ellis, *The Task of Social Hygiene* (London: Constable, 1912), pp. 88ff.

30. Havelock Ellis, *The Problem of Race Regeneration* (London: Cassell, 1909); "Eugenics and St. Valentine," *Nineteenth Century and After*, 59 (1906), pp. 779-87; *New Age*, 11 April 1908, p. 469.

31. Pearson cited in Pearson, "Pearson" (1938), p. 172; see also W.C.D. Whetham, "Inheritance and Sociology," *Nineteenth Century and After*, 65 (1909), pp. 85-87; Rev. R.F. Horton, *National Ideals and Race Regeneration* (London: Cassell, 1912), pp. 37-38; C.W. Saleeby, *Parenthood and Race Culture: An Outline of Eugenics* (London: Cassell, 1909).

32. Forrest, *Galton*, p. 250; Pearson, "Pearson" (1938), p. 238.

33. See C.W. Saleeby, "Racial Poisons: Alcohol," *Eugenics Review*, 2 (1910-1911), pp. 30-52; Charles H. Harvey, *The Biology of British Politics* (New York: Scribners, 1904).

34. *Problems in Eugenics: Papers Communicated to the First International Eugenics Congress* (London: Eugenics Education Society, 1912); see also *Nature*, 89 (1912), p. 558.

35. A.P. Reid, *Stirpiculture or the Ascent of Man* (Halifax: T.C. Allen, 1890), p. 5. On the common belief of late nineteenth-century Canadian alienists that degenerative taints were passed on by heredity, see S.E.D. Shortt, *Victorian Lunacy: Richard M. Bucke and the Practice of Late Nineteenth-Century Psychiatry* (Cambridge: Cambridge University Press, 1986), pp. 98-99.

36. *Public Health Journal*, 5 (1914), p. 219.

37. E.W. McBride, *An Introduction to the Study of Heredity* (London: Williams and Norgate, 1924), pp. 249, 245. McBride, who returned to England to become professor of zoology at the Imperial College of Science and Technology, was also author of *Embryology* (London: Benn, 1926) and *Evolution* (London: Benn, 1927). See M. Ridley, "Embryology and Classical Zoology in Great Britain," in T.J. Horton *et al.*, eds., *A History of Embryology* (Cambridge: Cambridge University Press, 1985), pp. 47, 61; Peter J. Bowler, "E.W. McBride's Lamarckian Eugenics and Its Implication for the Social Construction of Scientific Knowledge," *Annals of Science*, 41 (1984), pp. 245-60.

38. See *Report of the Eleventh Meeting of the National Council of Women, 1904* (London: Heal, 1905), pp. 118-21; *Report of the Twelfth Meeting of the National Council of Women* (Toronto: Johnston, 1906), pp. 72-78; *National Council of*

Women Yearbook, 1918-1919 (Toronto: Bryant, 1919), p. 52.

39. Reported in Colin K. Russell, "Feeble-mindedness," *Social Welfare*, 1 April 1920, p. 176.

40. *Journal of Heredity*, 2 (1911), pp. 29-33.

41. J.G. Adami, "The True Aristocracy," *Eugenics in Race and State* (Baltimore: Williams and Williams, 1923), pp. 273-89.

42. *Nature*, 10 September 1927, p. 354.

43. Gary Werskey, *The Visible College* (London: Allen Lane, 1978), pp. 66-67.

44. Joseph Levitt, *Henri Bourassa and the Golden Calf: The Social Program of the Nationalists of Quebec, 1900-1914* (Ottawa: Les editions de l'Université d'Ottawa, 1969), pp. 21-23.

45. Jean Charles Falardeau, ed., *Étienne Parent, 1802-1874* (Montréal: La Presse, 1975), pp. 254-56.

46. William Schneider, "Towards the Improvement of the Human Race: The History of Eugenics in France," *Journal of Modern History*, 54 (1982), pp. 268-91.

47. *The Women's Institute Quarterly*, 1 (1915), p. 12. On Ravenhill, see her *Eugenic Education for Women and Girls* (London: King, 1908) and *Memoirs of an Educated Pioneer* (Toronto: Dent, 1951).

48. *The Women's Institute Quarterly*, 1 (1916), p. 137; see also 2 (1916), p. 9.

49. V.M. Jackson, *Problems in Human Heredity* (Winnipeg: Jackson, 1937), pp. 28, 32. Jackson also authored *Fur and Game Resources of Manitoba* (Winnipeg: Saults and Pollard, 1926). On his interest in birth control, see Winnipeg *Free Press*, 8 June 1932, p. 4.

50. H.S. Patton, "Progress and Measurement," *Canadian Forum*, 2 (1921-1922), p. 456. Patton, one of the rare early critics of eugenics in Canada, was author of *Grain Growers Cooperation in Western Canada* (Cambridge, Mass.: Harvard University Press, 1926) and later professor of economics at Michigan State University.

51. Suzanne Zeller, *Inventing Canada: Early Victorian Science and the Idea of a Transcontinental Nation* (Toronto: University of Toronto Press, 1987). On the crisis of faith precipitated by the challenge of the new biological sciences, see Ramsay Cook, *The Regenerators: Social Criticism in Late Victorian English Canada* (Toronto: University of Toronto Press, 1985).

52. Helen MacMurchy, *The Feeble-minded in Ontario: Ninth Report, 1914* (Toronto: Ontario Provincial Secretary, 1915), p. 22; *Tenth Report, 1915*, p. 17.

Chapter 2

1. On the United States, see Hamilton Cravens, *The Triumph of Evolution*; Mark Haller, *Eugenics: Hereditarian Attitudes in American Thought* (Rutgers: Rutgers University Press, 1963); Ludmerer, *Genetics and American Society*; Bannister, *Social Darwinism*; Kevles, *In the Name of Eugenics*. On Britain, see Jones, *Social Darwinism and English Thought*; Searle, *Eugenics and Politics in Britain*; Donald A. Mackenzie, *Statistics in Britain, 1865-1930: The Social Construction of Scientific Knowledge* (Edinburgh: Edinburgh University Press, 1981).

2. See, for example, S.E.D. Shortt, "The New Social History of Medicine: Some Implications for Research," *Archivaria*, 10 (1980), pp. 12-13; Ronald Hamowy, *Canadian Medicine: A Study in Restricted Entry* (Vancouver: Fraser Institute, 1984).

3. It is important to note that in Canada, where support for public health was slow to mobilize, doctors played a relatively more active role than their counterparts in Britain and the United States in pushing for health regulations. See Heather MacDougall, "Public Health in Toronto Municipal Politics, the Caniff Years, 1883-1890," *Bulletin of the History of Medicine*, 55 (1981), pp. 186-202; "Epidemics and the Environment: The Early Development of Public Health Activity in Toronto, 1832-1872," in R.A. Jarrell and A.E. Roos, eds., *Critical Ideas in the History of Canadian Science, Technology, and Medicine* (Ottawa: HSTC Publishing, 1983), pp. 135-51; "'Enlightening the Public': The Views and Values of the Association of Executive Health Officers of Ontario, 1886-1903," in Charles Roland, ed. *Health, Disease, and Medicine: Essays in Canadian History* (Toronto: Hannah Institute, 1984), pp. 436-64; "Public Health and the 'Sanitary Idea' in Toronto, 1866-1890," in Wendy Mitchinson and Janice Dickin McGinnis, eds., *Essays in the History of Canadian Medicine* (Toronto: McClelland and Stewart, 1988), pp. 62-87.

4. On American developments, see Barbara Rosenkrantz, *Public Health and the State: Changing Views in Massachusetts, 1842-1936* (Cambridge, Mass.: Harvard University Press, 1972), pp. 75ff; Judith Walzer Leavitt, *The Healthiest City: Milwaukee and the Politics of Health Reform* (Princeton: Princeton University Press, 1982), pp. 241-44.

5. For similar findings elsewhere, see Donald Mackenzie, "Eugenics in Britain," *Social Studies of Science*, 6 (1976), pp. 499-532; Linda Clark, *Social Darwinism in France* (University, Alabama: University of Alabama Press, 1984), p. 155.

6. J.G. Adami, "Eugenics," *Canadian Medical Association Journal* [hereafter *CMAJ*], 2 (1912), p. 980.

7. Best exemplified by the creation in 1920 of the federal Department of Health. See Janice Dickin McGinnis, "From Health to Welfare: Federal Government Policies Regarding Standards of Public Health for Canadians, 1918-1945" (Ph.D. thesis, University of Alberta, 1980).

8. See J.G. Adami, "Medicine and War," *CMAJ*, 10 (1920), pp. 881-900; Robin Glen Keirstead, "The Canadian Military Experience During the Great War, 1914-1918" (M.A. thesis, Queen's University, 1982).

9. Kathleen McConnachie, "Methodology in the Study of Women in History: A Case Study of Helen MacMurchy, M.D.," *Ontario History*, 75 (1983), pp. 61-70; Veronica Strong-Boag, "Canada's Women Doctors: Feminism Constrained," in Linda Kealey, ed., *A Not Unreasonable Claim: Women and Reform in Canada, 1880s-1920s* (Toronto: Women's Press, 1979), pp. 109-30.

10. On MacMurchy's obituary, see *CMAJ*, 69 (1953), p. 651.

11. C.A. Hodgetts, "Infantile Mortality in Canada," *CMAJ*, 1 (1911), p. 727. On the urban context, see Terry Copp, *Anatomy of Poverty* (Toronto: McClelland and Stewart, 1974), pp. 93-100; Michael J. Piva, *The Condition of the Working Class in Toronto, 1900-1921* (Ottawa: University of Ottawa Press, 1979), pp. 113-23.

12. MacMurchy, *Maternal Mortality in Canada: A Report of an Enquiry Made by the Department of Health* (Ottawa, 1928), p. 5. See also her reference to "the Army of the Baby that never Has Been" in "The Baby's Father," *Public Health Journal* [hereafter *PHJ*], 9 (1918), p. 315.

13. MacMurchy, *Infant Mortality* (Toronto: King's Printer, 1910, 1911, 1912).

14. MacMurchy, *Infant Mortality* (1911), pp. 4-5. See also Piva, *Working Class*, pp. 123-25.

15. Suzann Buckley, "Efforts to Reduce Infant and Maternal Mortality in Canada Between the Two World Wars," *Atlantis*, 2 (1977), p. 76; see also Buckley, "Ladies or Midwives? Efforts to Reduce Infant and Maternal Mortality," in Kealey, ed., *A Not Unreasonable Claim*, pp. 131-50.

16. MacMurchy, *Infant Mortality* (1912), p. 61.

17. *Ibid.*, p. 31.

18. *Ibid.*, p. 16.

19. *Ibid.*, p. 16-17.

20. *Ibid.*, p. 28. See also her statement that "a test of good citizenship is the ability to make a good home and stay there." MacMurchy, *The Feeble-Minded in Ontario: 9th Report* (Toronto: Ontario Provincial Secretary, 1915), p. 13.

21. MacMurchy, *Infant Mortality* (1910), p. 33.

22. Buckley, "Efforts to Reduce Infant and Maternal Mortality," pp. 78-81.

23. M.C. Urquhart and K.A.H. Buckley, *Historical Statistics of Canada* (Cambridge: Cambridge University Press, 1965), p. 40.

24. On the international situation, see Dame Janet Campbell, *Some Maternity and Child Welfare Problems* (London: National Baby Week Council, 1925); Sam Schapiro and Edward C. Schlesinger, *Infant, Perinatal, Maternal, and Childhood Mortality in the United States* (Cambridge, Mass.: Harvard University Press, 1968), pp. 143-49.

25. MacMurchy, "Maternal Mortality," *Social Welfare* [hereafter *SW*], 6 (1923), pp. 28-30; see also Elizabeth MacCallum, "The Canadian Mother," *SW*, 6 (1924), pp. 248-50.

26. Dominion of Canada, *Report of the Department of Health for 1927* (Ottawa: King's Printer, 1928), p. 65.

27. See also MacMurchy, "Maternal Mortality," *CMAJ*, 17 (1927), pp. 1434-38.

28. On the popularization of MacMurchy's concerns, see Bertha E. Hall and Anne E. Wilson, "Must 1532 Mothers Die?" *Chatelaine* (July, 1928), pp. 6-7, 57, 66-67; Mary E. Power, "Public Health Education," *Canadian Public Health Journal* [hereafter *CPHJ*], 21 (1930), pp. 251-52.

29. MacMurchy, *Maternal Mortality*, p. 27. On MacMurchy's focus on the "medical" causes of death, see Suzann Buckley, "The Search for the Decline of Maternal Mortality: The Place of Hospital Records," in Mitchinson and McGinnis, eds., *Essays*, pp. 151-54.

30. W.B. Hendry, "Maternal Welfare," *SW*, 13 (1931), p. 180.

31. W. Benge Atlee, "Are Women Sheep?" *Canadian Home Journal*, 34 (1931), p. 9.

32. Atlee, "The Menace of Maternity," *Canadian Home Journal*, 29 (1932), p. 9.

33. *Ibid.*

34. Lesley Biggs, in "The Response to Maternal Mortality in Ontario, 1920-1940"

(M.A. thesis, University of Toronto, 1983), convincingly argues that these figures were not simply a result of high-risk cases being directed to urban hospitals.

35. E.W. Montgomery, "Maternal Mortality," *CPHJ*, 21 (1930), pp. 219-25.

36. Suzann Buckley, "From Prescriptions to Misconceptions: How to Reduce Maternal Mortality in Canada," unpublished 1985 paper, p. 7.

37. MacMurchy, "What We Can to Do for Posterity," *Canadian Therapeutist and Sanitary Engineer*, 1 (1910), p. 305.

38. But for those concerned with the problem, see Solomon Kobrinsky, "Abortion and Their Treatment," *CMAJ*, 15 (1925), pp. 789-91.

39. J. Wyllie, "Sex Differences in the Mortalities of Childhood and Adult Life," *CPHJ*, 24 (1933), p. 535.

40. F.W. Jackson and R.D. Jeffries, "A Five Year Study of Maternal Mortality in Manitoba, 1928-1932," *CPHJ*, 25 (1934), p. 105.

41. J.T. Phair and A.H. Sellers, "A Study of Maternal Deaths in the Province of Ontario," *CPHJ*, 25 (1934), p. 566.

42. *Need Our Mothers Die?* (Ottawa: Canada Welfare Council, 1935), pp. 6, 36-37, 43. Investigations of the New York Academy of Medicine indicated that 17.8 per cent of all maternal mortality cases were due to abortion. See Iago Galdston, *Maternal Deaths: The Ways to Prevention* (New York: Commonwealth Fund, 1937), pp. 66-70.

43. A similar line was taken by doctors who glibly argued that abortion deaths would be best countered by "education in moral fortitude, in social responsibility, and in the physiology of sex." F.W. Jackson, N.R. Rawson, and E. Couture, "Maternal Mortality in Manitoba, 1933-1937," *CPHJ*, 31 (1940), p. 321. For a recent overview of the issue, see Angus McLaren and Arlene Tigar McLaren, "Discoveries and Dissimulations: The Impact of Abortion Deaths on Maternal Mortality in British Columbia," *B.C. Studies*, 64 (1984-85), pp. 3-26.

44. The national rate dropped from 4.0 (1940) to 2.8 (1943). See *A Study in Maternal, Infant and Neonatal Mortality in Canada* (Ottawa: Bureau of Statistics, 1945); *Maternal Mortality in Ontario, 1921-1966* (Toronto: Ontario Department of Health Special Report No. 39, 1968), pp. 3, 10. See also Buckley, "Prescriptions."

45. Toronto *Globe*, 7 October 1910, pp. 1, 9; 21 October 1910, p. 1; Toronto *Daily Star*, 21 October 1910, p. 6; 26 October 1910, p. 12.

46. Toronto *Daily Star*, 7 November 1910, p. 7.

47. Huestis, "Medical Inspections in Schools," *Canadian Nurse*, 1 (1905), p. 69; see also Toronto *Daily Star*, 25 April 1912, p. 2.

48. MacMurchy, *Report on the Care of the Feeble-Minded* (Ontario Sessional Papers, 1912), p. 13.

49. The Montreal activities were sparked by Professor Carrie Derick. See MacMurchy, "Medical Inspections in Schools," *CMAJ*, 3 (1913), pp. 111-14.

50. A.P. Knight, "Medical Inspections in Schools," *Queen's Quarterly* [hereafter *QQ*], 15 (1907-08), p. 143.

51. *Ibid.*, p. 138.

52. Hastings's 1905 Ontario Medical Association talk cited by Knight, "Inspections," p. 145. See also Hastings's reference to slums as "hot beds for germination of disease, vice and crime." Piva, *Working Class*, p. 138.

53. Toronto *Daily Star*, 22 January 1913, p. 2.

54. Ottawa *Gazette*, 19 December 1910, p. 3.

55. Knight, "Inspections," p. 140.

56. Toronto *Daily Star*, 28 May 1912, p. 9; see also Charles G. Fraser, "The Feeble-Minded and the Public Schools," *PHJ*, 7 (1916), pp. 237-38.

57. For an overview, see Neil Sutherland, *Children in English Canadian Society* (Toronto: University of Toronto Press, 1976), pp. 71-78.

58. Paul Adolphus Bator, "'Saving Lives on the Wholesale Plan': Public Health Reform in the City of Toronto, 1900-1930" (Ph.D. thesis, University of Toronto, 1979), pp. 218-41.

59. Mrs. Willoughby Cummings reported that in 1896 Dr. Rosebrugh raised the issue within the NCW, which petitioned the government in 1899 for the custodial care of feeble-minded women. *PHJ*, 5 (1914), pp. 229-30.

60. Carol Bacchi, "Race Regeneration and Social Purity: A Study of the Social Attitudes of Canada's English-Speaking Suffragettes," *Histoire sociale/Social History*, 11 (1978), pp. 460-73; Veronica Jane Strong-Boag, *The Parliament of Women: The National Council of Women of Canada, 1893-1929* (Ottawa: National Museum of Man, 1976). For comparisons with American developments, see William Leach, *True Love and Perfect Union: The Feminist Reform of Society* (New York: Basic, 1980), p. 13.

61. Hamilton cited in Bacchi, "Race Regeneration," p. 462.

62. On Derick, see National Council of Women, *12th Annual Report* (Toronto: Johnstone, 1905), pp. 72-78; *National Council of Women Yearbook 1918-19* (1919), p. 52. For attacks on Derick's views, see *America: A Catholic Review of the Week*, 11 (19 February 1910), p. 515; 11 (12 March 1910), p. 602.

63. *The Yearbook of the National Council of Women 1915* (1915), p. 241.

64. Alexander Johnson cited in *Report of the 8th Annual Meeting* (Ottawa: Taylor and Clarke, 1901), p. 141. Johnson, formerly of Hamilton, Ontario, was head of the extension department at the school for the feeble-minded at Vineland, New Jersey. See Johnson's autobiography, *Adventures in Social Welfare* (Fort Wayne, Indiana: author, 1923); *PHJ*, 5 (1914), pp. 209-11.

65. National Council of Women, *13th Report* (Toronto: Johnstone, 1907), pp. 56, 58; *18th Report* (Toronto: Parker, 1911), pp. 41-43. MacMurchy was first influenced by European eugenicists, in part due to her attendance at the Second International Congress for School Hygiene in 1907 in London and the Third International Congress in 1910 in Paris. By the time the next meeting was held in Buffalo, New York, she was clearly very much under the sway of American eugenicists. See note 74 below.

66. Harvey G. Simmons, *From Asylum to Welfare* (Downsview: National Institute on Mental Retardation, 1982).

67. See, for example, Dr. H.L. Brittain, "Feeble-Mindedness," *PHJ*, 7 (1916), pp. 495-96.

68. M.C. Maclean cited in Sutherland, *Children*, p. 74.

69. MacMurchy, *The Almosts* (Boston: Houghton Mifflin, 1920), p. 22.

70. MacMurchy, *The Feeble-Minded in Ontario: 9th Report, 1914* (1915), p. 5.

71. MacMurchy, *The Almosts*, p. 173.

72. MacMurchy, *The Feeble-Minded in Ontario: 2nd Report* (1908), p. 7.

73. Dr. Walter E. Fernald cited in MacMurchy, *The Feeble-Minded in Ontario: 10th Report, 1915* (1916), p. 19.

74. MacMurchy relied heavily on the work of Henry H. Goddard of the school for the feeble-minded at Vineland, New Jersey, and Dr. Walter E. Fernald of the school for the retarded in Waverley, Massachusetts, for "evidence" of the social problems caused by biological defect. She was also aware by 1916 of the interest taken in such issues by wealthy American families such as the Harrimans and the Rockefellers. On the Rockefellers' support of eugenic research, see Barry Mehler and Garland E. Allen, "Sources in the Study of Eugenics, #2: The Bureau of Social Hygiene Papers," *Mendel Newsletter*, 16 (1978), pp. 6-15.

75. See, for example, Victoria *Times*, 18 November 1920, p. 6.

76. See Suzann Buckley and Janice Dickin McGinnis, "Venereal Disease and Public Health Reform in Canada," *Canadian Historical Review*, 63 (1982), pp. 345-47, 350-52.

77. MacMurchy cited *ibid.*, p. 350. On MacMurchy's support for anti-vice crusades, see Toronto *Daily Star*, 10 June 1913, p. 17.

78. MacMurchy, *The Feeble-Minded in Ontario: 10th Report* (1915), pp. 32-33; see also A.P. Reid, "Heredity and Public Health," *PHJ*, 4 (1913), p. 225; Gordon S. Mundie, "Feeble-Minded Children," *PHJ*, 5 (1914), pp. 166-67.

79. MacMurchy, *The Feeble-Minded in Ontario: 2nd Report* (1908), p. 19.

80. MacMurchy, *The Feeble-Minded in Ontario: 10th Report*, p. 8.

81. A.P. Knight, "Family Stock," *QQ*, 16 (1908-09), pp. 141-48; on the Jukes, see also A.P. Reid, "Eugenics," *PHJ*, 4 (1913), p. 284-86; and for a more recent appraisal, N.H. Rafter, ed., *White Trash: The Eugenic Family Studies* (Boston: Northeastern University Press, 1988).

82. MacMurchy, *The Feeble-Minded in Ontario: 2nd Report*, p. 19.

83. MacMurchy, *The Feeble-Minded in Ontario: 5th Report* (1911), p. 15.

84. MacMurchy, *The Feeble-Minded in Ontario: 9th Report* (1915), p. 13.

85. MacMurchy, *The Feeble-Minded in Ontario: 8th Report* (1914), p. 10.

86. Winnipeg *Free Press*, 11 October 1916, p. 9; 1 November 1916, p. 9; 8 November 1916, p. 11; 15 November 1916, p. 11.

87. *PHJ*, 2 (1911), pp. 58-59; see also Harold White, "School Medical Services – Vancouver," *PHJ*, 19 (1928), pp. 222-29.

88. See Toronto *Daily Star*, 12 March 1911, p. 22; MacMurchy, *The Feeble-Minded in Ontario, 8th Report*, p. 12.

89. MacMurchy, "Education of the Backward Child," *SW*, 1 (1919), pp. 246-47, 280-81; MacMurchy, *The Feeble-Minded in Ontario: 9th Report*, p. 5.

90. MacMurchy, *The Feeble-Minded in Ontario: 9th Report*, p. 9; MacMurchy, "The Mentally Defective Child," *PHJ*, 6 (1915), p. 85.

91. For Shortt, see *PHJ*, 5 (1914), pp. 227-28; for Brooking, *ibid.*, pp. 212-18; for Clarke, *ibid.*, 9 (1918), pp. 97-98; for Hincks, *ibid.*, 9 (1918), pp. 102-05.

92. MacMurchy, *The Feeble-Minded in Ontario: 9th Report*, p. 5.

93. *Ibid., 10th Report*, p. 5.

94. *Ibid., 2nd Report*, p. 15.
95. Atherton, "The Causes of Degeneracy of the Human Race," *Canada Lancet* [hereafter *CL*], 41 (1907-08), p. 100.
96. Bruce, "Mental Sanitation," *CL*, 40 (1906-07), p. 976.
97. Bell, "Social Maladies," *QQ*, 16 (1908-09), p. 52.
98. MacMurchy cited by Atherton, "Degeneracy," p. 101.
99. *Canada Law Journal*, 48 (1912), p. 207; see also J.B. Downey, *PHJ*, 4 (1913), p. 125.
100. *Canada Law Journal*, 48 (1912), pp. 207-08.
101. National Council of Women, *The Yearbook of the National Council of Women, 1915* (Toronto: NCW, 1915), p. 237; see also Robert M. Dickie, "War and the Survival of the Fit," *QQ*, 20 (1912-13), pp. 194-213.
102. Such demands were both a cause and effect of the inflation in the reported numbers of the feeble-minded. In 1900 they were thought to represent about 0.3 per cent of the population; by 1914 about 3 per cent, a tenfold increase. See Peter H. Bryce, "Medical Inspections in Schools," *PHJ*, 7 (1916), pp. 59-62.
103. *The Prevalence of Venereal Disease in Canada* (Toronto: University of Toronto Press, 1917), p. 20.
104. Reid, "Eugenics," *PHJ*, 4 (1913), p. 286.
105. Woodsworth, Winnipeg *Free Press*, 15 November 1916, p. 11.
106. Miller, "Preventive Pathology," *QQ*, 30 (1922-23), p. 143.
107. Clarke cited in Bator, "Health," pp. 230-31. A major provincial investigation resulted in Justice Hodgins's *Report of the Royal Commission on the Care and Control of the Mentally Defective and Feeble-Minded* (1919) but little was actually done in following up its recommendations of segregation and special education. See *PHJ*, 11 (1920), p. 126.
108. An important vehicle for such advice was MacMurchy's Little Blue Book Series of manuals produced for the Department of Health. *The Canadian Mother's Book*, originally published in 1923, was by 1931 distributed to 700,000 readers.
109. In 1934 MacMurchy was awarded a CBE, in 1939 she became a life fellow of the Academy of Medicine, and in 1949 she was named by Hobart and William Smith College – on the hundredth anniversary of Elizabeth Blackwell's graduation as North America's first woman doctor – as one of the ten leading women physicians in the world. *CMAJ*, 69 (1953), p. 651.
110. MacMurchy, *Sterilization? Birth Control? A Book for Family Welfare and Safety* (Toronto: Macmillan, 1934), p. 5.
111. *Ibid.*, p. 81.
112. *Ibid.*, p. 124.
113. *Ibid.*, p. 149.
114. *Ibid.*, p. 128. Marie Stopes, the English birth-controller, reported that in fact many women distrusted the medical profession and came to her for help because she was *not* a doctor. Stopes, *"The First Five Thousand" Being the First Report of the First Birth Control Clinic in the British Empire* (London: John Bale, 1925), p. 26.
115. MacMurchy, *Sterilization*, p. 148.

Chapter 3

1. Helen MacMurchy, "Defective Children," *Social Service Congress: Ottawa 1914* (Toronto: SSC, 1914), p. 101.

2. Social Service Congress, *Canada's Child Immigrants* (Toronto: SSC, 1924), pp. 16, 33. See also Neil Sutherland, *Children in English Canadian Society* (Toronto: University of Toronto Press, 1976), p. 73.

3. Howard Palmer, ed., *Immigration and the Rise of Multiculturalism* (Toronto: Copp Clarke, 1975), pp. 4-12.

4. Howard Palmer, "Reluctant Hosts: Anglo-Canadian Views of Multiculturalism in the Twentieth Century," in *Multiculturalism as State Policy* (Ottawa: Queen's Printer, 1976), pp. 84-97. For the best contemporary expression of this ideology, see Ralph Connor [Charles William Gordon], *The Foreigner* (Toronto: Westminster, 1909).

5. W.D. Scott, "Immigration and Population," in *Canada and Its Provinces* (Toronto: Glasgow, Brook, 1914-17), VII, pp. 531, 561, 565, 568, 569, 570.

6. James S. Woodsworth, *Strangers Within Our Gates or, Coming Canadians* (Toronto: Methodist Mission, 1909), p. 92; see also Terry L. Chapman, "The Early Eugenics Movement in Western Canada," *Alberta History*, 25 (1977), pp. 9-17; Marilyn Barber, "Nationalism, Nativism, and the Social Gospel: The Protestant Church Response to Foreign Immigration in Western Canada, 1897-1914," in Richard Allen, ed., *The Social Gospel in Canada* (Ottawa: National Museum of Man, 1975), pp. 186-226.

7. David J. Hall, *Sir Clifford Sifton* (Vancouver: University of British Columbia Press, 1981-85), I, pp. 262-69, II, pp. 66-72, 300-02. Immigration was a branch of the Department of Agriculture until 1892 when it was hived off to the Department of the Interior. A separate Department of Immigration and Colonization existed from 1917 to 1938 when it was subsumed under the Department of Mines.

8. Donald Avery and Peter Neary, "Laurier, Borden and a White British Columbia," *Journal of Canadian Studies*, 12 (1977), pp. 24-34; Donald Avery, *"Dangerous Foreigners": European Immigrant Workers and Labour Radicalism in Canada, 1896-1932* (Toronto: McClelland and Stewart, 1979).

9. Robert F. Harney and Harold Troper, *Immigrants: A Portrait of the Urban Existence, 1890-1930* (Toronto: van Norstrand Reinhold, 1975), ch. 4.

10. Carl Berger, *The Sense of Power: Studies in the Ideas of Canadian Imperialism, 1867-1914* (Toronto: University of Toronto Press, 1970), pp. 117, 131, 148-52.

11. J.R. Conn, "Immigration," *QQ*, 8 (1900), pp. 119, 129.

12. House of Commons, *Debates*, 12 April 1901, pp. 2933-34; 14 July 1903, p. 6563.

13. House of Commons, *Debates*, 7 February 1910, p. 3134; 23 January 1914, p. 140.

14. MacMurchy, *The Feeble-Minded in Ontario: 5th Report, 1910* (1911), p. 52.

15. Not all doctors were so damning of immigrants. See, for example, J.M. Shaver, "Civic Problems Caused by Immigrants," *PHJ*, 7 (1916), pp. 433-37.

16. Bator, "'Saving Lives on the Wholesale Plan,'" p. 219.

17. *CMAJ*, 2 (1912), p. 980.

18. "Defectives and Insane Immigrants," *CL*, 42 (1908-09), p. 62.

19. "Medical Inspection of Public Schools," *Canadian Journal of Medicine and Surgery* [hereafter *CJMS*], 21 (1907), p. 73.

20. "Medical Inspection in Schools," *PHJ*, 7 (1916), pp. 59-62; see also Peter H. Bryce, *The Value to Canada of the Continental Immigrant* (Toronto, 1928).

21. "Why is the Immigrant Act Not Enforced," *CJMS*, 25 (1909), pp. 251-53.

22. On American developments, see Samuel B. Thielman, "Psychiatry and Social Values: The American Psychiatric Association and Immigration Restriction, 1880-1930," *Psychiatry*, 48 (1985), pp. 299-310.

23. MacMurchy, *The Feeble-Minded in Ontario: 5th Report*, p. 32.

24. MacMurchy, *The Feeble-Minded in Ontario: 8th Report, 1913* (1914), pp. 17-18. See also *9th Report*, pp. 10-11; William W. Lee, "Effects of Immigration on National Health," *PHJ*, 4 (1913), pp. 134-36.

25. MacMurchy, *The Feeble-Minded in Ontario: 10th Report, 1915* (1916), pp. 32-33.

26. *Proceedings of the American Medico-Psychological Association* [hereafter *PAMPA*], 4 (1905).

27. *CL*, 41 (1907-08), pp. 944-45.

28. *PHJ*, 6 (1915), p. 558.

29. "Medical Inspection in the Schools," *QQ*, 15 (1907-08), p. 140.

30. *Canadian Practitioner and Review* [hereafter *CPR*], 33 (1908), pp. 477-78; *CL*, 42 (1908-09), p. 140.

31. "Social Maladies," *QQ*, 16 (1908-09), p. 50; see also A.H. Desloges, "Immigration," *PHJ*, 10 (1919), pp. 1-5.

32. House of Commons, *Debates*, 2 May 1917, p. 994.

33. *PAMPA*, 7 (1908), pp. 106-07.

34. See *Canadian Journal of Public Health*, 40 (1949), p. 84.

35. *Ontario Sessional Papers*, 74 (1886), pp. 128-32.

36. *Ontario Sessional Papers*, 32 (1899), pp. 20-21.

37. *Report of the Registrar General*, 9 (1903), p. 8.

38. *Ontario Sessional Papers*, 32 (1899), p. 21.

39. "Feeble-Mindedness and Social Environment," *American Journal of Public Health*, 8 (1918), p. 656.

40. Dominion of Canada, *Sessional Papers*, 25 (1910), p. 110.

41. "Ethical Problems Underlying the Social Evil," *CJMS*, 35 (1914), p. 269.

42. Peter H. Bryce, *The Illumination of Joseph Keeler, or, On to the Land* (Boston: AJPH, 1915).

43. "Infant Mortality," *SW*, 2 (1919), pp. 5-6.

44. *Report of the Registrar General*, 19 (1910), p. 6.

45. "The Undesirable Immigrant," *CPR*, 33 (1908), p. 477.

46. "The Canadian Immigration Policy," *Canadian Magazine*, 30 (1907-08), p. 358.

47. *Maclean's* (December, 1914), p. 56.

48. Prescott F. Hall, *Immigration and Its Effects Upon the United States* (New York: Holt, 1913). For a similar concern expressed by William Tait, professor of psychology at McGill, that immigrants were driving the best Canadians out of their own country, see *Canadian Journal of Mental Health* [hereafter *CJMH*], 3 (1921), pp. 272-73.

49. Manpower and Immigration, *A Report of the Canadian Immigration and Popula-*

tion Study Two: The Immigration Program (Ottawa: Info Canada, 1974), pp. 1-6.

50. J.D. Pagé, "Trachoma and Immigration," *Dominion Medical Monthly*, 25 (1905), p. 306; see also *PHJ*, 4 (1913), pp. 641-46.

51. Zlata Godler, "Doctors and the New Immigrants," *Canadian Ethnic Studies*, 9 (1977), p. 8.

52. "The Medical Inspection of Immigrants," *PHJ*, 3 (1912), p. 435.

53. Those excluded were mainly refused entry because of lack of funds. See W.G. Smith, "Immigration: Past and Future," *CJMH*, 1 (1919).

54. *CPR*, 33 (1908), p. 477.

55. *PHJ*, 4 (1913), p. 455.

56. "Immigration of the Mentally Unfit," *PHJ*, 6 (1915), p. 554.

57. Helen MacMurchy, "The Mentally Defective Child," *PHJ*, 6 (1915), p. 85.

58. J.D. Pagé, "Immigration and the Mentally Unfit," *PHJ*, 6 (1915), pp. 554-58; see also MacMurchy, *The Feeble-Minded in Ontario: 9th Report*, pp. 10-11.

59. G.R. Searle, *Eugenics in Britain*, pp. 38-41.

60. Woodsworth, *Strangers*, p. 264. On the American experience, see John Higham, *Strangers in a Strange Land: Patterns of American Nativism, 1860-1925* (New York: Atheneum, 1955); Barbara Miller Solomon, *Ancestors and Immigrants* (Cambridge, Mass.: Harvard University Press, 1956), pp. 146-57.

61. MacMurchy, *The Feeble-Minded in Ontario: 9th Report*, p. 11.

62. Avery, *"Dangerous Foreigners,"* pp. 81-82; Barbara Roberts, *Whence They Came: Deportation from Canada, 1900-1935* (Ottawa: University of Ottawa Press, 1988).

63. On Asians, see Howard Palmer, "Patterns of Racism: Attitudes Towards the Chinese and Japanese in Alberta, 1920-1950," *Histoire sociale/Social History*, 13 (1980), pp. 137-60; H.F. Angus, "Canadian Immigration: The Law and Its Administration," *American Journal of International Law*, 28 (1934), pp. 74-89; Peter Ward, *White Canada Forever: Popular Attitudes and Public Policy Towards Orientals in British Columbia* (Montreal: McGill-Queen's University Press, 1978). On American blacks, see Harold Troper, *Only Farmers Need Apply* (Toronto: Griffin House, 1972), pp. 121ff.

64. McGinnis, "From Health to Welfare: Federal Government Policies Regarding Standards of Public Health For Canadians, 1918-1945."

65. Sheard cited in Janice Dickin McGinnis and Suzann Buckley, "Venereal Disease and Public Health Reform," *Canadian Historical Review*, 63 (1982), pp. 345-46.

66. House of Commons, *Debates*, 2 May 1917, p. 992.

67. O.C.J. Withrow, "Mentally Defective Recruits for Army Service," *PHJ*, 8 (1917), pp. 109-11; Tom Brown, "Shell Shock in the Canadian Expeditionary Force, 1914-1918: Canadian Psychiatry in the Great War," in Charles Roland, ed., *Health, Disease, and Medicine: Essays in Canadian History* (Toronto: Hannah Institute, 1984), pp. 436-64.

68. *CMAJ*, 8 (1918), pp. 551-52.

69. Clarke, "The Defective Immigrant," *PHJ*, 7 (1916), pp. 462-65; see also Clarke, "Immigration," *PHJ*, 10 (1919), p. 441.

70. Bryce, "Medical Inspection in the Schools," *PHJ*, 7 (1916), pp. 59-62.

71. W.G. Smith, *A Study in Immigration* (Toronto: Ryerson Press, 1920), pp. 9, 11, 13; see also Clarke, "Mental Hygiene," *PHJ*, 13 (1922), p. 538.

72. Smith, *Immigration*, pp. 55, 169, 324. Smith was a professor of psychology at the University of Toronto.

73. *Ibid.*, p. 242; also pp. 317, 324.

74. *Ibid.*, pp. 369, 400.

75. See, for example, Jasper Halpenny, "Immigration," *CJMH*, 1 (1919), pp. 224-26.

76. "Annual Report of the CNCMH," *CJMH*, 2 (1920), p. 74.

77. *CJMH*, 2 (1920), p. 266.

78. See E.D. MacPhee, "Research on Mental Hygiene," *PHJ*, 14 (1923), pp. 339-43; *CMAJ*, 8 (1918), p. 538; H.H. Laughlin, *Biological Aspects of Immigration* (Washington, D.C.: Government Printing Office, 1920).

79. Kevles, *In the Name of Eugenics*, pp. 82-83, 97.

80. Franz Samelson, "Putting Psychology on the Map: Ideology and Intelligence Testing," in Allen R. Buss, ed., *Psychology in Social Context* (New York: Irvington, 1979), pp. 103-68; Michael Sokal, ed., *Psychological Testing and American Society* (New Brunswick, N.J.: Rutgers University Press, 1987).

81. Carl C. Brigham, *A Study of American Intelligence* (Princeton: Princeton University Press, 1923), pp. 119, 177, 208-09. In 1930 Brigham admitted the fallaciousness of the arguments advanced in *A Study*.

82. Haller, *Eugenics: Hereditarian Attitudes in American Thought*, pp. 155-57; Kenneth Ludmerer, "Genetics, Eugenics and the Immigration Restriction Act of 1924," *Bulletin of the History of Medicine*, 41 (1972), pp. 59-81.

83. Peter Sandiford, "The Inheritance of Talent Among Canadians," *QQ*, 35 (1927), p. 2. Elsewhere he wrote, "The eugenists are right so far as they stress the importance of stock, for, as every farmer knows, if one desires well-favoured offspring the best procedure is to start with first class parents." *Foundations of Educational Psychology: Nature's Gift to Man* (Toronto: Longmans, 1938), p. 42.

84. Sandiford was a student of the Columbia University psychometrician E.L. Thorndike, who also worked on twins. See Sandiford, *The Mental and Physical Life of School Children* (London: Longmans, 1913), p. 13; "Education," *PHJ*, 7 (1916), pp. 496-97; "I.Q.," *CJMH*, 3 (1922), p. 40; A.H. Wingfield and Peter Sandiford, "Twins and Orphans," *American Journal of Educational Psychology*, 19 (1928), pp. 420-21. See also Wingfield's book-length attempt to prove that intelligence was an inherited trait, *Twins and Orphans: The Inheritance of Intelligence* (Toronto: Dent, 1928).

85. Sandiford, "Inheritance," p. 8.

86. Sandiford, *Comparative Education* (Toronto: Dent, 1918), p. 431.

87. Sandiford, "Inheritance," p. 17. Sandiford's findings were critiqued in Helen Reid and Charles Herbert Young, *The Japanese Canadians* (Toronto: University of Toronto Press, 1938), pp. 135-36. On school testing elsewhere, see Gillian Sutherland, *Ability, Merit, and Measurement: Mental Testing and English Education, 1880-1940* (Oxford: Clarendon Press, 1984); Clarence J. Karier, "Testing for Order and Control in the Corporate Liberal State," in N.J. Block and Gerald Dworkin, eds., *The I.Q. Controversy* (New York: Pantheon, 1977), pp. 154-80.

88. Sandiford, "Inheritance," p. 18; see also E. Jamieson and P. Sandiford, "The Mental Capacity of Southern Ontario Indians," *Journal of Educational Psychology*, 19 (1928), pp. 536-51. Canada did produce one of the most notable critics of claims

made for racial differences in intelligence – Otto Klineberg. After obtaining his B.A. at McGill, Klineberg pursued graduate work at Columbia and was much influenced by Franz Boas. Klineberg demonstrated that the fact that northern U.S. blacks obtained higher test scores than southern blacks was due not to the more intelligent moving north, as the eugenicists claimed, but to their improved social and educational environment. H.A. Tanser, a Canadian student of psychology, sought to counter Klineberg's findings. Tanser argued that since the IQ scores of blacks who had lived in Kent County, Ontario, since the 1850s were fifteen to twenty points lower than those of whites, there was a basis for believing in "innate racial inferiority." See Otto Klineberg, *A History of Psychology in Autobiography*, 6 (1974), pp. 163-82; H.A. Tanser, *The Settlement of Negroes in Kent County, Ontario and A Study of the Mental Capacity of Their Descendants* (Chatham: Shepherd Publishing, 1939). Curiously enough, Tanser's obscure study, which was cited by the racist journal *Mankind Quarterly* in 1960 as providing proof of black inferiority, was republished in 1970 by the Negro Universities Press of Westport, Connecticut.

89. Sandiford, "Research in Education," *University of Toronto Quarterly*, 3 (1934), pp. 314, 315, 319.

90 On support of testing, see Colin K. Russell, *CMAJ*, 8 (1918), p. 551; William D. Tait, "Science and Education," *Scientific Monthly*, 29 (1929), pp. 132-36; Eric Clarke (son of Charles K. Clarke), "Mental Hygiene in Toronto Schools," *PHJ*, 13 (1922), pp. 126-30; Clarence Hincks, *PHJ*, 9 (1918), pp. 102-05; Chester E. Kellogg, "Mental Tests and Their Use," *Dalhousie Review* [hereafter *DR*], 2 (1922-23), pp. 490-99. E.J. Pratt noted that low standards of living seemed to affect intelligence: "Mental Tests in Toronto," *PHJ*, 12 (1921), p. 150; H.B. Moyle of the Ontario Hospital at Mimico warned that IQ tests only revealed "school acquirement," not raw intelligence, and so posed the danger of labelling a still developing child. "Childhood," *CJMH*, 3 (1921), p. 257.

91. On the women's organizations and eugenics, see Bacchi, "Race Regeneration and Social Purity"; Barbara Roberts, "A Work of Empire: Canadian Reformers and British Female Immigrants," in Kealey, ed., *A Not Unreasonable Claim*, p. 189. On domestics, see *A Conference of the Canadian Council of Immigration of Women* (Ottawa: King's Printer, 1928); Strong-Boag, *The Parliament of Women*, p. 248.

92. *The Yearbook of the National Council of Women* (Toronto: NCW, 1915), pp. 237, 241.

93. Marilyn Barber, "The Women Ontario Welcomed: Immigrant Domestics for Ontario Homes, 1870-1930," in Alison Prentice and Susan Mann Trofimenkoff, eds., *The Neglected Majority: Essays in Canadian Women's History*, vol. II (Toronto: McClelland and Stewart, 1985), pp. 112-13.

94. On Whitton, see Patricia T. Rooke and R.L. Schnell, *Discarding the Asylum: From Child Rescue to the Welfare State in Canada, 1800-1950* (New York: University Press of America, 1983), p. 247; see also Rooke and Schnell, "Child Welfare in English Canada, 1920-1948," *Social Service Review*, 55 (1981), pp. 484-506; and on the place of eugenics in the rise of social work, see Roy Lubove, *The Professional Altruist: The Emergence of Social Work as a Career* (Cambridge, Mass.: Harvard University Press, 1968), pp. 66-69.

95. Charlotte Whitton, "Mental Deficiency as a Child Welfare Problem," National Archives of Canada (NAC), MG 30 E 256 vol. 19.

96. Rooke and Schnell, *Discarding the Asylum*, p. 237. On the child immigrants, see Joy Parr, *Labouring Children: British Immigrant Apprentices, 1869-1924* (London: Croom Helm, 1980).

97. Social Service Council of Canada, *Canada's Child Immigrants* (Ottawa: SSCC, 1924); see also Mrs. J. Breckinridge McGregor, *"Several Years After": An Analysis of the Histories of a Selected Group of Juvenile Immigrants Brought to Canada in 1910 and in 1920 by British Emigration Societies* (Ottawa: CCCW, 1928), p. 5.

98. *Report of the New Brunswick Child Welfare Society, 1928-29* (Ottawa: CCCW, 1929), p. 205. The journal *Social Welfare* carried a steady stream of articles denigrating immigrants. See, for example, 1 (1919), pp. 130, 138-39; 2 (1920), pp. 175-77.

99. *United Farmers of Alberta*, 26 February 1924, p. 12; 2 February 1925, p. 20; 16 April 1927, p. 5. Agnes MacPhail, Canada's first woman Member of Parliament, followed Whitton's line in saying too many immigrants ended up in "jails, asylums, and hospitals." House of Commons, *Debates*, 7 June 1928, p. 3885; 27 May 1929, p. 2874.

100. J.D. Pagé, "Medical Aspects of Immigration," *PHJ*, 19 (1928), pp. 366-73; D.A. Clark, "Medical Aspects of Immigration," *PHJ*, 17 (1926), pp. 371-73.

101. "Our Immigration Laws," *CMAJ*, 17 (1927), p. 349. On deportations and rejections (the vast majority of which were due to civil rather than medical problems), see the *Annual Report of the Department of Immigration*, 1918-1938.

102. Palmer, "Reluctant Hosts," p. 91.

103. McGinnis, "From Health to Welfare," pp. 50-54.

104. Avery, *"Dangerous Foreigners,"* pp. 106-11; Mary Vipond, "Nationalism and Nativism: The Native Sons of Canada in the 1920s," *Canadian Review of Studies in Nationalism*, 9 (1982), pp. 81-95. On Bennett, see House of Commons, *Debates*, 7 June 1928, p. 3925.

105. Select Standing Committee on Agriculture and Colonization, *Minutes and Proceedings* (Ottawa: King's Printer, 1928).

106. On Jacobs, see House of Commons, *Debates*, 7 June 1928, pp. 3895-97; 27 May 1929, pp. 2894-95; on Luchkovich, 27 May 1929, p. 2903; on Woodsworth, 7 June 1928, pp. 3900-01.

107. Robert England, *The Threat to Disinterested Education* (Toronto: Macmillan, 1937), p. 10; *The Central European Immigrant in Canada* (Toronto: Macmillan, 1929), p. 198. See also his *The Colonization of Western Canada* (London: King, 1936); "Continental Immigration," *QQ*, 36 (1929), pp. 719-28; J. Murray Gibson, "The Foreign Born," *QQ*, 27 (1920), pp. 331-50, L. Hamilton, "Foreigners in the Canadian West," *DR*, 17 (1938), pp. 448-60; D. Walter Murray, "Continental Europeans in Western Canada," *QQ*, 38 (1931), pp. 63-75; Watson Kirkconnell, "Western Immigration," *Canadian Forum* (July, 1928), pp. 706-07. On those desiring more restrictions, see Duncan McArthur, "What is the Immigration Problem?" *QQ*, 35 (1928), pp. 603-14; W.A. Carrothers, "The Immigration Prob-

lem," *QQ*, 36 (1929), pp. 517-31; A.S. Whitely, "What Need of Immigration," *DR*, 9 (1929), pp. 225-29.

Chapter 4

1. The eugenicists seemed to have anticipated Foucault's insight that Victorian sexual repression in fact brought about incitation and that better control was made possible by instruction and intervention. See Michel Foucault, *The History of Sexuality, vol. I, An Introduction* (New York: Pantheon, 1978); Jeffrey Weeks, *Sexuality and Its Discontents: Meanings, Myths and Modern Sexualities* (London: Routledge and Kegan Paul, 1985). On "moral panics" in early twentieth-century Canada, see Mariana Valverde, "'The Age of Light, Soap, and Water': Moral Reform in English Canada," unpublished manuscript, 1988.

2. For "unwholesome sources" of sexual information, see Rev. F.L. Orchard, "Sex Education," *SW* (June, 1919), pp. 222-23; for an attack on old "taboos and phobias," see H. Benge Atlee, "Education and Human Problems," *DR*, 13 (1933-34), pp. 218-19.

3. *Yearbook of the National Council of Women of Canada* (1907), pp. 83-84; (1912), p. 56; (1915), p. 267; (1918-19), p. 67; (1928), p. 89; *Western Women's Weekly*, 14 February 1918, p. 1; 14 December 1918, p. 12; 24 May 1919, p. 12; see also Strong-Boag, *The Parliament of Women*, p. 272.

4. Miss Fotheringham, "Sex Education," *The Canadian Nurse*, 6 (1910) , p. 277. On the books recommended by the NCW, see its *Yearbook* (1919), p. 67.

5. Beatrice Bridgen, "One Woman's Campaign for Social Purity and Social Reform," in Richard Allen, ed., *The Social Gospel in Canada* (Ottawa: National Museum of Man, 1975), p. 44; Joan Sangster, "The Making of a Socialist Feminist: The Early Career of Beatrice Brigden, 1888-1941," *Atlantis*, 13 (1987), pp. 13-28.

6. Report of the Sex Hygiene Council, 24 April 1916, in Hugh Dobson Papers, United Church of Canada Archives; Harold White, "School Medical Services – Vancouver," *PHJ*, 19 (1928), pp. 222-29; Norah Lewis, "Physical Perfection for Spiritual Welfare: Health Care for the Urban Child, 1900-1939," in P.T. Rooke and R.L. Schnell, eds., *Studies in Childhood History: A Canadian Perspective* (Calgary: Detselig, 1982), pp. 154-57.

7. Peter Sandiford, "Sex Education," *PHJ*, 13 (1922), pp. 59-62, 118, 174, 215; 16 (1925), pp. 386-90; *Tell Your Children the Truth* (Toronto: Canadian Social Hygiene Council, 1926).

8. Margaret Prang, "'The Girl God Would Have Me Be': The Canadian Girls in Training, 1915-1939," *Canadian Historical Review*, 66 (1985), pp. 168-69.

9. Michael Bliss, "Pure Books on Avoided Subjects: Pre-Freudian Sexual Ideas in Canada," *Historical Papers* (1970), pp. 107-08.

10. Authur W. Beall, *The Living Temple: A Manual on Eugenics for Parents and Teachers* (Toronto: Penhale, 1933), p. 41.

11. *Ibid.*, p. 65.

12. *Ibid.*, p. 67.
13. On late nineteenth-century campaigns against masturbation in Canada, see Rev. W.J. Hunter, *Manhood: Wrecked and Rescued* (Toronto: William Briggs, 1894); Alexander Milton Ross, *Memoirs of a Reformer (1832-1892)* (Toronto: Hunter Rose, 1893), pp. 215-17. It was a sign of the times that B.G. Jefferis and J.L. Nichols, *Search Lights on Health or, Light in Dark Corners* (Toronto: Nichols, 1896), reappeared in the 1920's entitled *Safe Counsel or, Practical Eugenics.*
14. Peter H. Bryce, "Ethical Problems Underlying the Social Evil," *CJMS*, 35 (1914), pp. 213-21.
15. Hett, *Industrial Banner*, 28 May 1920, p. 2; 4 June 1920, p. 4; see also 21 May 1920, p. 1.
16. "Sex Education," *PHJ*, 15 (1924), pp. 258-62.
17. Jay Cassel, *The Secret Plague: Venereal Disease in Canada, 1838-1939* (Toronto: University of Toronto Press, 1987); Alan M. Brandt, *No Magic Bullet: A Social History of Venereal Disease in the United States Since 1880* (New York: Oxford University Press, 1985), pp. 25-29.
18. Buckley and McGinnis, "Venereal Disease and Public Health Reform in Canada," pp. 337-53. The lead in linking venereal disease, delinquency, and crime was given by the American Bureau of Social Hygiene, founded in 1913 by John D. Rockefeller.
19. Hastings, "The Consequences of Prostitution and Suggested Remedies," *Social Service Council of Canada: Ottawa 1914* [hereafter *SSC*] (Toronto: SSC, 1914), p. 214.
20. Emily Murphy, *The Black Candle* (Toronto: T. Allen, 1922), p. 307. Equally alarmist reports were made in Quebec by Dr. A.H. Desloges, general superintendent of the province's insane asylums. See Andrée Lévesque, "Le Bordel: milieu de travail controlé," *Labour/Le Travail*, 20 (1987), pp. 13-31.
21. MacMurchy, *The Feeble-Minded in Ontario: 9th Report*, p. 20.
22. C.K. Clarke in Conservation Commission of Canada, *The Prevalence of Venereal Disease in Canada* (Toronto: University of Toronto Press, 1917), p. 4.
23. Margaret Patterson, "The Care of Convicted Criminals," *SSC*, p. 230. For a similar pattern of blaming the victim, see Charlotte Whitton's assertion that up to three-quarters of unmarried mothers were feeble-minded: "Unmarried Parenthood," *SW* (April, 1920), p. 186.
24. J.J. Heagerty, "Venereal Disease in War," *CJPH*, 30 (1939), p. 567; Sir Andrew MacPhail, "The Medical Services," *Official History of the Canadian Forces in the Great War, 1914-1919* (Ottawa: Acland, 1925), pp. 287-94; E.H. Beardsley, "Allied Against Sin: American and British Responses to Venereal Disease in World War One," *Medical History*, 20 (1976), pp. 189-203.
25. *The Prevalence of Venereal Disease in Canada*, p. 20; see also J.G. Adami, *SW* (September, 1919), p. 285; (October, 1919), pp. 11-12; (December, 1919), p. 77.
26. Bates was also general director of the Health League of Canada. On the activities of the CSHC, see *SW* (February, 1919), p. 15; (March, 1919), p. 129; (June, 1919), p. 211; (June, 1920), p. 249; (May, 1926), pp. 160-61. In addition to *An Open Letter to Young Men* and *Healthy Happy Womanhood*, the CSHC distributed the interna-

tional eugenic classics of Cyril Burt, A.E. Wiggam, Paul Popenoe, and Havelock Ellis. See Bates, "Social Hygiene," *PHJ*, 19 (1928), p. 130.

27. A.C. Jost, "Social Hygiene," *SW* (December, 1924), p. 47. On the continued use of the threat of disease to repress youth, see Isabel Dingman, "Your Teen Age Daughter," *Chatelaine* (October, 1934), p. 63.

28. Direct government involvement in the anti-venereal disease campaign declined when federal funding of the National Council for Combatting Venereal Disease was ended during the depression. See Buckley and McGinnis, "Venereal Disease," p. 352; McGinnis, "From Health to Welfare," ch. 3.

29. *CL*, 42 (1908-09), pp. 402-03. Even earlier, Alexander Graham Bell had made a plea for the deaf to refrain from marrying. Bell, who in 1906 would be a member of the Eugenics Committee of the American Breeders Association, began in 1890 his own eugenic experiment by attempting to breed a "super race" of sheep in Baddeck, Nova Scotia. See Bell, "Marriage," *Science*, 17 (20 March 1891), pp. 160-63.

30. *CMAJ*, 8 (1919); see also W.A. Lincoln, *SW* (November, 1918), pp. 31-32; Nellie McClung, *In Times Like These* (Toronto: McLeod, 1915), pp. 138-39. On marriage restrictions in America, see Michael Grossberg, *Governing the Hearth: Law and Family in Nineteenth Century America* (Chapel Hill: University of North Carolina Press, 1985).

31. *SW* (March, 1921), p. 149. See also *SW* (May, 1926), pp. 168-70; P.T. Rooke and R.L. Schnell, *No Bleeding Heart: Charlotte Whitton, A Feminist on the Right* (Vancouver: University of B.C. Press, 1987), p. 43; J.J. Heagerty, "Medical Certificates for Marriage," *SW* (September, 1924), pp. 242-43.

32. Revised Statutes of Alberta, 1935, ch. 51; Revised Statutes of Saskatchewan, 1936, ch. 89; Revised Statutes of British Columbia, 1938, ch. 33.

33. See also Jaimie Snell and Cynthia Comacchio Abeele, "Combatting Nuptiality: Restricting Access to Marriage in Early Twentieth Century English-Speaking Canada," *Canadian Historical Review*, 69 (1988), pp. 466-89.

34. Bliss, "Pure Books," p. 89. In Quebec as late as the 1940's the Francophone reader who found inadequate such theological treatises as Adèle Harbour, *Le Mariage* (Montréal: Valiquette, 1940), might well have had to rely on turn-of-the-century classics like Sylvanus Stall, *Ce que tout homme marié devrait savoir* (Genève: Jeheber, 1947), and Sylvanus Stall and Mary Wood Allen, *Ce que toute jeune fille devrait savoir* (Genève: Jeheber, 1947).

35. On the introduction of eugenic concerns, see Winfield Scott Hall, *Sexual Knowledge* (Toronto: McClelland, Goodchild, and Stewart, 1916). Hall's works were recommended by the NCW.

36. *SW* (June, 1925), p. 172; for the Social Service Council's recommended books, see *SW* (January, 1929), p. 85.

37. Exner, *The Question of Petting* (New York: Association Press, 1932), p. 19. On the use of such books by Protestant ministers in marriage counselling, see the Hugh Dobson Papers, United Church of Canada Archives.

38. Morris Siegel, *Constructive Eugenics and Rational Marriage* (Toronto: McClelland and Stewart, 1934), pp. 62-77.

39. *Ibid.*, p. 112.
40. *Ibid.*, p. 124.
41. *Ibid.*, p. 134.
42. Morris Siegel, *Population, Race, and Eugenics* (Hamilton: author, 1939), pp. 59-75.
43. Maurice N. Eisendrath, "Children: By Chance or Choice," *The Never Failing Stream* (Toronto: Macmillan, 1939), pp. 166-71. Anti-Semites nailed a swastika on Eisendrath's door on Halloween, 1937. See Lita-Rose Betcherman, *The Swastika and the Maple Leaf: Fascist Movements in Canada in the 1930's* (Toronto: Fitzhenry and Whiteside, 1975), p. 105; and on the question of anti-Semitism and eugenics, see also G.R. Searle, *Eugenics and Politics in Britain* (Leyden: Noordhof International, 1976), pp. 40-41.
44. A.H. Tyrer, *Sex, Marriage and Birth Control* (Toronto: Marriage Welfare Bureau, 1936), pp. 31, 52.
45. *Ibid.*, p. 53.
46. Tyrer, unaware that a Canadian society was being formed, initially sought help for his activities from the British Eugenics Society. See correspondence of 26 December 1930, 9 January 1931, Eugenics Society Papers, Contemporary Medical Archives Centre, Wellcome Institute for the History of Medicine, D 52. In later editions of *Sex, Marriage and Birth Control*, Tyrer acknowledged the assistance of David B. Harkness, who in 1932 was president of the Eugenics Society of Canada. Tyrer also produced two cloying sex education tracts that were distributed by the Marriage Welfare Bureau: *Your Child Needs Your Help* and *"Where Did We Come From, Mother Dear?"* On Tyrer's career, see his autobiography, *And a New Earth* (Toronto: Elliott Press, 1941), and Angus McLaren and Arlene Tigar McLaren, *The Bedroom and the State: The Changing Practices and Politics of Contraception and Abortion in Canada, 1880-1980* (Toronto: McClelland and Stewart, 1986), pp. 93-98.
47. On Kaufman's activities, see McLaren and McLaren, *The Bedroom and the State*, pp. 103-23.
48. Canadians were not unique in shying away from the discussion of fertility control. See Charlotte Whitton's report that the Child Welfare Committee of the League of Nations section that dealt with "Biological Education" was split by the fear of some that sex education would lead to a discussion of birth control. *SW* (June, 1928), pp. 196-98. See also Michael S. Teitelbaum and Jay M. Winter, *The Fear of Population Decline* (New York: Academic Press, 1985).
49. On Kirkconnell and multiculturalism, see Howard Palmer, "Reluctant Hosts: Anglo-Canadian Views of Multiculturalism in the Twentieth Century," in *Multiculturalism as State Policy* (Ottawa, 1976), p. 96; and Watson Kirkconnell, *A Slice of Canada: Memoirs* (Toronto: University of Toronto Press, 1967).
50. Kirkconnell, *International Aspects of Unemployment* (London: Allen and Unwin, 1923), p. 78.
51. *Ibid.*, p. 79.
52. *Ibid.*, p. 80.
53. *Ibid.*, p. 36.
54. F.C.S. Schiller, "The Case for Eugenics," *DR*, 4 (1924-25), p. 409.

55. Lincoln, "The Little Ones," *SW* (December, 1918), p. 54; and see also Peter H. Bryce, "Feeble-Mindedness and Social Environment," *American Journal of Public Health*, 8 (1918), p. 656.

56. MacMurchy, *Sterilization*, p. 88.

57. J.A. Lindsay, "Sex in Education," *DR*, 10 (1930-31), p. 154.

58. William D. Tait, "Some Feminisms," *DR*, 10 (1930-31), pp. 53-54.

59. *Ibid.*, p. 55.

60. *SW* (September, 1923), pp. 43-44.

61. J.J. Heagerty, "Birth Control," *SW* (December, 1924), pp. 57-59.

62. MacMurchy, *Sterilization*, pp. 148, 149.

63. *Maclean's* (June, 1916), p. 28.

64. Kirkconnell, *Unemployment*, p. 50.

65. Heagerty, "Birth Control," *SW* (December, 1914), p. 59.

66. Hilda Ridley, "A Revaluation of Motherhood," *DR*, 9 (1929), p. 216.

67. Veronica Strong-Boag, "Wages for Housework: Mothers' Allowances and the Beginning of Social Security in Canada," *Journal of Canadian Studies*, 14 (1979), pp. 24-34. On the British experience, see John MacNicol, *The Movement for Family Allowances, 1918-1945: A Study in Social Policy Development* (London: Heineman, 1980), pp. 75ff. It should be noted that many of the eugenic-minded were fearful that pensions could be counter-productive if they supported "bonused breeding" and undermined discipline and self-control. See Rooke and Schnell, *Whitton*, pp. 79, 121; Gordon Bates, "Social Hygiene," *PHJ*, 19 (1928), p. 130.

68. *Canadian Forum* (March, 1925), pp. 174-75.

69. *Health Bulletin*, 15 (August, 1924), pp. 2-4; see also the London *Times*, 16 August 1924, p. 9. Hastings was also reported to have made a plea for birth control to the Health Officers' Association of Ontario meeting in 1924; see *Birth Control Review*, 8 (1924), p. 210.

70. *Toronto Star*, 27 April 1927, p. 17.

71. On Stephens's career, see McLaren and McLaren, *The Bedroom and the State*, pp. 61-66.

72. See Vancouver *Daily Province*, 14 March 1928, p. 1; 15 March, p. 1; 16 March, pp. 1, 6; 17 March, p. 1; 20 March, p. 1; Vancouver *Sun*, 13 March 1928, p. 8; 15 March, p. 8; 20 March, p. 8; Emily Murphy, "Companionate Marriage from the Point of View of the Mother and Child," *Chatelaine* (May, 1928), pp. 3-4, 56-58. Companionate marriage was also condemned by Bishop Sweeney of Toronto and Judge Raney of York County; see Toronto *Globe and Mail*, 21 September 1938, and clipping of 9 December 1930 in Withrow Papers. For the defence, see Judge Ben Lindsey, "Are Marriage Vows Sacred?" *Maclean's*, 15 April 1923, p. 37; Judge Ben Lindsey and Wainwright Evans, *The Companionate Marriage* (New York: Boni and Liveright, 1927); David C. Adie, "Trends in Family Life," *SW*, 9 (September, 1927), pp. 508-13. On Telford's activities, see McLaren and McLaren, *The Bedroom and the State*, pp. 65-66.

73. See the Withrow Papers, Public Archives of Ontario, Acc. 14892; *Toronto Star*, 6 May 1925; see also 9 May 1925 and the *Birth Control Review*, 9 (1925), p. 236.

74. Toronto *Telegram*, 20 May 1927, p. 11; see also R.M. MacIver, "Fertility Trends,"

in Louis Dublin, ed., *Population Problems in the United States and Canada* (Boston: Houghton Mifflin, 1926), pp. 286-308.

75. Toronto *Telegram*, 5 May 1927, p. 1; 7 May 1927, p. 18.

76. As a result of his prison experiences Withrow wrote *Shackling the Transgressor: An Indictment of the Canadian Penal System* (Toronto: Nelson, 1933) and *Poems from Prison* (Toronto: author, 1937). After 1933 he again provided his patients with contraceptives and advice on sex matters; he corresponded with and eventually met Marie Stopes. See Withrow Papers.

77. Florence Huestis was also a member of the National Council for the Prevention of Venereal Disease and the Hygiene Club. D.M. Lebourdais, in addition to his medical and writing interests, was general secretary of the Association of Ontario CCF Clubs. Rabbi Maurice Eisendrath was also a supporter of the League.

78. On Skey's life, see his file in the University of Toronto Archives, A 73-0026/422/49.

79. W.G. Nicholson, "Marriage and Birth Control," *SW* (January, 1931), p. 77.

80. Board of Evangelism and Social Service, *The Meaning and Responsibilities of Christian Marriage* (Toronto: United Church of Canada, 1932), p. 8.

81. Toronto *Globe and Mail*, 4 January 1937, p. 10. Zeidman, head of the Scott Mission – a Toronto philanthropic organization – had a projected radio talk on the subject of birth control banned by the CBC. See the Board of Evangelism and Social Service, United Church of Canada Archives, file 77 (1937), box 7. W.P. Reekie of the Saskatchewan Child Welfare League, in writing to the English Eugenics Society in 1932, had similarly assumed a fusing of eugenic and religious concerns. "We are now considering the founding of a specific mission on a nation-wide scale, the purpose of which would be to unite the light of science and the faith and motives of religion in the task of race building. We believe that in this task religion without science and science without religion are alike lame – that both natural law and spiritual grace are gifts from one Father to enable his children to travel an upward road." Reekie to Eugenics Society, 15 April 1932; see also Reverend J.G. Joyce to Eugenics Society, 25 January 1932, Eugenics Society Papers, D:52, Contemporary Medical Archives Centre. The English regarded this desire to reconcile religion and eugenics as a peculiarly North American preoccupation.

82. Emily Murphy, "Birth Control: Its Meaning," Vancouver *Sun*, 27 August 1932, p. 5. See also "Mothers and Birth Control," Emily Murphy Papers, City of Edmonton Archives. The Vancouver *Sun*, which had condemned Telford in 1928, was lauding his activities in 1933. See its editorial of 11 July 1933, p. 4.

83. On the transcripts of the trial, see the Dorothea Palmer Papers, University of Waterloo, Special Collections; for interpretations of the trial, see Diane Dodd, "The Birth Control Movement on Trial, 1936-37," *Histoire sociale/Social History*, 32 (1983), pp. 381-400; Gerald Storz and Murray Eaton, "Pro Bono Publico: The Eastview Birth Control Trial," *Atlantis*, 8 (1983), pp. 51-60; and McLaren and McLaren, *The Bedroom and the State*, pp. 116-20.

84. Kaufman to Mr. F.T. Cook, 9 September 1937, C.J. Gamble Papers, Countway Library, 958; see also Kaufman to Paul Kellogg, 23 February 1937, Social Welfare History Archives, University of Minnesota.

85. Kaufman to Charles Gamble, 21 July 1937, Gamble Papers, 958.

86. Kaufman to Guy Burch, 26 February 1941, Gamble Papers, 961.

87. For Kaufman's own account of the trial, see *Birth Control Trial* (Kitchener: PIB, 1937).

88. Palmer Papers, file 16; see also C.E. Silcox, "Eastview and the Public Good," *Canadian Forum*, 14 (May, 1937), p. 50.

89. Palmer Papers, file 23; see also W.L. Hutton, "Tendencies in Human Fertility," *CMAJ*, 30 (1934), pp. 73-77.

90. Palmer Papers, file 24. Chisolm was later to be deputy minister of health (1944-46) and director-general of the World Health Organization (1948-53).

91. It was symptomatic of the eugenic concerns of the birth-controllers that the organization set up to take over the running of the Toronto birth control clinic established by Kaufman was called the Toronto League for Race Betterment. It was led by Mrs. J. Wesley Bundy, Margaret Addison, Gladys Brandt, and Grace Orde. See the Toronto *Globe and Mail*, 12 January 1936.

92. The best account of their ideas is contained in Dora Forster, *Sex Radicalism as Seen by the Emancipated Woman of the New Time* (Chicago: Moses Harman, 1905). I have documented their Canadian careers in an as yet unpublished paper, "Eugenics and Sex Radicalism in Early Twentieth-Century Canada."

93. See Hal D. Sears, *The Sex Radicals: Free Love in High Victorian America* (Lawrence, Kansas: Regents Press, 1970); Leslie Fishbein, *Rebels in Bohemia: The Radicals of the Masses, 1911-1917* (Chapel Hill: University of North Carolina Press, 1982); Judith R. Walkowitz, "Science, Feminism, and Romance: The Men and Women's Club, 1885-1889," *History Workshop*, 21 (1986), pp. 37-59; Lucy Bland, "Marriage Laid Bare: Middle-Class Women and Marital Sex, c. 1880-1914," in Jane Lewis, ed., *Labour and Love: Women's Experiences of Home and Family, 1850-1940* (Oxford: Basil Blackwell, 1986), pp. 123-46.

94. *B.C. Federationist*, 6 February 1914, p. 5; 21 March 1919, p. 3; *The Voice*, 12 May 1911, p. 3; *One Big Union Bulletin*, 6 November 1924, p. 2; *Western Producer*, 6 January 1927, p. 12; 10 February 1927, p. 12; 3 March 1927, p. 12. Further letters on the subject ran through to November, 1927.

95. On the continuing interest of segments of the British left in eugenics, see Michael Freeden, "Eugenics and Progressive Thought: A Study in Ideological Affinity," *Historical Papers*, 22 (1979), pp. 645-71; Greta Jones, "Eugenics and Social Policy Between the Wars," *Historical Journal*, 25 (1982), pp. 717-28; Diane Paul, "Eugenics and the Left," *Journal of the History of Ideas*, 25 (1984), pp. 567-90.

96. It was not the intention of the eugenicists that contraception should free woman from her "natural" role; on the contrary, they assumed that birth control would help shore up heterosexuality and family life. On the repressiveness of much of early twentieth-century sexology, see Margaret Jackson, "Sexual Liberation or Social Control," *Women's Studies International Forum*, 6 (1983), pp. 1-18; Sheila Jeffreys, *The Spinster and Her Enemies* (London: Pandora, 1985).

97. Ernest M. Best, *SW* (1935), p. 118. Best was referring to Luther Burbank, a member of the original 1906 Committee on Eugenics established by the American Breeders Association and to the work done in the mid-1930's on in vitro fertilization by the Nobel laureate Herman Muller and Gregory Pincus (who later helped develop the

contraceptive pill). This vision, of course, had been already critiqued by Aldous Huxley in *Brave New World* (London, 1932). See Kevles, *In the Name of Eugenics*, pp. 188-90.

98. Best, *SW* (1935), p. 118.

Chapter 5

1. *CMAJ*, 29 (1933), p. 260. It is true that if both parents are retarded there is a good chance their offspring will also be retarded. Recent studies have suggested if both parents have an IQ of less than 70, 40 per cent of the offspring will be retarded; if only one parent, 15 per cent of the offspring will be retarded: and if both parents are normal, 1 per cent of the offspring will be retarded. But this still means that 83 per cent of the retarded have normal parents. If sterilization were going to be employed to eliminate the retarded it would be necessary to sterilize the normal. See Michael Craft, ed., *Tredgold's Mental Retardation*, 12th edition (London: Baillière, 1979), pp. 367-68.

2. *CMAJ*, 29 (1933), pp. 443-45; also *CMAJ*, 30 (1934), p. 210.

3. *CMAJ*, 11 (1921), pp. 823-25; 16 (1926), pp. 1233-38; 17 (1927), pp. 1526-28; 19 (1928), p. 586; 29 (1933), pp. 306, 657; 30 (1934), pp. 190, 195.

4. *CMAJ*, 30 (1934), p. 77; also *CMAJ*, 33 (1935), p. 192.

5. *CMAJ*, 21 (1929), pp. 72-74; also *CMAJ*, 32 (1930), p. 91.

6. On Alberta, see Terry L. Chapman, "The Early Eugenics Movement in Western Canada," *Alberta History*, 25 (1977), pp. 9-17.

7. Statutes of the Province of British Columbia, 1933, "An Act Respecting Sexual Sterilization," ch. 59, 7 April 1933.

8. On Manitoba, see Brian L. Ross, "An Unusual Defeat: The Manitoba Controversy over Eugenical Sterilization in 1933," unpublished paper, Institute for the History and Philosophy of Science and Technology, University of Toronto, 1981; on Ontario, see Chapter Seven below.

9. *The Law for the Prevention of Hereditarily Diseased Offspring* (Berlin, 1935).

10. See William L. Morton, *The Progressive Party in Canada* (Toronto: University of Toronto Press, 1950); for the international context, see D. Pickens, *Eugenics and the Progressives* (Nashville: Vanderbilt University Press, 1969); Richard Hofstadter, *The Progressive Movement* (Englewood Cliffs, N.J.: Prentice-Hall, 1963); Michael Freeden, "Eugenics and Progressive Thought: A Study in Ideological Affinity," *The Historical Journal*, 22 (1979), pp. 645-71.

11. Patricia Rooke and R.L. Schnell, *Discarding the Asylum: From Child Rescue to the Welfare State in Canada (1800-1960)* (Lanham, Md.: University Press of America, 1983), pp. 278-81; see also John Gabbay and Charles Webster, eds., "Mental Handicap and Education," *Oxford Review of Education*, 9 (1983).

12. Norah Lewis, "Physical Perfection for Spiritual Welfare: Health Care for the Urban Child," in Rooke and Schnell, eds., *Studies in Childhood History*, pp. 138-50; Diane L. Matters, "Public Welfare Vancouver Style, 1910-1920," *Journal of Canadian Studies*, 14 (1979), pp. 3-15.

13. On Dauphinée and Lindley, see Canadian National Committee for Mental Hygiene [hereafter CNCMH], *Mental Hygiene Survey of the Province of British Columbia* (Toronto: CNCMH, 1920), p. 19.

14. On Goddard, see Stephen Jay Gould, *The Mismeasure of Man* (New York: Norton, 1981), pp. 158-74.

15. Law Reform Commission of Canada [hereafter LRCC], *Sterilization: Implications for Mentally Retarded and Mentally Ill Persons, Working Paper 24* (Ottawa, 1980), p. 10.

16. *Ibid.*, p. 16.

17. James S. Woodsworth played a central role in popularizing eugenic fears in a series of articles he wrote for the *Winnipeg Free Press*, 11 October 1916, p. 9; 1 November 1916, p. 9; 8 November 1916, p. 11; 15 November 1916, p. 11. In the last article he stated: "Sterilization has been proposed. But general sentiment is so strong against such a radical measure that its adoption is not practicable." See also Zlata Godler, "Doctors and the New Immigrants," *Canadian Ethnic Studies*, 9 (1977), pp. 6-18.

18. On Hincks, see Dr. J.G. Fitzgerald and Dr. Grant Fleming, *Report of a Survey made of the Canadian National Committee for Mental Hygiene in 1932* (Ottawa: CNCMH, 1932).

19. Hincks reported that 3.56 per cent of the Vancouver school population was "mentally abnormal," and 72 per cent of the asylum population foreign born. CNCMH, *Mental Hygiene*, pp. 14-18, 48-50.

20. On Hincks's continued campaign to arouse the Canadian public to the danger of feeble-mindedness, see "Mental Hygiene Provisions in Public Health Programs," *CJPH*, 36 (1945), pp. 89-95; "Man's Last Spectre," *Proceedings of the Royal Canadian Institute* (1936), pp. 65-75.

21. The phrase "sterilization of the unfit" entered the vocabulary in 1888-89. See F.B. Smith, *The People's Health, 1830-1910* (London: Croom Helm, 1979), p. 120.

22. C.P. Blacker, *Eugenics: Galton and After* (London: Duckworth, 1952); Karl Pearson, *The Life of Francis Galton* (Cambridge: Cambridge University Press, 1914-1930); Haller, *Eugenics*; Charles Webster, ed., *Biology, Medicine and Society* (Cambridge: Cambridge University Press, 1981).

23. As early as 1861 Joseph Workman of the Toronto Asylum had written, "Insanity would die out if the sane avoided intermarrying with insane stock." *American Journal of Insanity* (January, 1861), p. 314, cited in Norman Dain, *Concepts of Insanity in the United States, 1789-1865* (New Brunswick, N.J.: Rutgers University Press, 1964), p. 241. R.W. Bruce was among the first in Canada to refer to the need for "asexualization" to supplement segregation; "Mental Sanitation," *CL*, 40 (1906-1907), p. 976.

24. J.H. Landman, *Human Sterilization: The History of the Sexual Sterilization Movement* (New York: Macmillan, 1932).

25. *The Champion* (January, 1914), pp. 11-12; see also *ibid.* (February, 1914), p. 6.

26. Bacchi, "Race Regeneration and Social Purity," pp. 460-74; Gillian Weiss, "'As Women and as Citizens': Clubwomen in Vancouver, 1910-1928" (Ph.D. thesis, University of British Columbia, 1983).

27. Strong-Boag, *The Parliament of Women*, pp. 353-70.

28. The United Farm Women of Alberta were the most outspoken proponents of sterilization and curbs on immigration. See, for example, *United Farmers of Alberta*, 1 December 1923, p. 8; 26 February 1924, p. 12.

29. Strong-Boag, *The Parliament of Women*, p. 318.

30. Elsie Gregory MacGill, *My Mother the Judge* (Toronto: PMA, 1955), p. 216; Howard Palmer, *Patterns of Prejudice: A History of Nativism in Alberta* (Toronto: McClelland and Stewart, 1982), pp. 112-13.

31. *Western Women's Weekly*, 8 February 1919, p. 8; 8 March 1919, p. 1; 6 December 1919, p. 1; 3 June 1922, p. 4.

32. *Western Women's Weekly*, 10 January 1918, p. 2.

33. *Western Women's Weekly*, 6 August 1921, p. 8. Explicitly anti-Asiatic sentiment was expressed by the British Progressive League; see *Western Women's Weekly*, 14 October 1922, p. 2.

34. Victoria *Daily Times*, 2 December 1925, p. 2; Vancouver *Sun*, 2 December 1925, p. 20.

35. *Journal of the Legislative Assembly (Session 1925)*, pp. 55, 37; see also Vancouver *Sun*, 19 November 1925, p. 2.

36. On the investigations of Dr. H.C. Steeves, see *Bulletin of the Vancouver Medical Association*, 1 March 1926, pp. 12-16.

37. On the history of institutional care and its growth in B.C., see *Report of the Mental Health Services, Sessional Papers: British Columbia*, II, 1953-1954, pp. 15-22.

38. Victoria *Daily Times*, 19 November 1925, p. 16.

39. E.J. Rothwell, *Report of the Royal Commission on Mental Hygiene* (Victoria, 1927).

40. *Ibid.*, cc 9.

41. Victoria *Daily Times*, 17 April 1926, pp. 1-2.

42. Vancouver *Daily Province*, 14 April 1926, p. 17.

43. Rothwell, *Report*, cc 17; see also Victoria *Daily Times*, 23 April 1926, p. 13; Vancouver *Daily Province*, 14 April 1926, p. 17.

44. Rothwell, *Report*, cc 53.

45. *Ibid.*, cc 9-10. A special submission of Paul Popenoe was included in the *Final Report of the Royal Commission on Mental Hygiene* (Victoria, 1928), appendix H. Because sterilization was compulsory in California, over 7,500 operations (more than half of the entire country) were performed in the state by 1932. See Harry H. Laughlin, *Eugenical Sterilization: 1926* (New Haven: AES, 1926); E.S. Gosney and Paul Popenoe, *Sterilization for Human Betterment* (New York: Macmillan, 1929); F.O. Butler, "A Quarter Century's Experience in Sterilization of Mental Defectives in California," *American Journal of Mental Deficiency*, IL (1945), pp. 1-6.

46. Victoria *Daily Times*, 17 April 1926, pp. 1-2. On the establishment of new services, see Richard James Clark, "Care of the Mentally Ill in British Columbia" (M.S.W. thesis, University of British Columbia, 1947), pp. 87-90.

47. On the lobbying of the Local Councils of Women, see Provincial Archives of British Columbia [hereafter PABC], Provincial Council of Women papers, Add. Mss 1961, box 1, file 1, 147, 171, 175; file 2, 5, 9-10. See also Vancouver *Sun*, 30 September 1926, p. 24.

48. Rothwell, *Report*, cc 9; Rothwell, *Final Report*, appendix H.

49. U.B.C. Special Collections, Vancouver Local Council of Women, box 1, files 2-3; box 4. On similar sentiments in Alberta, see *United Farmers of Alberta*, 1 February 1926, p. 20.

50. Rothwell, *Report*, cc 25.

51. Vancouver *Morning Star*, 7 March 1928, p. 1.

52. *Mental Defect and Social Welfare: Joint Report of the Committees on the Family and Child Welfare of the Social Service Council of Canada* (Ottawa: SSC, 1926), p. 27. Schofield called the resolution "the most unthought out piece of legislation ever asked for." Victoria *Daily Times*, 30 September 1926, p. 6; see also Victoria *Daily Times*, 17 April 1926, pp. 1-2; Victoria *Daily Times*, 12 October 1926, p. 6.

53. Timothy J. Christian, "The Mentally Ill and Human Rights in Alberta," unpublished University of Alberta paper, n.d., p. 9. See also K.J. McWhirter and J. Weijer, "The Alberta Sterilization Act: A Genetic Critique," *University of Toronto Law Journal*, 19 (1969), pp. 424-31; Terry Chapman, "The Early Eugenics Movement in Western Canada," *Alberta History*, 25 (1977), pp. 14-16.

54. Nellie McClung, *The Stream Runs Fast: My Own Story* (Toronto: Thomas Allen, 1945), p. 180; see also Byrne Hope Sanders, *Emily Murphy: Crusader* (Toronto: Macmillan, 1945), pp. 186-88.

55. Christian, "The Mentally Ill," pp. 13-20, 25-29. For contemporary defences of sterilization, see the *United Farmers of Alberta*, 3 January 1927, p. 16; 1 June 1927, p. 22; 1 February 1932, p. 25; C.A. Barrager *et al.*, "Sexual Sterilization: Four Years Experience Under the Act of Alberta," *CMAJ*, 31 (1934), p. 435. It should also be noted that in 1919 Alberta passed an Act Respecting Mentally Defective Persons that allowed for the compulsory institutionalization of the mentally defective even without the consent of parents and guardians. Alberta, *Revised Statutes*, ch. 21, 1919.

56. Vancouver *Sun*, 3 September 1932, p. 3.

57. *Ibid.*, 10 September 1932, p. 4.

58. *Ibid.*, 17 September 1932, p. 2.

59. *Ibid.*, 27 August 1932, p. 5; 24 September 1932, p. 5.

60. So, for example, the 1922 National Convention of Local Councils of Women discussed an issue of the *Birth Control Review* under the topic of "objectionable printed matter and films." *Western Women's Weekly*, 21 October 1922, p. 2.

61. *B.C. Federationist*, 21 November 1924, p. 1; 26 December 1924, p. 1.

62. Victoria *Daily Times*, 17 April 1926, pp. 1-2.

63. Vancouver *Sun*, 6 April 1932, p. 1.

64. *Ibid.*, 24 November 1926, p. 16.

65. *Ibid.*, 25 May 1927, p. 8.

66. *Ibid.*, 8 November 1927, p. 8; see also 31 December 1928, p. 8.

67. *Ibid.*, 3 April 1933, p. 4.

68. Victoria *Daily Times*, 1 April 1933, p. 5.

69. *Labour Statesman*, 20 February 1925, p. 3.

70. Vancouver *Sun*, 1 June 1927, p. 8.

71. *Ibid.*, 21 March 1929, p. 8. For other left-wing attacks on eugenics, see the *One Big Union Bulletin*, 28 May 1931, p. 2; *Canadian Tribune*, 27 April 1940, p. 2.

72. *Journal of the Legislative Assembly* (Session 1933), LXII, pp. 101-15.

73. Victoria *Daily Colonist*, 1 April 1933, p. 2.

74. Vancouver *Daily Province*, 1 April 1933, p. 3.

75. Vancouver *Sun*, 6 April 1933, pp. 1, 5.

76. *Ibid.*, 7 April 1933, p. 12.

77. Vancouver *Daily Province*, 7 April 1933, p. 13; Victoria *Daily Colonist*, 7 April 1933, p. 5.

78. On the protests of the Catholic Women's League and the Knights of Columbus, see the Vancouver *Sun*, 6 April 1933, p. 1; 25 May 1933, p. 14.

79. *Ibid.*, 24 April 1933, p. 9; Vancouver *Daily Province*, 23 April 1933, p. 2. Pius XI had condemned sterilization in 1930: "Public magistrates have no direct power over the bodies of their subjects. Therefore, where no crime has taken place and there is no cause present for grave punishment, they can never directly harm or tamper with the integrity of the body, either for the reason of eugenics or for other reason. . . ." Cited in MacMurchy, *Sterilization*, p. 16. See also Dr. Letitia Fairchild, *The Case Against Sterilization* (London, n.d.).

80. Vancouver *Sun*, 15 February 1934, p. 6.

81. *Statutes of the Province of British Columbia (1933)*, "An Act Respecting Sexual Sterilization," ch. 59 (7 April 1933).

82. See the *Canadian Parliamentary Guide* for the appropriate years.

83. Vancouver *Daily News*, 3 April 1933, p. 6.

84. Vancouver *Daily Province*, 1 November 1933, p. 22.

85. Victoria *Daily Times*, 6 January 1934, pp. 1-2.

86. Vancouver *Sun*, 20 June 1934, p. 9.

Chapter 6

1. MacMurchy, *The Feeble-Minded in Ontario: 9th Report*, p. 5.

2. Harvey Simmons, *From Asylum to Welfare* (Downsview: National Institute on Mental Retardation, 1982), p. 74.

3. See E.R. Johnstone, "The Feeble-Minded," *PHJ*, 5 (1914), pp. 209-11; MacMurchy, *The Feeble-Minded in Ontario: 8th Report*, p. 19.

4. Simmons, *From Asylum to Welfare*, pp. 75-76.

5. MacMurchy, *The Feeble-Minded in Ontario: 10th Report*, p. 35.

6. T.H. Wills, *CJMH*, 1 (1919), p. 237. See also MacMurchy, *The Feeble-Minded in Ontario: 8th Report*, p. 12.

7. F.E. Hodgins, *The Care and Control of the Mentally Defective and Feeble-Minded: Ontario Royal Commission* (1919). See also *PHJ*, 11 (1920), p. 126.

8. David MacLennan, "Beyond the Asylum: Professionalization and the Mental Hygiene Movement in Canada, 1914-1928," *Canadian Bulletin of Medical History*, 4 (1987), pp. 7-24.

9. "Democracy and Mental Hygiene," *CJMH*, 3 (1921), pp. 272-73; see also "Science and Education," *The Scientific Monthly*, 29 (1929), pp. 132-36.

10. On Hincks (1885-1964), see the C.M. Hincks Papers at the Canadian Psychiatry

Archives at the Queen Street Hospital, Toronto. The Archives contain three unpublished accounts of Hincks's life: C.M. Hincks, "Prospecting for Mental Health: An Autobiography" (1962); Charles G. Roland, "Clarence Meredith Hincks, 1885-1964: A Biography" (1966); and John D. Griffin, "The Chronicle of a National Voluntary Movement: The Canadian Mental Health Association" (1981).

11. John D. Griffin, "The Amazing Careers of Hincks and Beers," *Canadian Journal of Psychiatry*, 27 (1982), p. 668. See also Clifford Beers, *A Mind that Found Itself: An Autobiography*, 25th edition (Garden City: Doubleday, 1965).

12. MacMurchy, *The Feeble-Minded in Ontario: 8th Report*, p. 22; MacMurchy, "The Mentally Defective Child," *PHJ*, 6 (1915), p. 85.

13. *PHJ*, 7 (1916), pp. 502-03.

14. Tom Brown, "Shell Shock in the Canadian Expeditionary Force, 1914-1918: Canadian Psychiatry in the Great War," in Charles G. Roland, ed., *Health, Disease and Medicine: Essays in Canadian History* (Toronto: Clarke Irwin, 1984), p. 308. See also *CMAJ*, 8 (1918), pp. 551-52; *CJMH*, 1 (1919), pp. 2ff.

15. *CMAJ*, 10 (1920), pp. 1061-64.

16. *Western Women's Weekly*, 8 March 1919, p. 1.

17. *CMAJ*, 8 (1918), pp. 634-38.

18. Evelyn Molson Russell, "The Canadian National Committee on Mental Hygiene," *CMAJ*, 8 (1918), p. 538.

19. *CJMH*, 2 (1920), p. 131; see also J.N. Barss, "The Delinquent," *SW*, 1 April 1920, p. 190; C.K. Clarke, "Juvenile Delinquency and Mental Defect," *CJMH*, 2 (1920), pp. 228-32; Maud A. Merrill, "Feeble-Mindedness and Crime," *DR*, 1 (1920-21), pp. 360-67.

20. See C.G. Roland, "Clarence Hincks in Manitoba, 1918," *Manitoba Medical Review*, 45 (February, 1966), pp. 107-13; C.M. Hincks, "Mental Hygiene," *CMAJ*, 11 (1921), pp. 823-25; *CJMH*, 2 (1920), pp. 1-57; 3 (1921), pp. 1ff, 314ff. For an overview of the CNCMH's activities, see J.G. Fitzgerald and Grant Fleming, *Report of a Survey Made of the Organization in 1932* (Ottawa: Metropolitan Life, 1932).

21. Roland, "Hincks: A Biography," p. 85; Theresa M.R. Richardson, "The Century of the Child: The Mental Hygiene Movement and Social Policy in the United States and Canada" (Ph.D. thesis, University of British Columbia, 1987).

22. Griffin, "Chronicle," part two; Mary J. Wright and C. Roger Myers, eds., *History of Academic Psychology in Canada* (Toronto: C.J. Hogrefe, 1982).

23. See Veronica Strong-Boag, "Intruders in the Nursery: Childcare Professionals Reshape the Years One to Five, 1920-1940," in Joy Parr, ed., *Childhood and Family in Canadian Society* (Toronto: McClelland and Stewart, 1982), pp. 160-79; Kathleen McConnachie, "The Canadian Mental Hygiene and Eugenics Movements in the Inter War Years," unpublished Ontario Institute of Education Paper, September, 1983.

24. Charles Martin, "The Mental Hygiene Movement in Canada," *The Canadian Nurse*, 25 (1929), p. 62; Alan Brown, "The G.P. and Preventive Pediatrics," *CPHJ*, 21 (1930), p. 269.

25. See C.M. Hincks, *SW* (1926), pp. 168-74; "Mental Hygiene and Childhood,"

CPHJ, 21 (1930), pp. 26-29; "Mental Hygiene," *Health* (1943), p. 19; "Sterilize the Unfit," *Maclean's*, 15 February 1946, pp. 19, 39-40, 42.

26. P.D. Ross, *Report of the Royal Commission on Public Welfare: 13 August 1930*, pp. 9, 44. See also *National Council of Women Yearbook: 1930*, p. 96. It was presumably Charlotte Whitton, writing as editor of *Child Welfare News*, who greeted the Ross report with the retort:

> Such a "flatfooted" declaration for sterilization was hardly to be anticipated in reference to a question still largely in the experimental stage, from a royal commission in one of Canada's oldest, and (according to general repute) most conservative provinces.

Subsequent accounts were less critical. See *Child Welfare News* (September, 1930), p. 22; (March, 1934), pp. 20-22; (July, 1935), pp. 4-5.

27. Charles J. Hastings to the Eugenics Society, 21 August 1924, Eugenics Society Papers, Contemporary Medical Archives Centre, Wellcome Institute. See also Eugenics Society to Hastings, 1 September 1924, 14 November 1924, Eugenics Society Papers; Charles J. Hastings, "Visions of the Ghost of Malthus," *Health Bulletin*, 15 (August, 1924), pp. 1-4. Professor William McDougal, the Harvard social psychologist, Professor R.A. Fisher, the English eugenicist, and Sir William Beveridge, the English economist, participated at the Toronto meeting; see London *Times*, 16 August 1924, p. 9c.

28. *Birth Control News* (August, 1924), p. 3.

29. C.C. Macklin to Lillian C. Armstrong, 11 March 1930, American Eugenics Society Papers, American Philosophical Society; see also Armstrong to Macklin, 17 December 1929. Macklin's contacts were not the sort of men drawn to public controversies. Fraser was a marine zoologist, Thompson a biologist, and Shaner and Grant professors of anatomy.

30. D.B. Harkness to Eugenics Society, 29 December 1930, Eugenics Society Papers. See also Harkness to Eugenics Society, 3 October 1931.

31. Eugenics Society to E.J. Urwick, 5 February 1931, Eugenics Society Papers.

32. E.J. Urwick, *The Social Good* (London: Methuen, 1927), p. 225. Urwick was a friend and colleague of R.M. McIver.

33. Hutton's and Kaufman's activities will be noted below. As regards Harkness (who presided as the ESC's first president in 1932), it is only necessary to note that he was a respected worker in Canadian welfare circles: in the 1920's, secretary of the Dominion Prohibition Committee, member of the Manitoba Social Service Council; in the 1930's, consultant to the Community Welfare Council of Ontario and author of *Courts of Domestic Relations* (Ottawa, 1924). Harkness was a colleague of Charlotte Whitton, who beat him out of the League of Nations' Assessorship. On the pervasive influence of eugenic ideas in social welfare work in the interwar period, see Andrew Jones and Leonard Rutman, *In the Children's Aid: J.J. Kelso and Child Welfare in Ontario* (Toronto: University of Toronto Press, 1981), p. 170; Rooke and Schnell, *No Bleeding Heart: Charlotte Whitton, A Feminist on the Right*.

34. The medical profession took the leading role in the ESC. Dr. J. Thornley Bowman, Dr. A. Brodey, Dr. F.J. Conboy, president of the Ontario Dental Association, Dr. D.V. Curry, medical officer of health of St. Catharines, Dr. C.B. Farrar of the

Toronto Psychiatric Hospital, Dr. S.L. Frawley, Dr. George Gibbon, Dr. J.E. Hagmeier, Dr. A.L. Hare, Dr. Clarence Hincks of the CNCMH, Dr. W.L. Hutton, medical health officer of Brantford, Dr. B.T. McGhie, Ontario deputy minister of hospitals, Dr. R.G. Ratz, Dr. James Roberts, Hamilton medical health officer, Dr. Morris Siegel of Hamilton, Dr. William P. Tew, and Dr. F.N. Walker were all members.

The second largest contingent in the ESC was made up of representatives of the welfare profession: Frank Blain of the Fort William Children's Aid Society, D.B. Harkness, consultant to the Community Welfare Council of Ontario, R.W. Hopper of Toronto's Crippled Children's Society, Miss Grace A. Jackson of the London Welfare Bureau, Mrs. H.J. Vallentyne of the Ontario School for the Blind at Brantford, and Quintin Warner, judge of London's Juvenile Court.

From academia the ESC drew the support of Roy Fraser, professor of biology at Mount Allison University, W.T. MacClement, professor of biology at Queen's University, T.F. McIlwraith, professor of anthropology at the University of Toronto, Madge Thurlow Macklin, professor of physiology at the University of Western Ontario, and T.R. Robinson, professor of psychology at the University of Toronto.

Religious leaders in the ESC included Reverend G. Raymond Booth, Rabbi M.N. Eisendrath, Canon Lawrence Skey, and Reverend Dr. George T. Webb. Big business was represented by C.H. Carlisle, president of Goodyear Tire and the Dominion Bank, A.R. Kaufman of the Kaufman Rubber Company of Kitchener, E.E. Reid, manager of the London Life Insurance company, and T.H. Yull, a London advertising executive. At least two politicians were members of the ESC: Dr. F.J. Conboy, mayor of Toronto from 1942-1944, and James Simpson, vice-president of the Dominion Trades and Labour Congress and mayor of Toronto in 1935. The legal profession contributed A.M. Harley of Brantford and F.W. Wegenast, counsel for the Canadian Manufacturers' Association and drafter of the Ontario Workmen's Compensation Act. And finally, from education came Mr. T.H. Wholton, principal of the Galt Collegiate Institute. *Eugenical News*, 17 (1932), p. 467; 20 (1935), p. 60; *Eugenics Review*, 30 (1938-39), pp. 54-55; D.B. Harkness to the Eugenics Society, 6 June 1932, Eugenics Society Papers.

35. On similar findings on the social profile of eugenicists elsewhere, see Donald Mackenzie, "Eugenics in Britain," *Social Studies of Science*, 6 (1976), pp. 499-532; "Karl Pearson and the Professional Middle Class," *Annals of Science*, 36 (1979), pp. 125-43.

36. See Hutton, "Growth of Sanitary Conscience," *CPHJ*, 20 (1929), pp. 17-20; see also *CPHJ*, 21 (1930), pp. 315-19. On Hutton's life, see the Dr. William L. Hutton Scrapbook, Ms 665, Public Archives of Ontario [hereafter Hutton Papers]; and the Brantford *Expositor*, 1 July 1927; 26 August 1977.

37. Brantford *Expositor*, 14 November 1935, p. 5.

38. W.L. Hutton to Marie Stopes, 10 March 1932, Stopes Papers, British Museum.

39. Toronto *Mail and Empire*, 29 May 1932, clipping in the Hamilton Birth Control Clinic Papers, Hamilton City Library [hereafter HBC].

40. Hutton, "Tendencies in Human Fertility," *CMAJ*, 30 (1934), p. 77; see also "The Inheritability of Feeble-Mindedness," *CMAJ*, 37 (1937), pp. 591-94.

41. Hutton cited in the *Canadian Tribune*, 27 April 1940, p. 2.
42. On Kaufman's life, see McLaren and McLaren, *The Bedroom and the State.*
43. A.R. Kaufman, *Report #1* (n.p., n.d.).
44. A.R. Kaufman, *Report No. 6: Sterilization Experience in Kitchener, May 15, 1934.* Kaufman also distributed a pamphlet, *Vasectomy Techniques* (Kitchener: PIB, n.d.).
45. See Kaufman to Gilbert Colgate, 14 February 1938, in the Clarence Gamble Papers, Countway Library.
46. Kaufman to Clarence Gamble, 5 July 1937, Gamble Papers.
47. Kaufman, *Sterilization.*
48. Kaufman, *Sterilization Notes, No. 7* (Kitchener: PIB, 1935).
49. Kaufman, *Sterilization Notes*, p. 3.
50. Kaufman to H.L. Mencken, 10 August 1937, Gamble Papers. Kaufman sent a copy of a Mencken article in a letter to Clarence Gamble, 15 December 1939, Gamble Papers.
51. Kaufman to Mencken, 10 August 1937, Gamble Papers.
52. Neelands cited in *One Big Union Bulletin*, 28 May 1931, p. 2; Harkness cited in *Eugenical News*, 17 (1932), p. 47.
53. Toronto *Mail and Empire*, 23 March 1932, HBC.
54. Toronto *Mail and Empire*, 4 June 1933, HBC.
55. London *Free Press*, 21 January 1933, p. 5.
56. London *Advertiser*, 19 January 1933. Fraser's autobiography reeks of that self-conscious religiosity that British eugenicists thought peculiar to Canadians. See Roy Fraser, *Happy Journey* (Toronto: Ryerson, 1958).
57. *Toronto Star*, 19 January 1933, second section, p. 21.
58. Industrial Schools Association of Toronto Records, Series B: Correspondence MU1409-1410, Box 2,3. Support was also expressed by Colonel H.D. Smith, president of the Kent Children's Aid Society, Toronto *Globe*, 2 February 1934.
59. On Bruce, who was Lieutenant-Governor from 1932 to 1937, see his autobiography, *Varied Operations* (Toronto: Longmans, 1958); Herbert A. Bruce Papers, Public Archives of Ontario [hereafter Bruce Papers].
60. Bruce, "Sterilization of the Feeble-Minded," in *Our Heritage and Other Addresses* (Toronto: Macmillan, 1934), p. 44.
61. Bruce, "The Propagation of the Unfit," *Our Heritage*, pp. 21-26. See the letters to the editor of the Toronto *Mail and Empire*, 3, 23 May 1933, Bruce Papers. A.W. Beall, Ontario's self-appointed expert on masturbation and eugenics, supported Bruce and asserted misfits violated "the inalienable rights of the rest of us." Toronto *Mail and Empire*, 30 May 1933, Bruce Papers.
62. On CMA support, see *Toronto Star*, 3 May 1933, Bruce Papers.
63. Toronto *Mail and Empire*, 4 May 1933, Bruce Papers.
64. Farrar, educated at Harvard and Johns Hopkins, was professor of psychiatry at the University of Toronto from 1925. See his biography in *CMAJ*, 103 (1970), p. 307; and his text, *Technique of Mental Examination and Classification of Mental Disease* (n.p., n.d.).
65. *PHJ*, 17 (1926), pp. 83-89.
66. *CMAJ*, 23 (1926), pp. 1233-38.

67. "Sterilization and Mental Hygiene," *CPHJ*, 22 (1931), p. 93.

68. "Sterilization of the Unfit," *Canadian Doctor*, 2 (January, 1936), pp. 16-17, 43.

69. *CMAJ*, 40 (1939), p. 279.

70. F.N. Walker, "Sterility Among Hybrids," *CMAJ*, 16 (1926), pp. 661-65.

71. *Toronto Star*, 5 February 1935, p. 25.

72. *CMAJ*, 33 (1935), p. 192.

73. Premier Mitchell Hepburn, General Correspondence, 1935, Box 335, Public Archives of Ontario.

74. "Canada's Lost Population," *Chatelaine* (April, 1934), pp. 22, 34.

75. "The Exceptional Child," *SW*, 15 (June, 1935), p. 118. On the predominance of hereditarians in social work, see *Second Conference on Social Work: Proceedings* (Toronto, April 28-May 1, 1930).

76. MacMurchy, *Sterilization*, pp. 3, 5.

77. *Toronto Star*, 14 November 1935, pp. 1-2; see also *ibid.*, 3 February 1936, p. 22.

78. *Ibid.*, 4 December 1935, p. 23; see also Toronto *Mail*, 4 December 1935, Bruce Papers.

79. *Toronto Star*, 5 December 1935, Hutton Papers.

80. Toronto *Telegram*, 4 February 1936, Hutton Papers.

81. *Toronto Star*, 3 February 1936, p. 22.

82. Toronto *Mail and Empire*, 2 May 1933; Toronto *Telegram*, 8 June 1933, Bruce Papers.

83. Brantford *Expositor*, 18 February 1936, p. 18.

84. Kaufman, *Sterilization Notes*, p. 3.

85. *Toronto Star*, 17 February 1936, p. 1.

86. *CMAJ*, 33 (1935), p. 192.

87. Bruce, "The Fruit of the Family Tree," in *Friendship: The Key to Peace* (Toronto: Macmillan, 1937), pp. 213-20. See also the text of his 3 September 1936 speech to the Municipal Association, "The Problem of the Feeble-minded," *Friendship*, pp. 271-83. Support for Bruce's views was expressed by R.E. Mills, director of the Children's Aid Society, and Judge Emerson Coatsworth of the Canadian Bar Association in letters to the Toronto *Mail*, 25 April 1936; by Dr. H.B. Anderson, past president of the Ontario Medical Association, in a letter to the *Toronto Star*, 25 April 1936; and in an article in *Maclean's*, 1 July 1936, pp. 14, 33.

88. William L. Hutton, *A Brief for Sterilization of the Feeble-Minded* (n.p., June, 1936).

89. Toronto *Mail*, 12 June 1936, Bruce Papers.

90. Toronto *Mail*, 5 August 1936, Hutton Papers.

91. Hervé Blais, *Les tendances eugénistes au Canada* (Montréal: L'Institut familial, 1942), p. 91.

92. *Toronto Star*, 23 July 1936, pp. 1-2.

93. Hamilton *Herald*, 8 June 1933; Hamilton *Spectator*, 7 June 1933, Bruce Papers.

94. Toronto *Mail*, 15 September 1936, Bruce Papers; Kaufman, *Sterilization Notes*, p. 8.

95. Toronto *Mail*, 12 September 1936, Bruce Papers.

96. Kaufman, *Sterilization Notes*, pp. 6-7; and see Toronto *Telegram*, 27 November

1936. Within the National Council of Women Elizabeth Shortt's report in support of sterilization had been accepted in 1926 but Mabel L. Hanington attempted to prevent the organization from going further. "I BEG that the Women's Council will at the present juncture refrain as an organization from pushing for premature legislation regarding sterilization." *National Council of Women Yearbook: 1927*, p 29; see also *1929*, p. 93; *1930*, pp. 96-97.

97. On the dubious legality of sterilization, see Edmund F. Newcombe, "Legal Aspects of the Operation for Sterilization," *CMAJ*, 41 (1939), pp. 205-06.

98. *Eugenics Review* [hereafter *ER*], 30 (1938-39), p. 54.

99. Brantford *Expositor*, 13 February 1937, pp. 1, 6; see also Toronto *Telegram*, 15 February 1937, Bruce Papers.

100. Toronto *Globe*, 4 January 1937, Hutton Papers.

101. *ER*, 30 (1938-39), p. 283.

102. Bruce in Eugenics Society of Canada, *The Future of Our Race: Series of Radio Addresses* (n.p., 1938), pp. 21, 23.

103. C.W.M. Hart, associate professor of anthropology at the University of Toronto, was an Australian who later taught at the University of Wisconsin. In his academic work he revealed little interest in population issues and the "eugenic" portion of his 1938 radio address was merely the assertion that the process of natural selection was interfered with by man. It is curious that Hart and not T.F. McIlwraith, his fellow anthropologist at Toronto who was a member of the ESC, participated in the program.

104. W. Burton Hurd, "Is There a Canadian Race?" *QQ*, 35 (1928), pp. 615-27; *Origin, Birthplace, Nationality and Language of the Canadian People* (Ottawa: Acland, 1929). See the critique made of Hurd's pessimism by A.S. Whitely, "The Peopling of the Prairie Provinces of Canada," *American Journal of Sociology*, 38 (1932), pp. 240-52.

105. W. Burton Hurd, "Population Movements in Canada, 1921-1931," Canadian Political Science Association, *Papers of the Sixth Meeting*, 6 (1934), p. 52. Hurd, in linking literacy and race, was following M.C. Maclean, *Illiteracy and School Attendance* (Ottawa: Acland, 1921), pp. 57-68. The later *Report on the Criminality Among Foreign Born in Canada* (Ottawa: Canadian Citizenship Bureau, 1957) found that in fact the conviction rate of the native-born was in general higher than that of the foreign-born.

106. W. Burton Hurd, "The Case for a Quota," *QQ*, 36 (1929), pp. 145-59. See also A.R.M. Lower, "The Case Against Immigration," *QQ*, 37 (1930), pp. 557-74; "External Policy and Internal Problems," *University of Toronto Quarterly*, 6 (1936-37), pp. 326-37; Mary Jean Vipond, "National Consciousness in English-Speaking Canada in the 1920s: Seven Studies" (Ph.D. thesis, University of Toronto, 1974), pp. 41-43.

107. See Hurd's reference to the "threat to our population quality" in his contribution to *Future of Our Race*, p. 15. He also viewed the higher French-Canadian fertility as creating "tension on the ties of Confederation." See W. Burton Hurd, "The Decline of the Anglo-Saxon Canadian," *Maclean's*, 50 (1 September 1937), pp. 13, 45.

108. On Hurd's hostility to cultural diversity, see *Seventh Census of Canada: 1931*

(Ottawa: Cloutier, 1942), pp. 571, 634, 683. Hurd carried on the concern for assimilation expressed in James T.M. Anderson, *The Education of the New Canadian* (Toronto: Dent, 1918), pp. 8, 25.

109. The report also contained a candid admission of the sexism inherent in the process of institutionalization: " . . . a large number of these girls would not find themselves in an institution for mental defectives if they had not become pregnant." *Report of the Royal Commission on the Operation of the Mental Hospital Act, 1938*, pp. 49, 51.

110. Simmons, *From Asylum to Welfare*, p. 125.

Chapter 7

1. Kenneth M. Ludmerer, *Genetics and American Society: A Historical Appraisal* (Baltimore: Johns Hopkins University Press, 1972), p. 187.

2. On the American Eugenics Society, see Barry Alan Mehler, "A History of the American Eugenics Society, 1921-1940" (Ph.D. thesis, University of Illinois, 1988), pp. 133-43; on Huskins's support of sterilization, see Toronto *Evening Telegram*, 18 January 1934, p. 1; on his later joining with Hogben, Haldane, Muller, and Huxley in opposing crude eugenic programs, see *Journal of Heredity* (hereafter *JH*), 30 (1939), pp. 371-73. On the 1932 International Congress of Eugenics, see *Eugenical News*, 17 (1932), pp. 135-41.

3. I would like to thank Barry Mehler for generously sharing with me his collection of documents relating to Madge Thurlow Macklin, hereafter cited as Macklin Papers. For short biographical sketches of Macklin, see Hubert C.Soltan, "Madge Macklin: Pioneer in Medical Genetics," *Western Ontario Medical Journal* (1967), pp. 6-11; Barry Mehler, "Madge Thurlow Macklin," in Barbara Sicherman *et al.*, eds., *Notable American Women: The Modern Period* (Cambridge, Mass.: Belknap, 1980), pp. 451-52.

4. Letter from Dr. Jessie L. King and Dr. ? to Dr. Katherine Blunt, 1915, Macklin Papers.

5. Murray Barr, *A Century of Medicine at Western* (London: University of Western Ontario Press, 1977), pp. 351-53, 364-65; Murray Barr *et al.*, "Charles Macklin," *CMAJ*, 82 (1960), p. 335.

6. "Madge Thurlow Macklin," *Goucher Alumnae News* (Summer, 1951), p. 17.

7. Biographical Checklist, Macklin Papers.

8. Barr, *A Century of Medicine*, pp. 360-61.

9. Dean of Medicine to Dr. C.C. Macklin, 9 August 1945, Macklin Papers.

10. Margaret W. Rossiter, *Women Scientists in America, Struggles and Strategies to 1940* (Baltimore: Johns Hopkins University Press, 1982), p. 141.

11. *Ibid.*, pp. 143, 160ff, 195-96, 292.

12. *Ibid.*, pp. 297ff.

13. *Ibid.*, p. 211.

14. London *Free Press*, 19 October 1938; New York *Herald Tribune*, 28 January 1957; New York *Times*, 28 January 1957, Macklin Papers.

15. Macklin, "What Every Mother Knows," *JH*, 25 (1934), p. 248. Canada produced two other women scientists who carried out pioneering work in genetics – Norma Ford Walker (1893-1968) at the Hospital for Sick Children, Toronto, and Lulu Odell Gaiser (1896-1965) at MacMaster University; see *Canadian Journal of Genetics and Cytology*, 7 (1965), pp. 361-62; 10 (1968), p. 775.
16. See Macklin, "Inheritance in Cancer, a Note on the Work of Maude Slye," *CMAJ*, 16 (1926), pp. 1119-20. On Slye, see John Parascandola, "Maude Slye," in Sicherman, *Notable American Women*, pp. 651-52.
17. Macklin, "A Conference on Heredity as Applied to Man," *Science*, 5 June 1931, p. 614.
18. Macklin, "The Hereditary Factor in Human Neoplasms," *Quarterly Review of Biology*, 255 (1932), p. 256; see also Macklin, "Familial Incidence of Cancer," in *A Symposium on Cancer* (Madison: University of Wisconsin Press, 1938), pp. 38-39.
19. New York *Times*, 29 May 1938, Macklin Papers.
20. Macklin, "The Increase in Cancer in Canada, 1901-1921," *Transactions of the Royal Society of Canada*, 26 (1932), sect. 5, pp. 161-67; "The Problem of the Increase of Cancer," *CMAJ*, 36 (1937), pp. 189-95.
21. Macklin, "What Price Longevity?" Macklin Papers; see also *Science*, 7 October 1932, p. 12.
22. Macklin, "The Relationship of Heredity to Life Insurance," *CMAJ*, 41 (1939), p. 504.
23. Macklin was naturally interested in the Dionne quintuplets as a startling demonstration of the powers of heredity. See Macklin, "A Visit to Corbeil," *JH*, 25 (1934), pp. 420-22; and "Quints Progress," *JH*, 29 (1938), pp. 289-90.
24. Macklin, "Life Insurance," pp. 502-03.
25. Macklin, "Familial Incidence of Cancer," p. 43.
26. Macklin, "Human Tumors and Their Inheritance," *CMAJ*, 27 (1932), pp. 182-87.
27. Macklin, "Familial Incidence," p. 39.
28. Macklin, "The Inheritance of Disease," *Lancet*, 2 (1932), pp. 208-09. See also "Pitfalls in Dealing With Statistics, Especially as Related to Cancer of the Lung," an address given to the American College of Chest Physicians, Atlantic City, 1947, in Macklin Papers.
29. Macklin, "Comparison of Number of Breast Cancer Deaths Observed in Relatives of Breast Cancer Victims and the Number Expected on the Basis of Mortality Rates," *Journal of the National Cancer Institute*, 22 (1959), p. 927.
30. Macklin, "Etiological Factors in Carcinoma of the Uterus, Especially Cervix," *Journal of the International College of Surgeons*, 21 (1954), p. 365.
31. Macklin, "The Value of Accurate Statistics in the Study of Cancer," *CPHJ*, 25 (1934), pp. 369-73.
32. Macklin, "Life Insurance," p. 502.
33. Macklin, "The Value of Medical Genetics to the Clinician," in Charles B. Davenport, ed., *Medical Genetics and Eugenics* (Philadelphia: Women's Medical College of Pennsylvania, 1940), pp. 131-32.
34. Macklin, "Primogeniture: Is It a Factor in the Production of Developmental Abnormalities?" *Lancet*, 1 (1929), p. 973.

35. Macklin, "Value of Medical Genetics," p. 136.

36. Macklin, "Do the Modes of Transmission of Tumors Vary?" *JH*, 30 (1939), pp. 396-400.

37. Macklin, "Pitfalls," p. 2.

38. Macklin, "The Relation of the Mode of Inheritance to the Severity of an Inherited Disease," *Human Biology*, 4 (1932), p. 69.

39. Macklin, "Primogeniture and Developmental Anomalies," *Human Biology*, 1 (1929), pp. 382-405.

40. Macklin, "The British National Human Heredity Committee," *CMAJ*, 35 (1936), pp. 432-33; see also "Education and Research in the Field of Inheritance of Disease," *CMAJ*, 32 (1935), p. 82.

41. See, for example, Macklin, "The Need for a Course in Medical Genetics in the Medical Curriculum," in Harry F. Perkins *et al.*, eds., *A Decade of Progress in Eugenics* (Baltimore: Williams and Williams, 1934), pp. 157-58. See also "Partial List of Addresses by Madge T. Macklin," Macklin Papers.

42. Cited in Soltan, "Madge Macklin," p. 6.

43. Macklin, "Eugenics and the Medical Profession," *CMAJ*, 17 (1927), p. 1526.

44. *Ibid.*

45. Macklin, "A Conference on Heredity," p. 614.

46. See Macklin's talk, "The Cult of the Abnormal," given to the Ontario Agricultural College, Guelph, Ontario, 17 March 1938, in Macklin Papers. Macklin was no doubt attracted by the eugenicist assertion that social problems needed to be attacked with the sort of surgical ruthlessness doctors employed when dealing with tumours. "It would by no means be a misnomer to call the American Eugenics Society a Society for the Control of Social Cancer," boasted Ellsworth Huntington in the Society's official "catechism," *Tomorrow's Children: The Goal of Eugenics* (New York: John Wiley, 1935), p. 46.

47. Macklin, "Increase in Mental Defect in the Province of Ontario Since 1871," *Eugenic News*, 19 (1934), pp. 96-97; also "Genetical Aspects of Sterilization of the Mentally Unfit," *CMAJ*, 30 (1934), pp. 190-95.

48. On Hutton, see *CMAJ*, 30 (1934), p. 73; on the birth rate, see Macklin, "A Decade of Progress in Eugenics," *SW*, 15 (1935), pp. 126-28.

49. See the report of Macklin's speech in the London *Advertiser*, 21 January 1933, Macklin Papers.

50. Macklin, "Mental Defect," p. 99.

51. Macklin, "Life Insurance," p. 505.

52. *Ibid.*

53. See the report of Macklin's speech in the London *Advertiser*, 21 January 1933, Macklin Papers.

54. Macklin, "Mental Defect," p. 99.

55. Macklin, "The New Deal in Education," *Ontario Education Association*, 73 (1934), p. 47.

56. *Ibid.*, p. 51.

57. Macklin, "One Anthropologist's Logic," *JH*, 23 (1932), p. 457.

58. Macklin, "New Deal," p. 51.

59. *Ibid.*, p. 52.

60. Speech cited in *Toronto Star*, 24 April 1934, in Macklin Papers.
61. Through the mid-1930's Macklin gave a series of pro-sterilization talks before service clubs in Kitchener-Waterloo, London, Guelph, Windsor, and other Ontario towns. For a typical report, see the Kitchener *Daily Record*, 29 March 1933, in Macklin Papers.
62. Macklin, "The Influence of Heredity on Disease," *CMAJ*, 31 (1934), pp. 117-18. For Penrose's view, see *The Biology of Mental Defect* (London: Sidgwick and Jackson, 1963).
63. Macklin, "Influence of Heredity," p. 118.
64. Macklin, "Genes and the Unconscious," *JH*, 26 (1935), p. 73.
65. *Ibid.*, p. 73.
66. Macklin, "Heredity and the Social Problem Group," *CMAJ*, 30 (1934), p. 310.
67. Macklin, "The Case for the Inheritance of Schizophrenia," *JH*, 30 (1939), p. 205.
68. Macklin, "Eugenical Sterilization," *JH*, 28 (1937), pp. 99-102.
69. Macklin citing Kallman in "Schizophrenia," p. 204.
70. Macklin, "The Need for a Course in Medical Genetics in the Medical Curriculum," *Edinburgh Medical Journal*, 40 (1933), p. 23.
71. Macklin, "Inherited Blindness," *CMAJ*, 16 (1926), p. 1367.
72. See the report of Macklin's trip to Germany in the London *Free Press*, 19 October 1938. Under the Nazis, Kurt Pohlisch served on the Committee on "Genetically Determined Illness," which sent 75,000 mental patients to their deaths. He was prosecuted, but acquitted, after the war for his part in what was code-named the T4 program. See Ernst Klee, *"Euthanasie" im NS-Staat: Die "Vernichtung lebensunwerten Lebens"* (Frankfurt: S. Fischer Verlag, 1983), pp. 175, 227, 242, 324, 421; Robert Proctor, *Racial Hygiene: Medicine Under the Nazis* (Cambridge, Mass.: Harvard University Press, 1988), pp. 188-89. North American doctors like Macklin were kept informed of events in Germany by the "Letter from Berlin" that appeared regularly in the *Journal of the American Medical Association*.
73. Eysenck cited in *Western Ontario Medical Journal* (January, 1968), p. 11. It is, of course, ironic that a man like Eysenck, who defends the new eugenics, should have made such a statement.
74. For a report of Macklin's speech, see the Brantford *Expositor*, 22 February 1935, p. 16.
75. Macklin, "Eugenics Congress," *JH*, 23 (1932), p. 389. For Macklin's concern regarding the economic burden levied on society by the care of the blind, see "Hereditary Blindness," *CMAJ*, 16 (1926), p. 1368. For her suggestion that the government take funds from social welfare programs and put them into genetic research, see "Heredity and the Social Problem Group," *CMAJ*, 30 (1934), pp. 309-10.
76. Macklin, "Hereditary Factor," p. 276.
77. Macklin, "Can We 'Breed Out' Cancer in the Human Race?" *Edinburgh Medical Journal*, 45 (1938), p. 593.
78. Macklin did argue that childhood cancer should be countered, for example, by having survivors of retinal glioma prevented from having children and by preventing parents who had one such child from having any more. See Macklin, "Hereditary Factor," p. 277.

79. Soltan, "Madge Macklin," p. 8. Women like MacMurchy and Macklin played an especially important role in eugenics no doubt because such a new "science" was not yet a closed male shop. See Sandra Harding, *The Science Question in Feminism* (Ithaca: Cornell University Press, 1986), p. 62.

Chapter 8

1. *Toronto Star*, 19 January 1933, second section, p. 1.
2. *Maclean's*, 15 March 1935, p. 64; and see also *Toronto Star*, 5 February 1935, p. 25.
3. A similar silencing of eugenicists occurred in the United States. The Eugenics Record Office at Cold Spring Harbor closed at the end of 1939, the Eugenics Research Association faded away, and the American Eugenics Society was in effect moribund from 1940 on. See Haller, *Eugenics*, p. 180.
4. H. Dyson Carter, "Blame it on Grandpa's Zygotes," *Saturday Night* [hereafter *SN*], 21 December 1940, p. 15; G. Ziener, "How Hitler Builds His Super Race," *Maclean's*, 15 October 1941, pp. 17, 43. See also David G. Johnston, "Nazi Use of Sterilization," *SN*, 19 July 1941; Pauline C. Shapiro, "A Reply to a Sociologist," *SN*, 2 August 1941, p. 19. Canadians' concern for what was happening in Germany did not, however, translate into a willingness to offer shelter to Jewish refugees; see Irving Abella and Harold Troper, *None is Too Many: Canada and the Jews of Europe, 1933-1948* (Toronto: Lester and Orpen Dennys, 1982).
5. A.R. Kaufman to Guy I. Burch, 26 February 1941, Gamble Papers. Kaufman's plan on how to counter Nazism was peculiar, to say the least. He wrote one American birth control advocate: "I would like to inform you confidentially that I wrote to [the] Honorable Anthony Eden some time ago that Birth Control literature should be scattered over the Axis countries because it is easier and more humane to limit our enemies through Birth Control than by shooting them in periodic wars." A.R. Kaufman to R.L. Dickinson, 29 July 1943, Gamble Papers.
6. *ER*, 32 (1940-41), pp. 47-49, 55.
7. William Hutton to Eugenics Society, 16 June 1940, Eugenics Society Papers, D 89, Contemporary Medical Archives Centre, Wellcome Institute for the History of Medicine [hereafter ESP].
8. D.B. Harkness to Eugenics Society, 15 June 1940, ESP. On the enthusiasm for Canada receiving the "right sort" of evacuated children, see Charlotte Whitton, *SN*, 12 April 1941, p. 26; Helen MacMurchy, *Canadian Home Journal* (June, 1940), pp. 36-37.
9. D.B. Harkness to Eugenics Society, 24 June 1940, ESP.
10. D.B. Harkness to Eugenics Society, 28 June 1940; Eugenics Society to D.B. Harkness, 29 July 1940, ESP. On the conditions in London, see George Ignatieff, *The Making of a Peacemonger* (Toronto: University of Toronto Press, 1985), pp. 59-60; Charles Ritchie, *The Siren Years: A Canadian Diplomat Abroad* (Toronto: Macmillan, 1974), pp. 57-60.
11. On the selection process, see "Homes in Canada: Organization of Scheme in

England," ESP, D 40. The English organizers included the eminent sociologist Richard Titmuss, who later produced a classic analysis of wartime Britain, *Problems in Social Policy* (London: Longmans, 1950). On the general evacuation, see also Carlton Jackson, *Who Will Take our Children?* (London: Methuen, 1985); Travis L. Crosby, *The Impact of Civilian Evacuation in the Second World War* (London: Croom Helm, 1986).

12. Eugenics Society to D.B. Harkness, 30 July 1940, ESP.

13. Eugenics Society to D.B. Harkness, 9 October 1940, ESP.

14. *ER*, 56 (1964), p. 131. For the names of the Canadian hosts who were made Life Fellows of the Eugenics Society, see *ER*, 38 (1946-47), pp. 6-7. On the arrival of the evacuees in Canada, see the Brantford *Expositor*, 23 August 1940, pp. 1, 10.

15. W.L. Hutton to Mrs. G. Collyer, 6 January 1941, ESP.

16. W.L. Hutton to C.F. Chance, 13 March 1941, ESP.

17. John Noonan, *Contraception: A History of its Treatment by Catholic Theologians* (Cambridge, Mass.: Harvard University Press, 1966), pp. 424-25. In Europe sterilization laws were passed with little debate in those countries – Denmark (1929), Germany (1933), Norway (1934), Sweden and Finland (1935), Estonia (1936), Iceland (1938) – where there was no serious Catholic opposition. See Nils Roll-Hansen, "The Progress of Eugenics," *History of Science*, 26 (1988), pp. 295-331.

18. A.R. Kaufman to Margaret Sanger, 18 October 1935, Sanger Papers, Library of Congress. See also A.R. Kaufman to Clarence Gamble, 21 July 1937, Gamble Papers.

19. A.H. Tyrer, *To the Protestant Ministers of Canada* (n.p., n.d.), p. 6. A copy of this pamphlet is in the United Church of Canada Archives. On Arcand, see Lita-Rose Betcherman, *The Swastika and the Maple Leaf: Fascist Movements in Canada in the 1920s* (Toronto: Fitzhenry and Whiteside, 1975), pp. 32-44.

20. Watson Kirkconnell, *Canada, Europe and Hitler* (Oxford: Oxford University Press, 1940), pp. 203-04; see also his *Twilight of Liberty* (Toronto: Oxford University Press, 1941), p. 75.

21. Watson Kirkconnell, *Seven Pillars of Freedom: An Exposure of the Soviet World Conspiracy and its Fifth Column in Canada* (Toronto: Burns and MacEachern, 1944), pp. 163-64. For a reply, see Tim Buck, *Canada Needs a Party of Communists* (Toronto: CPC, 1943), p. 9. For an uncritical account of Kirkconnell, see J.R.C. Perkin and J.B. Snelson, *Morning in His Heart: The Life and Writings of Watson Kirkconnell* (Windsor, N.S.: Lancelot Press, 1985).

22. "Sociology," *America*, 19 February 1910, p. 515. Probably the best-known attack on eugenics written in English was G.K. Chesterton, *Eugenics and Other Evils* (London: Cassell, 1922), a collection of essays actually written before Chesterton's conversion to Catholicism. See also *Catholic Register*, 3 November 1938, p. 4; *Maclean's*, 1 April 1946, p. 73.

23. H.C. Miller, "L'Hygiène mentale se rattache aux oeuvres sociales de prévention," *Proceedings of the First Annual Meetings: Canadian Conference on Social Work* (Montreal: CCSW, 1928), pp. 168-71; *Le Devoir*, 20 July 1931, p. 2.

24. C. Forest, "Que faut-il penser de l'eugénisme?" *Revue dominicaine*, 36 (1930), pp. 272-83, 356-67.

25. Antonio Barbeau, *Sous les plantanes de Cos* (Montréal: Bernard Valiquette, 1942), pp. 22-80.

26. Gaston Lapierre, "Les campagnes internationales actuelles d'eugénisme," *Revue trimestielle canadienne*, 21 (1935), pp. 363, 368.

27. Louis-Marie Lalonde had studied at Harvard (where he obtained a Ph.D. in 1928) with the botanist M.L. Fernald and the eminent geneticists E.M. East and W.E. Castle. See *Canada français* [hereafter *CF*], 24 (1936-37), pp. 71-75; L.M. Lalonde, *Hérédité: manuel de génétique* (La Trappe: L'Institut agricole d'Oka, 1936), pp. 404, 416-17, 434. See also Marcelle Lepage, "Bon sang ne peut mentir," *CF*, 27 (1940), pp. 526-35. On the difficulty genetics had in establishing itself in France, see Richard M. Burian, Jean Gayon, and Doris Zallen, "The Singular Fate of Genetics in French Biology, 1900-1940," *Journal of the History of Biology*, 21 (1988), pp. 357-402.

28. Blais, *Les Tendances eugénistes au Canada*, pp. 161-62. See also Blais, "L'Eugénique au Canada," *Culture*, 2 (1941), pp. 324-37, and the review of his book carried in *CF*, 30 (1942-43), p. 637.

29. Blais, *Les Tendances*, p. 147.

30. Henri Martin, "La Dépopulation," *Semaine Sociale du Canada; 1923* (Montréal: L'Action française, 1924), pp. 142, 152; see also *L'Action française*, 10 (septembre, 1923), p. 144.

31. Gaston Lapierre, "La Limitation des naissances et les lois de stérilisations," *Le quartier latin*, 7 mars 1941, p. 4; L. Ferland, "Le Prix d'une vie," *CF*, 25 (1938), pp. 923-33; Mgr. Wilfred Lebon, "L'Encyclique sur le mariage chrétien," *CF*, 18 (1930-31), pp. 513-21; Edouard Jordan and J. Viollet, *Eugénisme et stérilisation* (Montréal: L'École sociale populaire, 1934), pp. 9, 19, 22; F.M. Drouin, *Autour de la famille: stérilisation et "Birth Control"* (Ottawa: Collège dominicaine, 1936), pp. 8, 12, 21.

32. See, for example, *Relations*, 1 (1941), p. 85; 5 (1945), p. 36.

33. Jacques Rousseau, *L'Hérédité et l'homme* (Montréal: Les éditions de l'arbre, 1945), pp. 197-210. Rousseau, who obtained a Ph.D. in botany from the Université de Montréal, was also the author of "La technique de l'observation en génétique," *Regards sur les sciences experimentales* (décembre, 1941), pp. 137-45. See also Paul Popenoe, "A French-Canadian Program of Eugenics," *Eugenical News*, 31 (1946), pp. 17-19.

34. Haller, *Eugenics*.

35. Kevles, *In the Name of Eugenics*, pp. 122-28, 164ff; Charles Rosenberg, *No Other Gods: On Science and American Social Thought* (Baltimore: Johns Hopkins University Press, 1976), pp. 96ff. In combatting the campaign for sterilizations in Manitoba Antoine d'Eschambault cited Haldane, Pearl, and Tredgold; see *Eugenical Sterilizations* (Winnipeg: Canadian Publishers, 1937), pp. 108-09.

36. *Report of the Departmental Committee on Sterilization* (Joint Committee on Sterilization, June, 1934); see also Michael Craft, ed., *Tredgold's Mental Retardation: 12th Edition* (London, 1979), pp. 4-8; R.C. Scheerenberger, *A History of Mental Retardation* (Baltimore, 1983), pp. 154-56.

37. Although they appear to have refrained from plunging into the Canadian debate over eugenics, it is of interest to note that two British authorities in the field –

Lionel Penrose and Enid Charles – were to spend the war years in Canada. Penrose, a renowned expert on mental defectiveness, served as director of psychiatric research at the University of Western Ontario and as consultant to the Ontario Department of Health from 1939 to 1945. Penrose, described by J.B.S. Haldane as the "greatest living authority on human genetics," made his hostility to eugenics clear: "There is no precise genesis of social efficiency, so that the idea that it can be prevented on the basis of genetical theory is essentially invalid." *The Biology of Mental Defect* (London: Birchall and Sons, 1963 [1949]), p. 289. To the dismay of eugenicists, Penrose returned to Britain in 1945 to assume the Galton Chair of Eugenics at University College, London.

Enid Charles, a noted feminist and brilliant mathematician, was the wife of the polymath and savage anti-eugenicist Lancelot Hogben. Charles was best known for *The Twilight of Parenthood* (London: Norgate and Williams, 1934), which provided ammunition for the argument that family allowances were necessary if the decline in the birth rate was to be curbed. She served as census research specialist at the Dominion Bureau of Statistics from 1942 to 1947. In responding to the sorts of fears expressed by Hurd concerning the changing racial composition of the country, she declared that "the biological aspects of 'racial origin' are a myth." *The Changing Size of the Family in Canada* (Ottawa: Bureau of Statistics, 1948), p. 54. On Charles and Hogben, see Gary Werskey, *The Invisible College* (London: Allen Lane, 1978), pp. 66-67, 104-09.

38. *CJPH*, 28 (1937), p. 152.
39. Toronto *Telegram*, 18 January 1934, p. 1.
40. *Toronto Star*, 19 August 1933, William Hutton Papers, Provincial Archives of Ontario.
41. *Canadian Doctor*, 2 (August, 1936), pp. 30-34.
42. Dr. Horne to H.S. Atkinson, 18 February 1935, Provincial Archives of Ontario, cited in Diane Dodd, "The Canadian Birth Control Movement" (M.A. thesis, Ontario Institute of Education, 1982), p. 88.
43. MacArthur, born in Buffalo and trained at Chicago, taught genetics at the University of Toronto from 1923 to 1948. He did important studies on chromosome mapping, working initially with fowl and tomatoes, but later interested himself in human genetics. He wrote articles with his wife Olive Turner MacArthur on twins and contributed to William Blatz *et al.*, *Collected Studies on the Dionne Quintuplets* (Toronto: University of Toronto Press, 1937). See the John W. MacArthur file in the University of Toronto Archives [hereafter UTA] and J.R. Drummond, "John Wood MacArthur, 1889-1950," *Royal Society of Canada Transactions*, 45 (1951), pp. 97-99.
44. *Toronto Star*, 17 March 1930, W.E. Gallie file, UTA.
45. *Toronto Star*, 20 March 1930, MacArthur file, UTA.
46. 15 March 1935 clipping, Hutton Papers.
47. *SW* (1937), p. 15.
48. *Ibid.* (1938), pp. 106-08.
49. R.O. Earl, "The Geneticist at Bay," *QQ*, 44 (1937), pp. 48-54. See also H.H. Newman, "Heredity, Environment and Twins," *QQ*, 47 (1940), pp. 429-36.
50. "The Problem of the Subnormal in the Community," *CJPH*, 28 (1937), p. 109.

51. In Britain – unlike Canada – there existed a pro-natalist eugenicist movement in favour of such legislation. See John MacNicol, *The Movement for Family Allowances, 1918-45: A Study in Social Policy Development* (London: Heineman, 1980), pp. 75-94. Although Leonard Marsh was clearly influenced by William Beveridge, there is no evidence of eugenic preoccupations in Marsh's *Health and Unemployment* (Toronto: Oxford University Press, 1938). Canada also failed to produce any notable social scientific rebuttal of eugenics. Franz Boas of Columbia University led American anthropologists in subjecting eugenics to scathing criticism. It is interesting to note that R.M. MacIver advanced eugenic arguments in defence of birth control while at the University of Toronto; after taking up a position at Columbia in 1927 he swung around to a clearly anti-eugenic stance. "What man has made man can make better. It is easier on the whole and less hazardous to experiment with environment than with heredity." R.M. MacIver, *The Contribution of Sociology to Social Work* (New York: Columbia University Press, 1931), p. 34.

52. On the interwar campaign of intellectuals in favour of state intervention, see Michiel Horn, *The League for Social Reconstruction* (Toronto: University of Toronto Press, 1980); Doug Owram, *The Government Generation: Canadian Intellectuals and the State, 1900-1945* (Toronto: University of Toronto Press, 1986); R. Douglas Francis, *Frank H. Underhill, Intellectual Provocateur* (Toronto: University of Toronto Press, 1986). On the political side, see J.L. Granatstein *et al.*, *Twentieth Century Canada* (Toronto: McGraw-Hill Ryerson, 1986), pp. 341ff; R. Bothwell *et al.*, *Canada Since 1945: Power, Politics and Provincialism* (Toronto: University of Toronto Press, 1981), pp. 66ff.

53. C.E. Silcox, "The Future of the Middle Class," *Food for Thought*, 3 (October, 1942), p. 7; see also *ibid.*, 3 (November, 1942), pp. 4-5; C.E. Silcox, "Are Family Allowances Constitutional?" *SN*, 7 October 1944, p. 11. On the support for allowances, see Dorothy H. Stepler, "Family Allowances for Canada," *Behind the Headlines*, 3 (1943); *Canadian Forum*, (September, 1944), pp. 123-24; Margaret Gould, *Family Allowances in Canada: Fact versus Fiction* (Toronto: Ryerson, 1945); George F. Davidson, "Family Allowances: An Installment in Social Security," *Canadian Welfare*, (September, 1944), pp. 6-11.

54. C.E. Silcox, *The Revenge of the Cradles* (Toronto: Ryerson, 1945), pp. 11, 23. In a similar vein Dr. Ruth Maclachlin asked post-war brides, "Do we want to repopulate the country from the alert, intelligent and therefore overcautious group, or shall we be content to have the less thoughtful, less responsible types of parents reproduce their kind?" "A Note to Brides: Don't Delay Parenthood," *Chatelaine* (May, 1946), p. 29.

55. Charlotte Whitton, "The Baby Bonus is a Dog in the Security Manger," *SN*, 3 March 1945, p. 6; Rooke and Schnell, *No Bleeding Heart: Charlotte Whitton, A Feminist on the Right*, pp. 79, 121, 123.

56. This did have its practical advantages: "vast numbers of condoms" were distributed to the troops to protect them from venereal disease. See J.W. Tice, "Venereal Disease in the R.C.A.F.," *CJPH*, 37 (1946), p. 53; Vancouver *Sun*, 18 May 1943, p. 3.

57. See Paul Popenoe and Roswell Johnson, *Applied Eugenics* (New York: Macmillan,

1920); E.S. Gosney and Paul Popenoe, *Sterilization for Human Betterment* (New York: Macmillan, 1929).

58. Paul Popenoe, "First Aid for the Family," *Maclean's*, 1 May 1947, p. 47. See also Popenoe, "First Aid for Unhappy Marriage," *Health* (September-October, 1946), pp. 5-6.

59. Clarence M. Hincks, "Sterilize the Unfit," *Maclean's*, 15 February 1946, p. 39. David B. Harkness, one-time president of the Eugenics Society of Canada, was still lamenting in 1945 Canadians' "lack of constructive planning and our tendency to drift." *The Nation Called Canada* (Toronto: Elliott Press, 1945), p. ix.

60. Hincks, "Sterilize the Unfit," p. 40. Hincks's figures on the number of recruits rejected was an exaggeration, but it is worthy of note that the sort of psychiatric screening that he, Clarke, and Withrow had sought in World War One was now employed in the Canadian Army. Lieutenant-General Andrew McNaughton supported the testing, which was carried out by Brigadier George Brock Chisolm, director-general of Medical Services, with the assistance of Hincks, William Line of the University of Toronto, and John Griffin, future head of the Canadian Mental Health Association. See W. Line and J. Griffin, "Personnel Selection in the Army," *CMAJ*, 48 (1943), p. 394; W.D. Ross, "Mental Hygiene and Reconstruction," *Public Affairs* (Summer, 1943), pp. 198-202; Francis Flaherty, "Army's Selection Methods Useful to Civilian Life," *SN*, 13 May 1944, pp. 10-11; M.F. Goldenberg, "How the Army Avoids Misfits," *Canadian Business* (May, 1943), pp. 62-64.

61. A.E. Grauer, *Hygiène publique: étude préparée pour la commission royale des relations entre le dominion et les provinces* (Ottawa: King's Printer, 1939), pp. 54, 120. Dr. Weir, the British Columbia Minister of Health, answered the accusation that B.C. envisaged a Nazi-like policy of compulsory sterilization with the unwise retort, "Unfortunately the right people in Germany are not always sterilized." Vancouver *Sun*, 23 April 1941, p. 14; 24 April, p. 2.

62. Christian, "The Mentally Ill and Human Rights in Alberta."

63. Provincial Archives of British Columbia, Provincial Secretary, Mental Health Services, GR 542, box 14, "Sterilization" (hereafter GR 542). The report was prepared by M. Stewart for A.L. Crease, the superintendent of Essondale, who forwarded it to deputy provincial secretary P. Walker on the assumption that sterilization would be discussed in the 1946 session of the legislature. Most of the medical diagnoses in the report were provided by Dr. E.J. Ryan.

64. Sterilization was by vasectomy for males and by salpingectomy for females.

65. Isobel Harvey to E.W. Griffith, 18 March 1944, GR 542.

66. A.L. Crease to P. Walker, 9 May 1944, GR 542.

67. On the costs of the provincial mental health system, see *British Columbia in the Canadian Confederation; A Submission to the Royal Commission on Dominion-Provincial Relations by the Government of British Columbia* (Victoria: King's Printer, 1938), p. 92.

68. Cases nine and fourteen.

69. Cases five, twenty-one, and twenty-six.

70. A.L. Crease to B.T. McGhie, Director of Hospital Services, Ontario, 1 May 1933, GR 542.

71. See the circular sent out to B.C. doctors by J. MacLachan, registrar of the College

of Physicians and Surgeons of B.C., 26 October 1945, GR 542. See also *CMAJ*, 40 (1939), pp. 205-06.

72. Cited in Harvey Simmons, *From Asylum to Welfare* (Downsview: National Institute on Mental Retardation, 1982), p. 117.

Epilogue

1. Cited in L.N. Penrose, *The Biology of Mental Defect* (London: Birchall, 1963), p. vii.

2. Board of Inquiry into the Cost of Living, *Report of the Board*, vol. 1 (Ottawa: King's Printer, 1915), p. 13, cited in Diane L. J. Matter, "'A Chance to Make Good': Juvenile Males and the Law in Vancouver, B.C. 1910-1915" (M.A. thesis, University of British Columbia, 1978), p. 5.

3. T.C. Douglas, "Youth and the New Day," *Research Review*, 1 (June, 1934), p. 3. *Research Review* also listed as recommended reading the works of Henry Pratt Fairchild, president of the American Eugenics Society.

4. Thomas, *The Making of a Socialist*, pp. 108, 174; McLeod and McLeod, *Tommy Douglas: The Road to Jerusalem*, pp. 40-41.

5. See the discussion of the problem offered in G.R. Searle, *Medical History*, 31 (1987), pp. 366-68; John MacNicol, "Eugenics and the Campaign for Voluntary Sterilization in Britain Between the Wars," *Social History of Medicine*, 2 (1989), pp. 147-70.

6. Gisela Bock, "Racism and Sexism in Nazi Germany," *Signs*, 8 (1983), pp. 400-21; Jeremy Noakes, "Nazism and Eugenics: The Background to the Nazi Sterilization Law of 14 July 1933," in R.J. Bullen, ed., *Ideas into Politics: Aspects of European History, 1880-1950* (London: Croom Helm, 1984), pp. 75-95; Paul Weindling, "Weimar Eugenics: The Kaiser Wilhelm Institute for Anthropology, Human Heredity, and Eugenics in Social Context," *Annals of Science*, 42 (1985), pp. 303-18; Robert Jay Lifton, *The Nazi Doctors: Medical Killing and the Psychology of Genocide* (New York: Basic, 1986); Benno Muller-Hill, *Murderous Science: Elimination by Scientific Selection of Jews, Gypsies, and Others, Germany 1933-1945* (New York: Oxford University Press, 1987); Sheila Faith Weiss, *Race Hygiene and National Efficiency: The Eugenics of Wilhelm Schallmeyer* (Berkeley: University of California Press, 1987).

7. For defences of the program, see David Gibson, "Involuntary Sterilization of the Mentally Retarded: A Western Canadian Phenomenon," *Canadian Psychiatric Association Journal*, 19 (1974), pp. 59-63; W.R.N. Black, *Mental Health in Alberta* (Edmonton: Human Resources, 1969).

8. *Toronto Star*, 16 December 1978, p. 1; K.L. Dickin and B.A. Ryan, "Sterilization and the Mentally Retarded," *Canada's Mental Health*, 31 (1983), p. 48; K.G. Evans, "Sterilization of the Mentally Retarded – A Review," *Canadian Medical Association Journal*, 123 (1980), pp. 1066-70.

9. Bernard M. Dickens, "Eugenic Recognition in Canadian Law," *Osgoode Law Journal*, 13 (1975), pp. 547-77; see also 11 (1973), p. 182.

10. Allan Chase, *The Legacy of Malthus* (New York: Knopf, 1977); Toronto *Globe and Mail*, 30 January 1989, p. A10.

11. Murray L. Barr, *A New Aspect of Genetics and Its Bearing on Mental Retardation* (Saskatoon: University of Saskatchewan, 1966); C.O. Carter, ed., *Developments in Human Reproduction and Their Eugenic, Ethical Implications* (New York: Academic Press, 1983); *Pre-Natal Diagnosis: To Be or Not To Be* (Toronto: CBC Color Film, 1981); M.A. Santos, *Genetics and Man's Future* (Springfield, Illinois: Thomas, 1981).

12. H.B. Holmes, B.B. Hoskins, and M. Gross, eds., *The Custom Made Child* (Clifton, NJ.: Humanities Press, 1980); Mary Anne Warren, *Gendercide: The Implications of Sex Selection* (Totowa, N.J.: Rowman and Littlefield, 1985); Myra Fooden *et al.*, eds., *Genes and Gender: IV. The Second X and Women's Health* (New York: Gorian Press, 1983); Rita Arditti *et al.*, *Test Tube Women* (London: Pandora, 1984); Thomas M. Shapiro, *Population Control Politics: Women, Sterilization, and Reproductive Choices* (Philadelphia: Temple University Press, 1985); Rona Achilles, "New Age Procreation," *Healthsharing* (Fall, 1985), pp. 10-14; Gena Corea, *The Mother Machine: Reproductive Technologies from Artificial Insemination to Artificial Wombs* (New York: Harper and Row, 1986).

Index

THE CANADIAN SOCIAL HISTORY SERIES